The
WESTMINSTER
SHORTER *and*
LARGER
CATECHISMS

Other works by Dr. Surrendra Gangadean & The Logos Foundation:

Philosophical Foundation: A Critical Analysis of Basic Beliefs

History of Philosophy: A Critical Analysis of Unresolved Disputes

Theological Foundation: A Critical Analysis of Christian Belief

Philosophical Foundation: Trivium Study Guide

The Logos Papers: To Make the Logos Known

*The Westminster Confession of Faith:
A Doxological Understanding*

*On Natural and Revealed Theology:
Collected Essays of Surrendra Gangadean*

*The Logos Curriculum:
Grammar Catechisms: Philosophical, Theological, and
Historical Foundations*

Fundación Filosofica: Un Análisis Crítico de Creencias Básicas

DOXOLOGICAL REFORMED COMMENTARY SERIES:

*The Book of Revelation: What Must Soon Take Place
Doxological Postmillennialism*

*The Book of Job: Deepening the Revelation of God's Glory for All Time
An Ironic Theodicy*

*The Epistle to the Romans:
The Righteousness of God Revealed from Faith to Faith
The Gospel According to St. Paul*

*The Biblical Worldview: Creation, Fall, Redemption
Genesis 1–3: Scripture in Organic Seed Form*

The

WESTMINSTER SHORTER *and* LARGER CATECHISMS

A Doxological Understanding

SURRENDRA GANGADEAN

A DIVISION OF THE LOGOS FOUNDATION

Phoenix, Arizona

The Westminster Shorter and Larger Catechisms: A Doxological Understanding

Copyright © 1993, 2023 Surrendra Gangadean

Logos Papers Press 2023
Phoenix, Arizona
logospaperspress.com
thelogosfoundation.org

Printed in the United States of America

Cover Design: Beth Ellen Nagle
Typesetting: Matthew P. Hicks & Brian J. Phelps
Front Cover Image: Jovannig/stock.adobe.com
Back Cover Image: Jankost/stock.adobe.com

Library of Congress Cataloging-in-Publication Data pending

Gangadean, Surrendra, 1943–2022.
    The Westminster shorter and larger catechisms: a doxological understanding
    Includes bibliographical references and footnotes.
    ISBN 979-8-9867472-8-6 (hardcover)
    ISBN 979-8-9867472-0-0 (paperback)
    ISBN 979-8-9867472-9-3 (e-book)

1. Westminster Standards 2. Theology—Westminster Shorter Catechism 3. Theology—Westminster Larger Catechism 4. Historic Christianity 5. Theology—Doxological I. Title

Ad Majorem Dei Gloriam!

For the Greater Glory of God

CONTENTS

Editor's Preface   xi

The Westminster Assembly: The Doxological Focus on the Glory
of God   xv

Introduction: The Westminster Confession of Faith, Its Relation to
Other Creeds, and Levels of Understanding   xvii

THE SHORTER CATECHISM

Chapter 1: Man's Chief End and the Word of God   3
     (Questions 1-3)

Chapter 2: God and His Decrees   9
     (Questions 4-8)

Chapter 3: Creation and Providence   15
     (Questions 9-12)

Chapter 4: The Fall of Man   21
     (Questions 13-19)

Chapter 5: The Covenant of Grace and the Person and Work
     of Christ   29
     (Questions 20-28)

Chapter 6: The Benefits of Christ's Work   39
     (Questions 29-38)

Chapter 7: The Moral Law: The Rule of Our Obedience   51
     (Questions 39-42)

Chapter 8: Preface and Commandments 1-4: Our Duty to God   55
     (Questions 43-62)

Chapter 9: Commandments 5-10: Our Duty to Man   69
     (Questions 63-81)

Chapter 10: Our Fallen Condition and the Consequence of Sin   81
     (Questions 82-84)

Chapter 11: Faith, Repentance, and the Ordinary Means
  of Salvation   83
  (Questions 85-88)

Chapter 12: Ordinary Means of Salvation: The Word of God   87
  (Questions 89-90)

Chapter 13: Ordinary Means of Salvation: The Sacraments   91
  (Questions 91-97)

Chapter 14: Ordinary Means of Salvation: Prayer   97
  (Questions 98-107)

THE LARGER CATECHISM

Chapter 15: Man's Chief End and the Word of God   109
  (Questions 1-6)

Chapter 16: God and His Decrees   119
  (Questions 7-14)

Chapter 17: Creation and Providence   131
  (Questions 15-20)

Chapter 18: The Fall of Man   141
  (Questions 21-29)

Chapter 19: The Covenant of Grace and the Person and Work
  of Christ   153
  (Questions 30-56)

Chapter 20: The Benefits of Christ's Work   179
  (Questions 57-90)

Chapter 21: The Moral Law: The Rule of Our Obedience   215
  (Questions 91-100)

Chapter 22: Preface and Commandments 1-4: Our Duty to God   227
  (Questions 101-121)

Chapter 23: Commandments 5-10: Our Duty to Man   247
  (Questions 122-148)

Chapter 24: Our Fallen Condition and the Consequence of Sin   269
  (Questions 149-152)

Chapter 25: Faith, Repentance, and the Ordinary Means
        of Salvation   273
        (Questions 153-154)

Chapter 26: Ordinary Means of Salvation: The Word of God   275
        (Questions 155-160)

Chapter 27: Ordinary Means of Salvation: The Sacraments   281
        (Questions 161-177)

Chapter 28: Ordinary Means of Salvation: Prayer   295
        (Questions 178-196)

APPENDICES

Appendix 1: The Distinctives of Westminster Fellowship   313

Appendix 2: The Doxological Focus of the Westminster
        Standards   315

Appendix 3: Historical Foundation:
        The Work of the Holy Spirit Leading the Church
        Into All Truth   317

Appendix 4: The Goal of the Knowledge of God   321

Appendix 5: Rational Presuppositionalism:
        Critically Examining Assumptions for Meaning   327

Appendix 6: The Clarity of General Revelation:
        God's Eternal Power and Divine Nature, and the
        Moral Law   333

Appendix 7: The Noetic Effect of Sin:
        The Effect of Moral Evil on the Mind of Man   337

Appendix 8: Postmillennial Eschatology:
        The Earth Shall Be Full of the Knowledge of God   345

Appendix 9: The Regulative Principle of Worship:
        According to the Revealed Will of God   351

Appendix 10: Discipleship at Westminster Fellowship   353

Appendix 11: Membership and Baptismal Vows   355

About the Author   357

EDITOR'S PREFACE

D R. SURRENDRA GANGADEAN (1943–2022), professor, pastor, husband, father, mentor, friend, and builder, was a giant in the faith, a Philosopher among philosophers, and a Theologian among theologians. He spent a lifetime refining the foundation for philosophy and theology and Historic Christianity. By recognizing the foundation, he was able to name the errors in the history of ideas due to the failure to have laid and built upon that sure foundation. He taught in the college classroom for 45 years, the seminary for over 25 years, and from the pulpit for almost 30 years. He taught Introduction to Philosophy, Logic, Ethics, Philosophy of Religion, Eastern Religions, World Religions, Introduction to Christianity, Introduction to Humanities, Philosophy of Art, The Great Books, Philosophical Theology, Biblical Worldview, Biblical History, Church History, Systematic Theology, Biblical Hermeneutics, and Existential Hermeneutics. In each of his encounters with notable thinkers and with his students, Dr. Gangadean heard, understood, and took intellectual challenges seriously. There was no known basic challenge he did not work through—first for himself, then with others in much discussion, and then in his teaching and writing. He was tenacious in going after a basic dispute or challenge, finding the assumptions underlying the challenge, and then attempting to respond and resolve the problem.

The Westminster Shorter and Larger Catechisms: A Doxological Understanding is an example of Dr. Gangadean's incisive analysis, which through clarity and economy of words, provides the most needed insights to understand, defend, and advance the faith. In writing a study guide for the Catechisms, Dr. Gangadean focused primarily on those doctrines that have been challenged since their formulation at the Westminster Assembly (1643–1648). Modernity, in its quest for universal knowledge claims, questioned 1) the relation between faith and reason, 2) the knowability of God and the proofs for God's existence, 3) the goodness of God in the face of evil, 4) the doctrine of original sin, 5) the justice of God, and 6) the justification for exclusivist claims of Christianity. This work is a much-needed response to these pressing challenges.

Other study guides have been written on the Catechisms, but they have yet to identify the doxological focus of the Westminster Standards to provide a comprehensive response. Understanding of the Reformed Faith is fourfold: traditional, soteriological, worldview, and doxological. Only the doxological understanding incorporates the assumptions and doctrines required to formulate answers that take into account the persistent and cumulative effect of challenges to the coherence of the faith since the rise of the Modern world. The doxological understanding affirms the doctrine of the clarity of general revelation and the inexcusability of unbelief (WCF 1.1), the use of reason (the light of nature and good and necessary consequences) to understand general and special revelation (1.1, 1.6), the doxological focus on the knowledge of the glory of God (SCQ. 1, 101; WCF 4.1, 5.1), divine sovereignty in creation–fall–redemption, and the law of God for all of life. Readers that engage diligently with this work will be able to trace how these assumptions and doctrines are woven systematically into every response. The concern for consistency in thought and analysis permeates Dr. Gangadean's work, and this study guide is no exception.

Here, the reader will find the truths of the Reformed Faith explained in their utmost clarity. The reader is spared lengthy expositions that often obscure and burden rather than illuminate. Instead, an engaging, sharp, and precise explanation challenges the reader to trace and uncover the use of reason through good and necessary consequences. Dr. Gangadean wrote increasingly succinctly; he intended to express depth of meaning with the brevity of words. He referred to this approach as "sutra style," which is the style of writing displayed in this work.

Dr. Gangadean wrote the Shorter Catechism portion of this work for the congregants at Westminster Fellowship in 1993–1994. His desire to see the continual growth of those under his care compelled him to write a study guide incorporating the doxological understanding to prepare God's people for works of service in the kingdom. Inspired by Dr. Gangadean's subsequent contributions, The Logos Foundation Editorial Board completed the Larger Catechism study guide in 2022 by using his other writings, sermons, and lectures to formulate a companion study guide to the Shorter Catechism. The Editorial Board makes no claim of originality. We desire to convey our understanding of the quality and content Dr. Gangadean taught us over the years. Any inaccuracies or errors are our sole responsibility. Eleven appendices were added to assist the reader in understanding the doctrines entailed in the Westminster Standards. They can be read before the main work or consulted throughout.

In addition to the Shorter and Larger Catechisms, a study guide of The Westminster Confession of Faith will be published to complement the doxological understanding of the Westminster Standards. The increasing number of works made available from Dr. Gangadean will shed light on his systematic, presuppositional, cumulative, and comprehensive approach to doctrine and life. These works, whether in philosophy, theology, or the humanities, are complementary, for they are written from the same methodology, assumptions, and the goal of taking thoughts captive for the glory of God.

—THE LOGOS FOUNDATION
EDITORIAL BOARD
Phoenix, Arizona
December 2022

THE WESTMINSTER ASSEMBLY
The Doxological Focus on the Glory of God

THE REFORMATION (1517–1648) ATTEMPTED to restore the Church to the Historic Christian Faith based upon the historically cumulative insight of earlier Church councils. It specifically responded to the challenges of sacramentalism and synergism addressed in the Councils of Jerusalem and Orange.

The Westminster Confession of Faith (WCF) built upon earlier creeds of the Reformation: Augsburg (Lutheran), Thirty-Nine Articles (Anglican), Belgic (French), Helvetic (Swiss), Heidelberg (German), and Dort (Dutch). It is the last and most conscious and consistent creed of the Reformation and of Church history.

The Westminster Standards (WCF and its Catechisms) affirm the clarity of general revelation and the inexcusability of unbelief,[1] the use of reason (the light of nature and good and necessary consequences) to understand general and special revelation,[2] the doxological focus on the knowledge of the glory of God,[3] divine sovereignty in creation–fall–redemption, and the law of God for all of life.

Reformation soteriology has been summed up in the *ordo salutis*—the order of the application of redemption: effectual calling (regeneration), conversion (repentance and faith), justification (based on Christ's righteousness received by faith alone), adoption (having all the privileges of children of God), sanctification (being made holy through knowing the truth), and glorification (the removal of all sin at death and the removal of death by the resurrection of the body).

In response to the challenge of Arminian semi-Pelagianism at Dort, WCF affirmed (from Dort) the doctrines of Total Depravity, Unconditional Election, Limited Atonement, Irresistible Grace, and Perseverance of the Saints.

---

1. *Westminster Confession of Faith 1.1.*

2. *WCF 1.1, 1.6.*

3. *Westminster Shorter Catechism Questions 1, 101; WCF 4.1, 5.1.*

The spirit of the theology of the Reformation has been summed up in the affirmation of the Five Solas: *Sola Scriptura* (by Scripture alone), *Sola Fide* (by faith alone), *Sola Gratia* (by grace alone), *Solus Christus* (by Christ alone), and *Soli Deo Gloria* (for the glory of God alone).

Uncritically held assumptions remain in the Church and have been the source of divisions in the Church, which have scandalized the world. The Church must acknowledge the nature of the spiritual warfare between belief and unbelief present at every level, enter into the process of much discussion by which the Holy Spirit leads the Church into all truth, and take every thought captive raised up against the knowledge of God from unbelief, both in the Church and in the world.

INTRODUCTION

The Westminster Confession of Faith,
Its Relation to Other Creeds,
and Levels of Understanding

WHAT IS A CONFESSION OF FAITH?

A *CONFESSION OF FAITH* IS A SUMMARY OF WHAT the pastor-teachers[1] have achieved in understanding the Scriptures in light of the challenges raised to the Church in history. The first of these challenges occurred in Acts 15, when Jewish believers raised questions about how we are to be saved in light of the transition from the Old to the New Testament. In response to this challenge, the pastor-teachers, along with the apostles, gathered together, and after much discussion, came to an agreement, which was sent out to the Church.[2] The process of much discussion by pastor-teachers is the ordinary way the Church grows in its understanding of doctrine and achieves the unity of the faith.

Today the Church is badly divided, indicating that it has not built on the work of the pastor-teachers in the past. In studying the work of the Westminster Divines, we can grow in our understanding of challenges that have been answered and of those that remain. Within Christendom, the three major denominational differences are Roman Catholicism, Eastern Orthodoxy, and Protestantism. Within each of

---

1. By pastor-teachers is meant the leaders of the Christian Faith who have engaged with the most pressing theological issues in the history of the Church. They have served as the instrument of the Holy Spirit to respond to challenges of the Faith. *So Christ himself gave the apostles, the prophets, the evangelists, the pastors and teachers, to equip his people for works of service, so that the body of Christ may be built up until we all reach unity in the faith and in the knowledge of the Son of God and become mature, attaining to the whole measure of the fullness of Christ* (Ephesians 4:11-13). The progress of the Faith in Church history is not merely the contributions of great men, but the work of the Holy Spirit working through men through the process of much discussion. All those involved are counted among the pastor-teachers.

2. *Acts 15:23-31.*

these there are many variations. The extent and depth of the divisions within the body should call us to engage more thoughtfully with the content of the Westminster Assembly. We must keep as a constant in our minds that in its statements, the Westminster Confession of Faith is either speaking positively in favor of a view or objecting to a challenge. The Confession, along with the accompanying Shorter and Larger Catechisms (together, The Westminster Standards), is the high-water mark of the Historic Christian Faith because it responded to all the relevant challenges up to its writing (1648). A thoughtful study of the Standards requires that we penetrate the material at the level of challenges and responses to the Faith.

It is the Lord's intention that the Church respond to challenges, through the process of much discussion by the pastor-teachers, as the ordinary means by which it grows in its understanding of the Faith and that by which fullness of the truth is to be attained. Our Lord said that he would "send the Holy Spirit to lead the Church into all truth."[3] As seen in Acts 15, it is attested that "it seemed good to the Holy Spirit and to us."[4] This is a paradigm example of how the Holy Spirit leads the Church into all truth.

Ordinary means are the God-ordained means to exercise dominion over an area of life or discipline. Ordinary means entail making use of the means provided by God to proceed in wisdom. Building on the historically cumulative insight achieved in Church history, through the work of the pastor-teachers, in response to challenges, is the God-ordained way to attain to maturity, fruitfulness, unity, and fullness in Christ.[5] If our goal in understanding the Faith is doxological, to give all glory to God, as opposed to merely soteriological (centered on salvation—in the minimal sense of justification, so that we may go to heaven), then we will see the need to become established in the Faith in its full sense of the term,[6] to attain to the full measure of the stature of Christ.[7] The councils and creeds of the Church that are consistent with

---

3. *John 16:13.*

4. *Acts 15:28.*

5. *Ephesians 4:11-13*; Surrendra Gangadean, "Paper No. 54: From Foundation to Fullness: A Biblical Worldview for Maturity, Fruitfulness, Unity, and Fullness," in *The Logos Papers: To Make the Logos Known* (Phoenix: Logos Papers Press, 2022).

6. Gangadean, "Paper No. 98: Faith and the Word of God: The Object of Faith," in *The Logos Papers.*

7. *Ephesians 4:13.*

the truth of God are the work of the Holy Spirit leading the Church into all truth—apart from this, we cannot expect to attain maturity in the Historic Christian Faith. In light of this context, it is fitting and proper that it is asked: what is our understanding of the Westminster Confession of Faith and Catechisms? And what is our understanding of the work of the Holy Spirit leading the Church into all truth up to the development of the Westminster Standards (1648)? The Standards is a comprehensive work that has built on what has come before and summarizes all that is true in previous councils and creeds. It is an enduring work that prepares us to address subsequent challenges in the modern world.[8]

RELATION OF THE WESTMINSTER CONFESSION TO PRECEDING CREEDS

A *creed* is a statement of belief, from the Latin word *credo*, which means, "I believe." The word *confession* is used synonymously with *creed*. The Westminster Confession of Faith and the Shorter and Larger Catechisms were written at the end of the Reformation period (1643–1648), which also coincided with the beginning of the Modern period (1648–1950). In summing up the most prominent challenges that came into the Church up to that time, they particularly addressed the challenge of the sacramental system of the Roman Catholic Church of Medieval Europe. Although the Westminster Assembly faithfully answered the challenges of its time, many more significant challenges have developed since (in 370+ years), from both Modernity (1648–1950) and Postmodernity (1950–present),[9] which the Church has yet to (in council or creed) meaningfully answer (systematically and comprehensively). Accordingly, the WCF is the last of the creeds and there is no other since that time that has attained to the lofty heights, in its degree of excellence, precision, and depth of thought, reached by the WCF.[10] Subsequent creeds,

---

8. Gangadean, "Paper No. 58: The Spiritual War (Part I): On the State of the Church and the World," in *The Logos Papers.*

9. Gangadean, "Paper No. 16: The Historic Christian Faith: The Holy Spirit Guides the Church into All Truth," in *The Logos Papers.*

10. Since the Westminster Confession of Faith is the highest expression of Historic Christianity, the founding pastor of Westminster Fellowship, Surrendra Gangadean, adopted the WCF as the doctrinal basis for WF. See Appendices 1–3 for a fuller explanation of the distinctives of WF.

such as The London Baptist Confession of 1689, used the majority of the content of the WCF, but set aside important components instead of building on it. The exclusion of these elements from the WCF has served as a source of division in the Reformed Faith since.[11]

The content of the confessions and creeds provide a cumulative development of the Historic Christian Faith. Each one responded to the most pressing challenges that divided the Faith in their time. As the gospel spread worldwide, believers had to contend with competing worldviews and faulty assumptions used to dilute, distort, and undermine the truth of the gospel. Contending with unbelief gave rise to the creeds and councils that constitute the Holy Catholic and Apostolic Faith. It is important that before addressing the content of the Westminster Shorter and Larger Catechisms, we gain an understanding of the main doctrines formulated in the creeds and councils that preceded the Westminster Standards. The creeds and confessions explained below

---

11. The London Baptist Confession of 1689 retained much of the WCF, yet proceeded to replace two significant epistemic statements. One deals with the relationship between general revelation (GR) and special revelation (SR), and the other speaks about the use of reason in interpreting the Scriptures. WCF 1.1 begins by affirming the clarity of general revelation (cGR) and proceeds to explain the need for Scriptures to provide knowledge of God's will for redemption. The WCF moves from GR to SR, thus setting the context for the need for redemption from the failure to know God in the created order. The Baptist Confession reverses the order and gives an implied primacy to SR over GR. The changed statement reads as follows: *"The Holy Scripture is the only sufficient, certain, and infallible rule of all saving knowledge, faith, and obedience, although the light of nature, and the works of creation and providence do so far manifest the goodness, wisdom, and power of God, as to leave men inexcusable"* (BC 1.1). This change reverses the logical and historical order acknowledged in the WCF. This move marks the tendency in theology, since the Baptist Confession, to appeal to SR as the more reliable source of knowledge, which by implication is seen as more clear and more certain than GR. As the challenges of the modern world mount, the Church has increasingly appealed to SR for its answers, yet that comes at the cost of neglecting GR and the clarity of God's existence contained therein.

The second statement regards the use of reason to interpret SR. The original statement in the WCF reads as follows: *"The whole counsel of God concerning all things necessary for His own glory, man's salvation, faith, and life, is either expressly set down in Scripture, or by good and necessary consequence may be deduced from Scripture"* (WCF 1.6). It was changed into the following: *"The whole counsel of God concerning everything essential for his own glory and man's salvation, faith, and life is either explicitly stated or by necessary inference contained in the Holy Scriptures."* (BC 1.6). The change from "good and necessary consequences" to "necessary inference" restrains interpretation to a more literal and textual basis. The larger and broader context of cGR in which Scripture is given is set aside for a SR context exclusively. "Good and necessary consequences" is an application of presuppositional thinking. In it, the less basic ideas are interpreted in light of the more basic ones. In the context of hermeneutics, the context of cGR is logically and historically prior to SR and, therefore, it is presupposed in the content transmitted in SR. As such, it must not be excluded.

have positively strengthened the formulation of the Faith; together, they constitute the Holy Catholic and Apostolic Faith.[12]

Historic Christianity makes explicit the teaching of Scripture and its practice in liturgy; it cannot be used to set aside the truth from either general revelation or from Scripture, which are more basic. Among the several councils in the history of the Church, not all the content in the confessions and creeds has undergone the same degree of discussion. Some theological topics were central, such as the Trinity in Nicea or the Incarnation in Chalcedon, and some related topics were not yet challenged at that time in history; hence, less attention was given to them. And therefore, their formulation does not carry the same weight as the most debated parts do. In other words, not everything contained in every creed or council underwent the process of much discussion. Some assumptions were not subject to intellectual scrutiny at that time in history. As such, those parts of a confession do not have the same degree of authority as compared to those portions that did undergo the process of much discussion. Theological topics that have not undergone much discussion allow for uncritically held assumptions to persist. Those assumptions are later, in the course of history, brought under scrutiny and give rise to the need to formulate a response that takes into account the intellectual challenges that have arisen in God's providence. Historic Christianity continues to respond to challenges as God makes them increasingly relevant in history. This is part of the process of the Holy Spirit leading the Church into all truth; the Church is to take every thought captive that raises itself up against the knowledge of God and make them subject unto Christ.[13]

The progress attained through creeds and councils remains. The fundamental truths reached and settled after much discussion are foundational to the Faith. Later confessions cannot set aside what has been agreed upon in Historic Christianity without addressing prior deliberation.[14] We are morally responsible for not lightly and thoughtlessly disregarding the work of God accomplished in history through the pastor-teachers. We should think long and hard (critically) before calling into question what has been agreed upon through the process

---

12. Gangadean, "Paper No. 16: The Historic Christian Faith: The Holy Spirit Guides the Church into All Truth," in *The Logos Papers*.

13. *2 Corinthians 10:4-5*.

14. Gangadean, "Paper No. 113: Historic Christianity: Contrasted to Popular Christianity," in *The Logos Papers*.

of much discussion. Historic Christianity includes more than the early councils and creeds listed below, but they contain the fundamental teachings, so they constitute building blocks of momentous importance.

The First Council at Jerusalem: Sacrament and Salvation

The first Church Council at Jerusalem (A.D. 51) dealt with the question of sacrament and salvation: is circumcision necessary for salvation? Against the teaching that one must be circumcised and obey the law to be saved, the Council answered: "We gave no such command."[15] Underlying this conflict was the error of literalism. Hebraic literalism, not distinguishing sign and reality, led to ceremonial legalism and has been a major stumbling block to faith past and present.[16] This council rejected the insistence that sacraments are necessary for salvation, and the Historic Christian Faith affirms this teaching.

The Apostles' Creed: Gnosticism and Dualism

The Apostles' Creed (A.D. 180) summarizes the Church's response to the challenge to the truth from the Greek worldview of epistemological gnosticism[17] (vs. the clarity of general revelation), metaphysical dualism (both matter and spirit are eternal), and ethical dualism (separating the soul from the hindrances of the body). Against metaphysical dualism, the Church affirms God as Creator of heaven and earth. God in the flesh (the Incarnation) is real, not apparent, and bodily existence continues forever (in the resurrection).

The Nicene Creed: The Trinity

At Nicea (A.D. 325), the Church summarized its understanding that God is one over and against misunderstanding, which has survived in several forms throughout history (Arianism, Socinianism, Deism, Unitarianism, Judaism, and Islam). What is one is a unity, and unity is

---

15. *Acts 15:24.*

16. Gangadean, "Paper No. 60: The Spiritual War (Part II): Church Councils and Settling Current Divisions in the Church," in *The Logos Papers*; Surrendra Gangadean, *The Westminster Confession of Faith: A Doxological Understanding* (Phoenix: Logos Papers Press, 2023). See Question 8.

17. Epistemological gnosticism is the belief that knowledge is only for some, not all human beings. The nature of this knowledge is esoteric rather than knowledge about the basic things regarding God and man, and good and evil.

a unity of diversity. God the Most High is a unity of the highest reality, that of Persons. "In the unity of the Godhead there be three persons, of one substance, power, and eternity: God the Father, God the Son, and God the Holy Ghost: the Father is of none, neither begotten, nor proceeding; the Son is eternally begotten of the Father; the Holy Ghost eternally proceeding from the Father and the Son."[18]

The Council of Carthage: The Canon of the New Testament Scripture

At the Council of Carthage (A.D. 397), the Church identified all the books and only the books that constitute the Scripture of the New Testament, the Word of God written, the rule of faith and life for all Christians. Scripture in every age must be spoken in the name of God (consistent with clear general revelation and with any prior special revelation). Scripture, as redemptive revelation, is given only by God, and being given by God, is kept pure and entire by God in every age so that nothing is to be added to it or taken away from it, contrary to all contradictory claims. Both the Old and New Testaments were received by the testimony of the Church.

The Council of Chalcedon: Christ Is God and Man

At the Council of Chalcedon (A.D. 451), the Church affirmed the doctrine of Christ as fully God and fully man. In the Incarnation, "two whole, perfect, and distinct natures, the Godhead and the manhood, were inseparably joined together in one person, without conversion, composition, or confusion."[19] The doctrine of Christ as God and man affects every aspect of understanding the person and work of Christ as Creator of all things, upholder of all things, redeemer of all things, and heir of all things.[20]

The Council of Orange: Sin and Salvation

At the Council of Orange (A.D. 529), the Church affirmed the doctrine of sin (man is fallen in Adam) and salvation (man is saved by grace) in

---

18. *WCF 2.3.*

19. *WCF 8.2.*

20. *Hebrews 1:1-3.*

response to Pelagian and semi-Pelagian error. The Church affirmed the distinction of liberty and ability in the four-fold state of man: 1) before the Fall, it was possible to sin; 2) after the Fall, it is not possible not to sin; 3) after regeneration, it is possible not to sin; 4) in man's glorified state, it is not possible to sin. While ability changes, liberty (doing what I want) does not change. Grace is given by God, sovereignly, as he wills. Grace is not dependent on man's willing, but by grace man is made willing. All acts by which we are saved—whether we "believe, will, desire, strive, labor, pray, watch, study, seek, ask, or knock"[21]—are by grace, the gift of God, not of ourselves, so that no man can boast.

THE FIVE SOLAS: Summary of the Reformation Principles

The Five Solas were derived from the creeds of the Reformation: The Westminster Confession built upon Augsburg (Lutheran), Thirty-Nine Articles (Anglican), Belgic (French), Helvetic (Swiss), Heidelberg (German), and Dort (Dutch).

Sola Scriptura: The Authority for Faith Is Scripture Alone

The authority of Scripture as special revelation is opposed to the authority of all other forms of special revelation (including the opinions of men or of private spirits). *Sola Scriptura* (SS) is not opposed to the use of reason in making good and necessary consequences, but assumes it. SS is not opposed to the clarity of general revelation, but assumes it. SS is not opposed to historically cumulative insight, the work of the Holy Spirit leading the Church into all truth, summed up in its creeds and confessions/councils, but anticipates it. SS requires all of the Scriptures and only the Scriptures, understood with good and necessary consequences, to be used in interpreting the Scriptures. Interpretation, therefore, is contextual, not literal or allegorical (in light of foreign assumptions).[22]

---

21. *Council of Orange, Canon 6.*

22. By foreign assumptions is meant the use of assumptions that are inconsistent with the biblical worldview of creation-fall-redemption, along with related and presupposed doctrines and beliefs.

Sola Fide: Justification Is by Faith Alone

Justification is based on a person having righteousness. This righteousness is from Christ, whose righteousness is perfect and complete, and not from oneself. Christ's righteousness is imputed to the believer. This act of imputation assumes that Adam's sin is imputed to all men and that man's sin is imputed to Christ. The righteousness of Christ is received by faith alone. Justification is not sanctification; imputation of righteousness is not infusion of righteousness; forgiveness of sin is not cleansing from sin, but cleansing flows from forgiveness.

Sola Gratia: Salvation Is by Grace Alone

Salvation is by grace alone, from beginning to end, without any admixture of human works. Both faith and works that glorify God are by grace. The grace of salvation is sovereignly bestowed, by God's predestination, apart from any condition in the person. The context of the bestowal of grace is summed up in the acronym TULIP.[23] In the order of application of redemption (*ordo salutis*), God's act of effectual calling (regeneration) precedes man's conversion (repentance and faith). Predestination is not opposed to but upholds freedom—properly understood as liberty to do what one desires, rather than ability to do otherwise.

Solus Christus: Salvation Is by Christ Alone

Salvation is through Christ alone, and not through Christ and the Church as mediator of grace. Salvation is through Christ alone and not through Christ and the merits or intercession or mediation of any other. Salvation is through Christ alone and not through Christ and any practice of penance in this life or in the next or through any supposed good deeds. Salvation is through Christ alone and not apart from Christ; there is no salvation without atonement, or without the vicarious atonement of Christ. Salvation is through Christ alone and in this life alone, after which is the final judgment, which vindicates the divine justice in judging man in unbelief.

---

23. Gangadean, "Paper No. 18: Salvation by Grace: The Sovereignty of God in the Salvation of Man" in *The Logos Papers*.

Soli Deo Gloria: All of Life Is for the Glory of God Alone

God's glory, which is intrinsic in his being, cannot be added to but is only manifest in, by, unto, and upon all his creatures.[24] God manifests his glory in all his works of creation and providence, which purpose is extended to the Fall of man.[25] Man's chief end is to glorify and enjoy God in all that by which he makes himself known, in all his works of creation and providence.[26] The purpose of the work of dominion in the creation mandate and of the work of Christ in making disciples of all nations is the knowledge of God, which is eternal life.[27] The outcome of Christ's work through the Church is that the earth will be filled with the knowledge of the Lord as the waters cover the sea.[28]

THE SYNOD OF DORT: The Sovereignty of God in the Salvation of Man

TULIP is an acronym for the five points addressed in the Canons of Dort.

Total Depravity

Sin affects the whole (total) heart of man so that no one seeks God, no one understands, and no one is righteous.[29] Sin (moral evil) has become rooted in self-deception and self-justification so that the curse of toil and strife, and old age, sickness, and death was imposed by God to restrain, recall from, and remove moral evil in man.[30] While sin is total in extent, sin varies in degrees (men are more or less conscious and consistent in their unbelief), and it may increase to ever-deeper depravity. The sin of not seeking results in culpable ignorance of what is clear about God and the moral law. Inconsistencies within one's understanding result in inconsistencies within one's feelings and within one's actions. The

---

24. *WCF 2.2.*

25. *WCF 4.1, 5.1, 6.1.*

26. *SCQ. 1, 101; WCF 4.1, 5.1.*

27. *Genesis 1:28; Matthew 28:20; John 17:3.*

28. *Isaiah 11:9.*

29. *Romans 3:10-11.*

30. *Genesis 3.*

understanding of fallen man (learned or unlearned) is deficient so that it is knowing the truth that makes one holy and sets one free.[31]

Unconditional Election

Election unto salvation is not based on any condition (past, present, or future) in man, but wholly on God's purpose, which is, in wisdom, to make his glory known. Election unto salvation is not apart from or against secondary causes such as seeking and understanding or repentance and faith; predestination is not of ends without means, but of both ends and means. Election of men presupposes the Fall (infralapsarianism) either to leave one in sin and death or to restore one to life and righteousness. Unconditional election is not arbitrary regarding justice; spiritual death is always due to sin, and mercy never sets aside justice, but satisfies justice through vicarious atonement by Jesus Christ. God has mercy on whom he chooses. Showing mercy to some is not unfair to others; what is unfair is to deny justice to any.

Limited Atonement

The intent and effect of Christ's atonement makes salvation actual for the elect, not merely possible for all, but actual for none. It is the revealed will of God that no one *should* sin and that all who sin *should* repent of sin and come to salvation. It is the decreed will of God to *permit* sin and the persistence of some in sin against calls to repentance. It is the decreed will of God (by promise) that good *will* overcome evil, that all nations *will* be blessed, that all nations *will* be discipled, that the earth *will* be filled with the knowledge of the Lord as the waters cover the sea.[32] It is by the decree of God that the limit of atonement *does* include the salvation of the whole world as the kingdom of God grows to its fullness. The decree of God to save the world reveals the length, breadth, depth, and height of the love of God for mankind."[33]

---

31. *John 17:17; 8:32.*

32. *Isaiah 11:9.*

33. *John 3:16; Ephesians 2:14-21.*

Irresistible Grace

The grace of salvation is prevenient to the time of one's salvation; it operates to preserve and prepare a person for salvation. Salvation begins with effectual calling in which a person is raised from spiritual death to life, which is to be regenerated by spiritual rebirth or to be recreated as a new creature in Christ. Regeneration is wholly of God and not from man, either positively (by man's will cooperating with God's will) or negatively (by man's will not resisting God's will). By regeneration, a person is made both willing and able to seek and to understand and to do the will of God so that regeneration precedes and *naturally* results in repentance and faith. The grace of salvation continues after regeneration throughout one's life to make a person willing and able to know and do the will of God.

Perseverance of the Saints

Those who are effectually called (regenerated) are kept by the power of God unto salvation. A person who is outwardly called (but not effectually called) may fall away from their profession of faith. A person who is effectually called may fall away for a time or be left to walk in darkness, but is never utterly destitute of the seed of God.[34] Assurance of salvation is not of the essence of faith; a true believer may lack assurance but may through the right use of ordinary means attain assurance.[35] Assurance based on false teaching or practice is presumptuous. Perseverance of believers is not *regardless* of sin, but a *perseverance* and growth in faith and righteousness.

LEVELS OF UNDERSTANDING
THE REFORMED FAITH

Four distinct levels of commitment to the Reformed Faith, from less to more deeply founded, are identified below in order that believers might become more conscious and consistent in understanding and seeing the need for a deeper foundation for the Historic Christian Faith.

---

34. *WCF 18.4.*

35. *WCF 18.3.*

1. *Traditional Reformed:* this level includes those brought up in Reformed churches as covenant children, having had exposure to the Reformed teaching, and who absorbed it by an acquaintance, not by explicitly examining the Reformed Faith. In other words, *Traditional Reformed* is a minimal level attained by upbringing, not thorough reflection. Many hold to the WCF in this way, in terms of traditional exposure to the content, and remain there. Although this is how some come to the Reformed Faith, one should go beyond this level of understanding.

2. *Soteriological Reformed:* this level emphasizes salvation and includes those who call themselves five-point Calvinists (TULIP). They hold to the *ordo salutis* (the order of application of salvation) and the Five Solas of the Reformation (*Sola Scriptura, Sola Fide, Sola Gratia, Solus Christus, Soli Deo Gloria*). This is a common way many become involved with the Reformed Faith as it centers primarily on the doctrine of salvation. While this understanding is necessary for our faith, its scope does not extend to the biblical worldview and the moral law as applied to culture.

3. *Worldview Reformed:* this level is more invested in the cultural implications of Reformed theology and is connected with the work of Abraham Kuyper's *Lectures on Calvinism.* It is a distinct level from *Soteriological Reformed* as it seeks to implement the ethical implications of the biblical worldview (creation–fall–redemption) to culture and its institutions and focuses on kingdom living. In the words of Abraham Kuyper, "there is not a square inch in the whole domain of our human existence over which Christ, who is Sovereign over all, does not cry: Mine!"[36] *Worldview Reformed* seeks the Lordship of Christ in all areas of life. However, it falls short of the *Doxological Reformed* level as it does not affirm the clarity of God's existence and the goal of filling the earth with the knowledge of God.

4. *Doxological Reformed:* this level is the deepest (most basic) and most comprehensive level of understanding the Reformed Faith. Doxology is giving glory to God. The doxological understanding of Reformed theology focuses on and magnifies the fullness of the knowledge of the

---

36. James D. Bratt, *Abraham Kuyper: A Centennial Reader* (Grand Rapids, MI: William B. Herdmans Publishing Company), 461.

glory of God as stated in Isaiah 11:9: "for the earth shall be full of the knowledge of the Lord as the waters cover the sea." The Westminster Standards emphasize the glory of God and the doxological focus of the Standards draws out the implications of this emphasis for all of life. Several statements from the Standards, taken together, are the basis for a doxological understanding of theology:

Westminster Confession of Faith (WCF) 1.1 emphasizes the clarity of general revelation and the inexcusability of man's unbelief: "Although the light of nature, and the works of creation and providence, do so far *manifest the goodness, wisdom, and power of God*, as to leave men inexcusable . . ."[37]

WCF 2.2 emphasizes the manifestation of God's glory in, by, unto, and upon the created order: "God hath all life, *glory*, goodness, blessedness, in and of himself; and is alone in and unto himself all-sufficient, not standing in need of any creatures which he hath made, nor deriving any glory from them, but only *manifesting His own glory* in, by, unto, and upon them."

WCF 3.3 emphasizes that God decrees all things for the praise of his glory: "By the decree of God, for the manifestation of *His glory*, some men and angels are predestinated unto everlasting life [to the praise of his *glorious* mercy]; and others foreordained to everlasting death [to the praise of his *glorious* justice]."

WCF 4.1 emphasizes that God created to make his glory known: "It pleased God the Father, Son, and Holy Ghost, for the *manifestation of the glory* of His eternal power, wisdom, and goodness, in the beginning, to create or make of nothing the world, and all things therein, whether visible or invisible, in the space of six days, and all very good."

WCF 5.1 emphasizes that God rules to make his glory known: "God, the great Creator of all things, doth uphold, direct, dispose, and govern all creatures, actions, and things, from the greatest even to the least, by His most wise and holy providence, according to His infallible foreknowledge, and the free and immutable counsel of His own will, to the *praise of the glory* of His wisdom, power, justice, goodness, and mercy."

---

37. Emphasis added here and on the following points.

WCF 6.1 emphasizes that God permitted the Fall and sin for his own glory: "Our first parents, being seduced by the subtlety and temptations of Satan, sinned in eating the forbidden fruit. This their sin God was pleased, according to His wise and holy counsel, to permit, having purposed to order it to *His own glory.*"

The doxological focus is further expressed in the Shorter Catechism. The answer to Shorter Catechism Question (SCQ) 1, regarding the chief end of man, is a summary statement of the doxological focus: "Man's chief end is to *glorify God*, and to enjoy him forever."[38]

The answer to SCQ. 46, regarding the First Commandment, emphasizes that we are to worship and glorify God accordingly: "The first commandment requireth us to know and acknowledge God to be the only true God, and our God; and to *worship and glorify* him accordingly."

Finally, the answer to SCQ. 101, regarding the First Petition of the Lord's Prayer, emphasizes that we are to glorify God in all that by which he makes himself known: "In the first petition, which is, *Hallowed be thy name*, we pray that God would enable us and others to *glorify* him in all that whereby he maketh himself known; and that he would dispose all things to his own *glory.*"

The preceding selections from the Confession and the three Shorter Catechism questions unfold the meaning of *Doxological Reformed*. The doxological focus is the most basic and, therefore, fundamental

---

38. Benjamin B. Warfield in his essay, "The First Question of the Westminster Shorter Catechism," draws attention to the doxological aim of this question. He states: "No Catechism begins on a higher plane than the Westminster 'Shorter Catechism.' Its opening question . . . sets the learner at once in his right relation to God. Withdrawing his eyes from himself, even from his own salvation, as the chief object of concern, it fixes them on God and His glory, and bids him seek the highest blessedness in him." He continues, "The Westminster Catechism cuts itself free at once from this entanglement with lower things and begins, as it centers and ends, under the illumination of the vision of God in His glory, to subserve which it finds to be the proper end of human as of all other existence, of salvation as of all other achievements. To it all things exist for God, unto whom as well as from whom all things are; and the great question for each of us accordingly is, How can I glorify God and enjoy him forever?" Warfield further explains that "The peculiarity of this first question and answer of the Westminster Catechisms, it will be seen, is the felicity with which it brings to concise expression the whole Reformed conception of the significance of human life."

understanding of the Westminster Standards, despite not being commonly identified or taught in many Reformed circles. The doctrine of the clarity of God's existence (clearly revealed in and understood from the creation) and the earth being filled with the knowledge of God is distinctive of the doxological level of Reformed theology. The focus/goal of all of human life is to know God and make him known.

—

THE
SHORTER
CATECHISM

—

Chapter 1

———

MAN'S CHIEF END AND
THE WORD OF GOD

QUESTION 1

What is the chief end of man?

Man's chief end is to glorify God, and to enjoy him forever.

1. What is meant by chief end?

The chief end of man means that there is one ultimate purpose to human existence that gives meaning and unity to life.

2. What is it to glorify God?

To glorify God is to know God in all that by which he makes himself known and to make his glory known to others.[1]

3. How does God make his glory known?[2]

God makes his glory known in all his works of creation and providence.[3] Man knows the glory of God through his work of dominion in God's creation.

---

1. *SC Question 46, 101.*

2. Gangadean, "Paper No. 112: Why General Revelation Is Basic in the Christian Worldview," in *The Logos Papers*; "Paper No. 117: Knowing and Making God Known," in *The Logos Papers*.

3. *WCF 4.1, 5.1.*

4. What is it to enjoy God?

To enjoy God is to behold the beauty of the LORD, which knowledge is eternal life.[4]

5. What errors are here to be avoided?

We become divided rather than united if we do not seek man's ultimate end. We become man-centered rather than God-centered if we do not seek to glorify God. We become otherworldly or this-worldly if we do not seek to know God through the work of dominion.

QUESTION 2

What rule has God given to direct us how we may glorify and enjoy him?

The Word of God, which is contained in the scriptures of the Old and New Testaments, is the only rule to direct us how we may glorify and enjoy him.

1. What do the Scriptures teach about the Word of God?[5]

We are taught in the Scriptures that there are seven senses of the Word of God. The Word of God is eternal (In the beginning was the Word);[6] the Word of God is revealed in all men as reason (the life of the Logos was the light of men);[7] the Word of God is revealed in all of his works of creation and providence (the Logos was in the world);[8] the Word of

---

4. *John 17:3*; Gangadean, *The Westminster Confession*. See Question 24; Surrendra Gangadean, *Philosophical Foundation: A Critical Analysis of Basic Beliefs*, Second Edition (Phoenix: Public Philosophy Press, 2022), 208-211.

5. Gangadean, "Paper No. 30: The Word of God: The Logos Is Truth," in *The Logos Papers*; "Paper No. 111: Common Christian Misconceptions About Reason: A Response," in *The Logos Papers*.

6. *John 1:1*.

7. *John 1:4; Psalm 8:5; Romans 1:20; WCF 1.1*.

8. *John 1:10*.

God is revealed in the Scriptures of the Old and New Testaments (He came to his own);[9] the Word of God is incarnate in Jesus Christ (the Word was made flesh);[10] Christ the Lord sends the Spirit to lead the Church into all Truth (He will guide you into all truth);[11] each believer is born again by the living Word of God, and each believer is sanctified by the Truth (Your Word is truth).[12]

2. What is the relation between reason and Scripture?[13]

Reason is the laws of thought, which makes all thought possible. Reason is necessary to understand the Word of God in creation and the Word of God in Scripture. Reason, as the laws of thought, is the self-attesting form of the Word of God.[14]

3. What is the relation between the Word of God in creation and in Scripture?

Creation clearly reveals God's eternal power and divine nature, so that man's unbelief is without excuse.[15] What is Scripture must be consistent

---

9. *John 1:11.*

10. *John 1:14.*

11. *John 16:13; Acts 15; Ephesians 4:10-16.*

12. *1 Peter 1:23; John 17:17.*

13. "THAT it is the right and the duty of all men to exercise their reason in inquiries concerning religion, is a truth so manifest, that it may be presumed there are none who will be disposed to call it in question.

    Without reason there can be no religion; for in every step which we take, in examining the evidences of revelation, in interpreting its meanings or in assenting to its doctrines, the exercise of this faculty is indispensable.

    When the evidences of Christianity are exhibited, an appeal is made to the reason of men for its truth; but all evidence and all argument would be perfectly futile, if reason were not permitted to judge of their force. This noble faculty was certainly given to man to be a guide in religion, as well as in other things. He possesses no other means by which he can form a judgment on any subject, or assent to any truth; and it would be no more absurd to talk of seeing without eyes, than of knowing any thing without reason.

    It is therefore a great mistake to suppose, that religion forbids, or discourages the right use of reason. So far from this, she enjoins it as a duty of high moral obligation, and reproves those who neglect to judge for themselves what is right." Archibald Alexander, *A Brief Outline of the Evidences of the Christian Religion* (Philadelphia, PA: Palala Press), 56.

14. There are several levels of "clear": self-attesting, self-evident, self-referentially absurd, and clear to reason. See Appendix 2, Question 14 in Gangadean, *Philosophical Foundation*, for a fuller exposition of each.

15. *Romans 1:18-20.*

with God's eternal power and divine nature. Scripture, as redemptive revelation given by God, assumes the existence of sin in the denial of clear general revelation.

4. What is the relation between Christ and the Scriptures?

Man, having denied the Word of God in himself, in the creation, and in Scripture, needs God's redemption. The Scriptures reveal God's purpose to redeem man through the work of Christ, who stands in man's place. Jesus Christ is the eternal Word of God incarnate who brings us forgiveness and brings us to the knowledge of God as promised in the Scriptures.

5. How can it be known that Scripture is the Word of God?[16]

Only the Scriptures of the Old and New Testaments are spoken in the name of God because only these Scriptures are consistent with what can be known of God from general revelation. Because of the reality of sin in man, Scripture could not have originated by man, but only by the will of God. The Spirit of God, illumining our minds by reason, enables us to understand the Word of God in creation and in Scripture.

QUESTION 3

What do the Scriptures principally teach?

The Scriptures principally teach, what man is to believe concerning God, and what duty God requires of man.

1. For what purpose were the Scriptures given?[17]

The Scriptures, as redemptive revelation, show how God is both just and merciful to man in sin. They were given to instruct and to correct us in order to prepare us for work through which God is glorified.

---

16. Gangadean, *The Westminster Confession.* See Questions 5-8.

17. Gangadean, "Paper No. 87: Scripture," in *The Logos Papers*; "Paper No. 112: Why General Revelation Is Basic in the Christian Worldview," in *The Logos Papers*.

2. What work is given to man?

From the beginning, man was given the work of dominion,[18] the cultural mandate, through which God is glorified. In Christ, the work is continued in the mission mandate[19] to bring all men to know God.

3. What is the relation between our knowledge of God and our duty?

Knowing God enables us to do our duty, and doing our duty, obeying God's law, enables us to increase in the knowledge of God.

---

18. *Genesis 1:26-28;* Appendix 4.

19. *Matthew 28:18-20.*

Chapter 2

GOD AND

HIS DECREES

QUESTION 4

What is GOD?

God is a Spirit, infinite, eternal, and unchangeable in his being, wisdom, power, holiness, justice, goodness, and truth.

1. How is the knowledge of God's nature possible?

God's nature is known through innate knowledge (by nature we have concepts about the nature of God)[1] and increased through his works of creation and providence.

2. What are the incommunicable attributes of God?[2]

Infinitude, eternality, and unchangeability are attributes of God which cannot be possessed by any creature.

---

1. Here, the concept of *sensus divinitatis* is to be understood as one having an innate sense of the qualities of infinite, eternal, and unchanging, which can only, upon analysis, be applied to God. This is in contrast to the view of a sense of dependence on a higher power or awareness of God as Creator and ruler.

2. Gangadean, *The Westminster Confession*. See Question 13.

3. What are some implications to be derived from the concept of God?

The clarity of general revelation, the sovereignty of God, the timelessness of God, God's omnipresence, and the nature of freedom are implications which we often fail to see.

QUESTION 5

Are there more Gods than one?

There is but one only, the living and true God.

1. What is affirmed in the unity of God?

There is no division within God and all aspects of life are equally under God, in contrast to polytheism.

2. What is a false view of the unity of God?

Unity does not deny diversity within God or affirm that God's being includes all being, in contrast to attributeless pantheism (*Nirguna Brahman*).

3. How are we to understand the oneness of God?

By the oneness of God,[3] we are to understand that both unity and diversity are ultimate in God and in his creation.

---

3. Surrendra Gangadean, *History of Philosophy: A Critical Analysis of Unresolved Disputes* (Phoenix: Public Philosophy Press, 2022), 40; Gangadean, *The Westminster Confession.* See Question 15.

QUESTION 6

How many persons are there in the Godhead?

There are three persons in the Godhead: the Father, the Son, and the Holy Spirit; and these three are one God, the same in substance, equal in power and glory.

1. How is the doctrine of the Trinity known?

The Trinity is known by the great events of the creation, the Incarnation, and Pentecost, and in many other passages throughout Scripture.

2. In what respect are Father, Son, and Holy Spirit equal?

The attributes of deity are affirmed of each person of the Trinity, an ontological trinitarianism (the same in essence).[4] This is set in contrast to various forms of subordination: Monarchianism, Arianism, Unitarianism, Deism, and Islam.

3. In what respects are the three persons different?

Each person of the Trinity has a different function, an economical trinitarianism.[5] There is a distinct order within the Trinity. This is set in contrast to modalism.

---

4. Gangadean, *The Westminster Confession*. See Question 15.

5. Gangadean, *The Westminster Confession*. See Question 15.

QUESTION 7

What are the decrees of God?[6]

The decrees of God are, his eternal purpose, according to the counsel of his will, whereby, for his own glory, he has foreordained whatsoever comes to pass.

1. What is the basis of God's sovereign rule over all?

God is Creator of all that exists and is self-existent and independent of the creation.[7] The creature is not self-existent, but wholly dependent on God for its being and continued existence. Denial of God's sovereignty is rooted in denial of creaturely dependence.

2. What are the common errors in denying God's sovereignty?

1) That ultimately things come about by chance or luck, that there is no plan of God, that if the will is free, it cannot be caused—e.g., in semi-Pelagian and Arminian Christianity, and in some philosophers (Kant and William James vs. Augustine, Luther, and Calvin).

2) That ultimately our lives are fated, that there is no freedom, that the outcome is not affected by our beliefs and desires—e.g., the Greek fates, in Islam, karma, astrology, and in teachers of hard (vs. soft) determinism (Marx and Freud).

3. How are these errors to be avoided?

The guide for life is not the decree of God, but the revealed will of God summed up in the Commandments. We are not to leave things to chance, nor are we to be resigned and fail to use ordinary means.

---

6. Gangadean, *The Westminster Confession*. See Questions 16–21.

7. Gangadean, *History of Philosophy*, 40.

4. What is the extent and purpose of God's decrees?[8]

The decrees extend not only to salvation, but to all that comes to pass; their purpose is for the revelation of God's wisdom, power, justice, and goodness.

QUESTION 8

How does God execute his decrees?[9]

God executes his decrees in the works of creation and providence.

1. How are God's decrees executed through his work of creation?

The decrees of God are not externally imposed upon the creature so as to nullify its nature, but come to expression through the nature of the creature. As God's nature is revealed in what he does, so what the creature does reveals its nature.

2. How are God's decrees executed through his work of providence?

God upholds, directs, disposes, and governs his creatures so that things come to pass according to their natures.

3. Is God bound by the nature of the thing created?

God, in his ordinary providence, makes use of means, yet is free to work above, without, and against them, at his pleasure, which is according to his own nature.

---

8. Gangadean, *The Westminster Confession*. See Question 16.

9. Gangadean, *The Westminster Confession*. See Questions 17-21.

Chapter 3

___

CREATION AND PROVIDENCE

QUESTION 9

What is the work of creation?

The work of creation is, God making all things of nothing, by the word of his power, in the space of six days, and all very good.

1. What is creation *ex nihilo*?[1]

By the Word of God, the substance of the universe and all that is in it came into being. This is set in contrast to contemporary naturalism, which claims the universe is self-existing,[2] dualism which claims matter eternally co-exists with spirit as in Platonic thought,[3] and spiritual monism of Eastern mysticism, which claims the world is unreal or a manifestation of God.[4]

---

1. Gangadean, *Philosophical Foundation*, 141-143; Gangadean, "Paper No. 142: The Biblical Worldview (Part II): Biblical Cosmology: Creation *Ex Nihilo*," in *The Logos Papers*; Gangadean, *The Westminster Confession*. See Question 22.

2. Gangadean, "Paper No. 78: Material Monism," in *The Logos Papers*; "Paper No. 90: Christianity and Secular Humanism: The Difference," in *The Logos Papers*.

3. Gangadean, "Paper No. 82: Dualism," in *The Logos Papers*.

4. Gangadean, "Paper No. 80: Spiritual Monism," in *The Logos Papers*.

2. What is special creation?

It is the acts of God subsequent to creation *ex nihilo* by which God formed and filled the earth with creatures made each after its own kind.[5] Special creation ended with the Sabbath day in contrast to theistic evolution.[6]

3. What is meant in saying the world was created very good?

The goodness of the creation consists in its revealing God's glory as he intended in creating and in the absence of all evil, both moral and natural.

QUESTION 10

How did God create man?

God created man male and female, after his own image, in knowledge, righteousness, and holiness, with dominion over the creatures.

1. What are the various aspects of man as the image of God?

Man is created a body/soul unity, a male/female unity, with a formal or larger aspect of the image of God, with a triune personality, and with dominion.[7]

---

5. Gangadean, *History of Philosophy*, 53; Gangadean, "Paper No. 143: The Biblical Worldview (Part III): Biblical Cosmology: Subsequent Creation by Forming and Filling," in *The Logos Papers*; Gangadean, *The Westminster Confession*. See Question 22.

6. Gangadean, "Paper No. 79: The Creation vs. Evolution Controversy," in *The Logos Papers*; "Paper No. 143: The Biblical Worldview (Part III): Biblical Cosmology: Subsequent Creation by Forming and Filling," in *The Logos Papers*.

7. Gangadean, "Paper No. 85: An Introduction to Christianity," in *The Logos Papers*; "Paper No. 87: Scripture," in *The Logos Papers*; Gangadean, *The Westminster Confession*. See Question 23.

2. What is meant by the body/soul unity?

Having a body is an integral part of being a human being. The rending of body and soul in death is removed in the resurrection. The visible body reveals the invisible soul and is the basis of anthropomorphism in speaking about God.

3. What is meant by the male/female unity?

Man was originally one being; woman was formed from man; what became two are to be united again in one flesh. Both maleness and femaleness equally reflect diverse aspects of what is united in God. The context of this unity is the pursuit of the good, which is the source of all unity.

4. What is meant by the larger aspect of the image of God?

The larger aspect of the image of God is that man is finite, temporal, and changeable in his being, wisdom, power, holiness, justice, goodness, and truth. This is equally true of all human beings, always. These attributes exist as formal capacities only and structure human consciousness of self and of God.

5. What is meant by the triune personality of man?

Man is created in knowledge, holiness, and righteousness, called the narrower aspect of the image of God. This aspect has specific content, was lost in the Fall and restored in regeneration. It reflects the structure of the human heart and is the basis of our diverse functions as prophet, priest, and king. The order in the Trinity is reflected in the order of these functions within each person and should be reflected between persons in any group.

6. What is the dominion that man is to exercise?

Man's work of dominion reflects God's dominion in creation; man is to form the creation by developing all the powers latent in the creation; man is to name the creation so as to know God who revealed his glory in creating; man is to fill everything in every way as the rule of God's kingdom over all. The task of dominion is for the entire race throughout history. The work will be completed when the earth is filled with the knowledge of God as the waters cover the sea.[8] The Sabbath given to man signifies the goal and completion of this work.

7. What two areas are involved in naming and ruling the creation?

Naming the natural and the human world is the work of the sciences and the humanities; ruling is the work of technology and all the human arts. Technology develops the powers latent in nature. The arts communicate the truth concerning the human condition and develop the powers latent in man.

QUESTION 11

What are God's works of providence?

God's works of providence are his most holy, wise, and powerful preserving and governing all his creatures, and all their actions.

1. What is the general providence of God?[9]

In general providence, God upholds everything by the word of his power and rules over all by the natural laws of creation.

2. What is the particular providence of God?[10]

In particular providence, God rules over men and nations by his moral law, withholding grace and permitting sin and death, and giving grace that brings righteousness and life as he pleases.

3. What is the end of God's holy rule?

God works all things to the praise of his glory.

---

8. *Isaiah 11:9.*

9. Gangadean, *The Westminster Confession*. See Questions 24-25.

10. Gangadean, *The Westminster Confession*. See Questions 26-29.

QUESTION 12

What special act of providence did God exercise towards man in the estate wherein he was created?

When God created man, he entered into a covenant of life with him, upon condition of perfect obedience; forbidding him to eat of the tree of the knowledge of good and evil, upon pain of death.

1. What was God's purpose in the covenant?[11]

God's purpose in the covenant was to establish mankind in life on the basis of obedience. By keeping this covenant, man would be changed by God from a condition in which it was possible to sin to one in which it would not be possible to sin.

2. What was signified by the two trees?

The two trees outwardly represented the two ways that are always before all men: the way of life and the way of death, good and evil, the knowledge of God, and the knowledge of good and evil.[12]

3. Did the covenant forbid mankind to have the knowledge of good and evil?

Only God determines what is good for a being based upon the nature of the being he creates. Good for man as a rational being is the use of his reason to the fullest, to understand the meaning of the world, which reveals the glory of God; thus, good for man is to possess the knowledge

---

11. Gangadean, *The Westminster Confession*. See Questions 35-38; Gangadean, "Paper No. 145: The Biblical Worldview (Part V): The Fall: The Covenant of Creation and the Temptation," in *The Logos Papers*.

12. Gangadean, "Paper No. 4: The Cornerstone: Good & Evil – Life & Death: The Beginning of the Foundation," in *The Logos Papers*.

of God.[13] What is forbidden as evil is man's self-determination of good and evil apart from his nature as a being created in the image of God.

---

13. Gangadean, *Philosophical Foundation*, 208-213.

Chapter 4

THE FALL OF MAN

QUESTION 13

Did our first parents continue in the estate wherein they were created?

Our first parents, being left to the freedom of their own will, fell from the estate wherein they were created, by sinning against God.

1. What does it mean to be left to the freedom of their own will?

It means that God is not the cause of man's sin, but permitted it; that God could have prevented their sin by upholding them in his grace.

2. What is the state of man that made it possible to sin?

Man is created changeable in knowledge, holiness, and righteousness, which changeable condition would have been altered by obedience through the covenant.

3. Why did God permit sin?[1]

God permitted sin, not by a bare permission merely, but was pleased according to his eternal plan, having purposed to deepen the revelation of his glory by his rule over sin.

---

1. Gangadean, "Paper No. 146: The Biblical Worldview (Part VI): The Fall: Sin," in *The Logos Papers*; "Paper No. 147: The Biblical Worldview (Part VII): The Fall: Death and Theodicy," in *The Logos Papers*; Gangadean, *The Westminster Confession*. See Question 30.

QUESTION 14

What is sin?[2]

Sin is any want of conformity unto, or transgression of, the law of God.

1. Are any of the commands of God arbitrary?

The commands of God are based on his nature and the nature of man, who is made in the image of God. No command of God is arbitrary, nor can God deny himself. Sin as moral evil always involves a denial of God's nature and a violation of our nature.

2. What generally is denied in sin?

In sin, there is generally a denial of who God is and what is good for man. This can be seen in the account of the Fall of man in the Garden of Eden, in what man must believe in coming to God, and in understanding what the Scriptures principally teach.

3. How else is sin described in Scripture?

Sin is described as denial of clear general revelation; as not seeking God, not understanding God, not doing righteousness; as shutting one's eyes, and closing one's ears, and hardening one's heart.

4. What are the two aspects of sin?

Sin is either by omission, what we fail to do, or by commission, what we do.

5. What common errors show misunderstanding of sin?

Antinomianism denies the universal and perpetual nature of the law as the way of life. Legalism denies the spiritual and total nature of the

---

2. Gangadean, *The Westminster Confession*. See Questions 30-34; Appendix 7.

law as the way of life. Both reduce the purpose of the law to that of justification, but differ over its continued necessity.

QUESTION 15

What was the sin whereby our first parents fell from the estate wherein they were created?

The sin whereby our first parents fell from the estate wherein they were created was their eating the forbidden fruit.

1. What is the significance of eating the forbidden fruit?

Eating the forbidden fruit signified a turning away from the way of life (the knowledge of God) to the way of death (determining good and evil for oneself).

2. What came before the outward act of eating the forbidden fruit?

In believing "you shall not surely die," man doubted God as Creator, infinite in truth; and in believing "you shall be as God knowing good and evil," man denied his creatureliness and finitude as made in the image of God.

3. What led man into unbelief?

Being left to himself, man did not continue to seek God; he did not pursue the way of life, the good as the knowledge of God. In not seeking, man failed to see what was clearly revealed about God in general revelation.

QUESTION 16

Did all mankind fall in Adam's first transgression?

*The covenant being made with Adam, not only for himself,
but for his posterity; all mankind, descending from him by
ordinary generation, sinned in him, and fell with him, in
his first transgression.*

1. What is original sin?

Original sin is the origin of all sin, historically and logically.[3]

2. How is Adam's sin the historical origin of all sin?

The guilt of Adam's sin is imputed to all those united to him by ordinary
generation by virtue of the covenant of life. By this guilt, the effect of
his sin on his nature is passed on so that all men are born spiritually
dead and must be regenerated to have life.

3. How is Adam's sin the logical origin of all sin?

The logical origin of all sin is the denial of God in the denial of clear
general revelation, which was the sin of Adam.

4. Is there any injustice in imputing the sin of Adam?

No, but where sin abounded, grace did much more abound in imputing
the righteousness of the last Adam.[4]

---

3. Gangadean, *The Westminster Confession*. See Questions 30-34; Appendix 7.

4. *Romans 5.*

QUESTION 17

Into what estate did the Fall bring mankind?[5]

The Fall brought mankind into an estate of sin and misery.

1. What is to be distinguished in man's estate of sin?

In sin, there is to be distinguished the change in the condition of man's entire heart, the narrower aspect of his nature, commonly called the depravity of our nature, and actual transgressions that proceed from this nature, whether by omission or by commission.

2. What is to be distinguished in man's estate of misery?

In human misery, there is to be distinguished spiritual death, which is the inherent consequence of sin,[6] and the miseries of this life, which are imposed upon man as a call to repentance from sin.[7]

---

5. Gangadean, "Paper No. 146: The Biblical Worldview (Part VI): The Fall: Sin," in *The Logos Papers*; "Paper No. 147: The Biblical Worldview (Part VII): The Fall: Death and Theodicy," in *The Logos Papers*; "Paper No. 148: The Biblical Worldview (Part VIII): Redemption: The First and Second Calls to Repentance," in *The Logos Papers*; "Paper No. 149: The Biblical Worldview (Part IX): Redemption: The Third Call to Repentance," in *The Logos Papers*; Gangadean, *The Westminster Confession*. See Questions 30-34.

6. *Genesis 2:17; Romans 6:23; Ephesians 2:1.*

7. *Genesis 2:25; 3:7, 9, 14-19.*

QUESTION 18

Wherein consists the sinfulness of that estate whereinto man fell?

The sinfulness of that estate whereinto man fell consists in the guilt of Adam's first sin, the want of original righteousness, and the corruption of his whole nature, which is commonly called original sin; together with all actual transgressions which proceed from it.

1. What is meant by our whole nature?

God created man finite, temporal, and changeable in knowledge, holiness, and righteousness, which is the narrower aspect of man's nature, also called the heart of man. The whole heart is affected by the Fall of man, not merely one or two aspects. The Fall does not affect the larger, formal aspect of man's nature, which is the essence of his humanness.

2. How is each aspect of the heart corrupted or changed by the Fall?

Man changed in knowledge from understanding the nature of God and believing that he exists to misunderstanding that nature and to unbelief. Man changed in holiness from desiring the knowledge of God as the good to desiring what pleases him in unbelief. Man changed in righteousness from doing what God commanded to doing what is pleasing in his own eyes.

3. How do actual transgressions proceed from this corrupt nature?

Having shut his eyes to the contradictoriness of his unbelief, and hardening himself to natural evil, which calls him to repentance, man, in self-deception and in self-justification, acts upon his unbelief and his unholy desires.

QUESTION 19

What is the misery of that estate whereinto man fell?

All mankind by their fall lost communion with God, are under his wrath and curse, and so made liable to all the miseries of this life, to death itself, and to the pains of hell forever.

1. What is it to lose communion with God?

The communion with God that was lost is having his Word remain in us and our obeying that Word.

2. What is spiritual death?

It is the wages of sin;[8] the inherent effect of the destruction of our nature in the denial of God; the effect of being given up to sin by God's wrath. It consists of meaninglessness, boredom, and the shame of guilt in all their manifestations. It is present now in this life, continuing in the next life, and is the essence of what hell is.[9]

3. What is natural evil?[10]

Natural evil is the miseries of this life, imposed upon man after the Fall by the curse, and is God's call to man to repentance. It consists of toil and strife, and old age, sickness, and physical death in all their manifestations.

---

8. *Genesis 2:17; Romans 6:23; Ephesians 2:1.*

9. Gangadean, *Philosophical Foundation*, 195-197; Gangadean, *The Westminster Confession.* See Questions 31-32.

10. Gangadean, "Paper No. 149: The Biblical Worldview (Part IX): Redemption: The Third Call to Repentance," in *The Logos Papers.*

Chapter 5

___

THE COVENANT OF GRACE AND THE PERSON AND WORK OF CHRIST

QUESTION 20

Did God leave all mankind to perish in the estate of sin and misery?

God having, out of his mere good pleasure, from all eternity, elected some to everlasting life, did enter into a covenant of grace, to deliver them out of the estate of sin and misery, and to bring them into an estate of salvation by a Redeemer.

1. Are there constraints on God's mercy?

God is not required to have mercy by anything outside of himself, but being infinite in goodness, he is pleased to have mercy. Yet his mercy is not arbitrary, but according to his eternal plan, which is to the praise of his glory. But his mercy is sovereign, having elected some to life, according as God has mercy on whom he will have mercy.[1]

2. How is man redeemed by the covenant of grace?[2]

Those who are fallen according to the covenant of works made with Adam must be redeemed by the terms of that covenant. The Redeemer

___

1. *Romans 9:16-18.*

2. Gangadean, "Paper No. 114: The Gospel: For Everyone," in *The Logos Papers*; "Paper No. 148: The Biblical Worldview (Part VIII): Redemption: The First and Second Calls to Re-

must perfectly obey in the place of Adam and must pay the penalty of sin due by that covenant. The grace of God does not negate but satisfies the justice of God. Yet the covenant is gracious in that God himself fulfills the terms of the covenant in the place of man. And there are not two covenants by which man is redeemed, but one covenant of grace, differently administered under the old and new covenants.

3. How is man brought into the estate of salvation?

Through union with the new covenant head, man's sins are pardoned. The power of sin and its misery is progressively removed, and man is thereby enabled to fulfill his task of dominion through which he achieves the goal of the knowledge of God, which is eternal life.[3]

QUESTION 21

Who is the Redeemer of God's elect?[4]

*The only Redeemer of God's elect is the Lord Jesus Christ,
who, being the eternal Son of God, became man, and so was,
and continues to be, God and man in two distinct natures,
and one person, forever.*

1. Is there any salvation apart from Christ?

Since all have sinned and come short of the glory of God in failing to acknowledge God's clear general revelation,[5] and since the wages of sin is death,[6] all men need salvation. There is no other name under heaven

---

pentance," in *The Logos Papers*; "Paper No. 149: The Biblical Worldview (Part IX): Redemption: The Third Call to Repentance," in *The Logos Papers*; "Paper No. 150: The Biblical Worldview (Part X): Redemption: Justification and Sanctification," in *The Logos Papers*.

3. *John 17:3.*

4. Gangadean, *The Westminster Confession*. See Questions 39-43.

5. *Romans 3:23.*

6. *Romans 6:23.*

given to men by which we must be saved.[7] Only he has perfectly obeyed God's will in all things, and only he has borne the penalty of sin by his death on the cross. There is only one mediator between God and men. There are not, therefore, many paths to God, nor can any person by his own works save himself.

2. Who is the Lord Jesus Christ?

The Lord Jesus Christ is the eternal Son of God who became man, so that he is both the Son of God and the Son of Man. In contrast to Eastern mysticism, he is not one of many incarnations of the divine, but the only incarnation of God. In contrast to Western humanism, he is not merely a wise human teacher, but God incarnate. In contrast to ancient Gnosticism, he is not merely a higher spiritual being appearing in the form of man, but God incarnate.

3. How can there be one person in two natures?

In Christ, two whole, perfect, and distinct natures, the Godhead and the manhood, were inseparably joined together in one person, without *conversion* (one nature does not change and become the other—God does not change into man or man into God), *composition* (Christ is not partly God and partly man), or *confusion* (each nature acts distinctly according to its own essence). Which person is very God, and very man, yet one Christ, the only mediator between God and man.[8]

QUESTION 22

How did Christ, being the Son of God, become man?

Christ, the Son of God, became man, by taking to himself a true body and a reasonable soul, being conceived by the power of the Holy Spirit, in the womb of the Virgin Mary, and born of her, yet without sin.

---

7. *Acts 4:12.*

8. *WCF 8.2.*

1. How can God become man?

God being infinite can take to himself the finite, but man being finite cannot take to himself the infinite. The infinite is not opposed to but is inclusive of the finite; the finite, however, is not inclusive of the infinite.

2. How is Christ truly man?

Christ has both a body and soul: he was conceived of the virgin Mary, of her substance; he grew in wisdom and stature; he was, as man, anointed by the Holy Spirit; he was tempted in all points as we are, yet without sin; he suffered under Pontius Pilate; he was crucified, dead, and buried.[9]

3. How is Christ man, yet without sin?[10]

Christ was conceived by the power of the Holy Spirit, in the womb of the virgin Mary. Only Christ, of those born of women, was not conceived by a human father, so the sin of Adam was not imputed to him. Only Christ, as sinless in nature, is able to undertake man's redemption.

QUESTION 23

What offices doth Christ execute as our Redeemer?[11]

Christ, as our Redeemer, executeth the offices of a prophet, of a priest, and of a king, both in his estate of humiliation and exaltation.

1. What is the origin of these offices?

Man, made in the image of God, in knowledge, holiness, and righteousness, was to function as prophet, priest, and king in God's creation.

---

9. See *The Apostles' Creed*.

10. Gangadean, *The Westminster Confession*. See Question 40.

11. Gangadean, *The Westminster Confession*. See Question 39.

Man is to love God with his whole heart, with all his mind, his soul, and his strength.[12]

2. What is the function of each office?

Man as prophet is to understand God's revelation, both in creation and in history and in the Scriptures, so as to attain to the fullness of the knowledge of God. Man as priest is to teach God's revelation, so as to bring all men to holiness, the sanctification that comes through knowing the truth. Man as king is to rule in God's creation, so as to bring all men to righteousness through obeying God's law in all things.

3. How does Christ execute these offices in humiliation and exaltation?

In his humiliation, Christ, by his perfect obedience, both active and passive, fulfills the law and accomplishes the redemption of those who are given to him. In his exaltation, Christ, seated at the right hand of God, rules over men and nations by his Word and Spirit to apply his redemption to those who are given to him.

4. Where in Scripture are these offices manifested?

These offices are manifested in the person and work of Moses as prophet, Aaron as priest, and David as king, and in those who continued these offices. They are also manifested in the various gifts Christ gives to every believer for the building up of his body, the Church.

QUESTION 24

How doth Christ execute the office of a prophet?

Christ executeth the office of a prophet, in revealing to us, by his Word and Spirit, the will of God for our salvation.

---

12. *Deuteronomy 6:5; Mark 12:30.*

1. What is the goal of Christ's work as prophet?

Christ, as prophet, brings his people to the knowledge of God, which is eternal life.[13]

2. How does Christ bring us to the knowledge of God?

God is a Spirit whom no man has seen nor can see.[14] Christ, the eternal Word of God, reveals God through his work as Creator, Ruler, and Redeemer. As the Word of God incarnate, Christ rules in history to bring his people, by his Spirit, to understand this revelation.

3. What does Christ reveal as the will of God for our salvation?

Christ, in the Scriptures, reveals our need for deliverance from the penalty and the power of sin by his work, by which also he brings us to understand God's law, so that by obeying it in all things we may know God in all that by which he makes himself known.

QUESTION 25

How doth Christ execute the office of a priest?

Christ executeth the office of a priest, in his once offering up of himself as a sacrifice to satisfy divine justice, and reconcile us to God and in making continual intercession for us.

1. What is the goal of Christ's priestly work?

Christ's priestly work brings his people to holiness, in which we are devoted to God in all of life.

2. How does Christ as priest bring us to holiness?

Christ brings us to holiness by removing the penalty of sin through the sacrifice of himself on the cross, and by removing the power of sin

---

13. *John 17:3.*
14. *1 Timothy 6:16.*

through the daily sanctifying work of his Word and Spirit, for which also he ever lives to make intercession for us.[15]

3. What is the goal of holiness?

The goal of holiness is the knowledge of God. God is the rewarder of those who diligently seek him.[16] Without holiness, no one shall see God.[17]

QUESTION 26

How doth Christ execute the office of a king?

Christ executeth the office of a king, in subduing us to himself, in ruling and defending us, and in restraining and conquering all his and our enemies.

1. What is the goal of Christ's work as king?

Christ as king brings his people to righteousness, to do justice in the earth, to exercise dominion over the creation and over sin.

2. How does Christ subdue us to himself?

Christ subdues us to himself by removing the enmity in our hearts by regenerating and sanctifying us by his Word and Spirit.

3. How does Christ rule and defend us?

Christ rules us by bringing us to know and to do his will revealed in the law of God. He defends us by his name, which is a strong tower for the righteous.[18]

---

15. *Hebrews 7:25.*
16. *Hebrews 11:6.*
17. *Hebrews 12:14.*
18. *Proverbs 18:10.*

4. How does Christ restrain and conquer all his and our enemies?

The enemy of Christ is sin, dwelling in the world, in our flesh, and in the devil. He restrains sin by his judgments on the earth. He conquers sin by the proclamation of the Word of God, which is the sword of the Spirit.

QUESTION 27

Wherein does Christ's humiliation consist?

Christ's humiliation consisted in his being born, and that in a low condition, made under the law, undergoing the miseries of this life, the wrath of God, and the cursed death of the cross; in being buried, and continuing under the power of death for a time.

1. How is Christ humiliated in every condition of his life?

In every condition of his life, Christ identifies more and more with man as a creature in his need, and with man as sinner in his misery.

2. Why did God become man?

Christ came as a substitutionary atonement for our sins, according to the Scriptures. All we like sheep have gone astray; we have turned everyone to his own way; and the Lord has laid on him the iniquity of us all.[19] He is the Lamb of God who takes away the sin of the world.[20]

3. How does Christ represent us in atonement?

Christ represents us in place of Adam in the covenant of grace. As in Adam all die, even so in Christ shall all be made alive. Since by man came death, by man came also the resurrection of the dead.[21]

---

19. *Isaiah 53:6.*

20. *John 1:29.*

21. *1 Corinthians 15:21-22.*

QUESTION 28

Wherein consisteth Christ's exaltation?

Christ's exaltation consisteth in his rising again from the dead on the third day, in ascending into heaven, in sitting at the right hand of the Father, and in coming to judge the world at the last day.

1. What does Christ's rising from the dead signify?

Christ's rising from the dead shows his triumph over sin and death by the perfect righteousness of his sinless life and by the full payment of the penalty of sin by his atoning death.

2. What is signified by Christ's ascending into heaven and his sitting at the right hand of the Father?

Christ's ascension and session show that he has been given all authority in heaven and earth and that he now exercises that authority in making disciples of all nations.

3. When does Christ come to judge the world?

Christ comes to judge individual men, nations, and churches suddenly; at any moment throughout history; but his final coming to judge all men will occur after he has overcome all opposition to his rule through the preaching of the gospel.

Chapter 6

THE BENEFITS OF
CHRIST'S WORK

QUESTION 29

How are we made partakers of the redemption
purchased by Christ?

*We are made partakers of the redemption purchased
by Christ, by the effectual application of it to us by his
Holy Spirit.*

1. Who is the Holy Spirit?

The Holy Spirit is the third person of the Trinity. He is a person, not a
force. He is God, not lesser in power or glory. He is third in the work
of the Trinity in that he proceeds from the Father and the Son.

2. What is the work of the Holy Spirit?

The Holy Spirit, as the Lord and giver of life, makes the work of Christ
effectual by regenerating the elect, and by dwelling in and with them,
to illumine their minds to understand God's Word, thereby enabling
them to carry out the work of Christ in discipling the nations.

3. What are some common misunderstandings of the person and
work of the Holy Spirit?

In deism, the reality of the Holy Spirit is denied; in Arminianism, the
priority of the work of the Holy Spirit is denied; in sacramentalism,

the immediateness of the work of the Holy Spirit is denied; in Pentecostalism, the ordinary means used by the Holy Spirit is denied.

QUESTION 30

How does the Spirit apply to us that redemption purchased by Christ?

*The Spirit applieth to us the redemption purchased by Christ,
by working faith in us, and thereby uniting us to Christ in
our effectual calling.*

1. What is faith?

Faith is a conviction based upon understanding. Faith rests on reason
as truth rests on meaning. Faith grows as understanding grows; faith
is tested as understanding is tested.[1]

2. What is the object and act of faith?

The object of faith is fundamentally concerned with the existence
and nature of God and all that is derived from this. The act of faith is
trusting in God according to his nature and the promises of Scripture
which are grounded in his nature.[2]

3. How does the Holy Spirit work faith in us?

The Holy Spirit works faith in us by regenerating and sanctifying us.
In regeneration, the life of God is restored in us, by which life we are

---

1. Gangadean, "Paper No. 8: Belief and Unbelief—The Spiritual War: Introductory Re-
marks," in *The Logos Papers*; "Paper No. 21: Faith and Reason in Christianity," in *The Logos
Papers*; "Paper No. 98: Faith and the Word of God: The Object of Faith," in *The Logos
Papers*; "Paper No. 128: Abraham's Faith: The Elements of Abraham's Faith in Offering up
Isaac," in *The Logos Papers;* "Paper No. 129: Faith and Reason in the Life of Abraham," in
The Logos Papers; Gangadean, *The Westminster Confession*. See Questions 62-64.

2. Gangadean, *Philosophical Foundation*, 124-127; Gangadean, "Paper No. 128: Abraham's
Faith: The Elements of Abraham's Faith in Offering up Isaac," in *The Logos Papers*; "Paper
No. 129: Faith and Reason in the Life of Abraham," in *The Logos Papers*.

brought to the conviction that God is, that we have sinned, and that we are redeemed by Christ. In sanctification, we are brought to know the truth by the illuminating work of the Spirit, by which truth we are set free.

QUESTION 31

What is effectual calling?[3]

Effectual calling is the work of God's Spirit, whereby, convincing us of our sin and misery, enlightening our minds in the knowledge of Christ, and renewing our wills, he doth persuade and enable us to embrace Jesus Christ, freely offered to us in the gospel.

1. What is to be distinguished in effectual calling?

The two parts of effectual calling are the inward work of the Holy Spirit called regeneration, and the outward effect of this work called conversion.

2. What is regeneration?

Regeneration is an act of the Holy Spirit in which a person is changed from a state of spiritual death to life.

3. What is conversion?[4]

Conversion is the outward effect of regeneration in which a person is convicted of sin, has repentance towards God, and has faith in Jesus as Lord.

---

3. Gangadean, *The Westminster Confession.* See Questions 49-52.
4. Gangadean, *The Westminster Confession.* See Questions 65-69.

4. How does the Holy Spirit bring us to the conviction of sin?

The Holy Spirit brings us to see that there is no life apart from God and that the misery of spiritual death is due to our unbelief.

QUESTION 32

What benefits do they that are effectually called partake of in this life?

They that are effectually called do in this life partake of justification, adoption, sanctification, and the several benefits, which in this life, do either accompany or flow from them.

1. What is the order of salvation?

The order of salvation (*ordo salutis*), is the order of the application of the redemption accomplished by Christ and applied by the Holy Spirit to those who are elected in Christ.[5]

2. What is the sequence of the order of salvation?

The sequence of the *ordo salutis* is first regeneration, then conversion, which is repentance and faith, then justification, adoption, sanctification, and finally, glorification at death.

3. How is the order of salvation to be understood?

While each benefit is inseparable in experience, yet each is to be distinguished from the other, and each is to be understood on the basis of the preceding benefit.

4. What common errors occur in understanding the *ordo salutis*?

Some common errors in the *ordo salutis* are the reversal of regeneration and conversion (confessional regeneration), omitting the necessity of

---

5. Gangadean, *The Westminster Confession.* See Question 19.

repentance (e.g., baptismal regeneration), confusing sanctification with justification (the sacramental system), and the denial of glorification at death (purgatory).

QUESTION 33

What is justification?[6]

Justification is an act of God's free grace, wherein he pardons all our sins, and accepteth us as righteous in his sight, only for the righteousness of Christ imputed to us, and received by faith alone.

1. What is revealed in the need for justification?

The need for justification shows that God has so made us that we are required to give an account for all our behavior.

2. What is the first error regarding justification?

The first error is that man can justify himself in his unbelief, either by seeking to deny the clarity of general revelation and the inexcusability of unbelief or by blaming another for his conduct.

3. What is the second error regarding justification?

The second error is that we can, by our own conduct, live up to the righteousness required by God's law. Legalism is the religious practice that reduces the requirements of the law to a set of outward rules and religious observances in order to achieve righteousness.

4. What is the third error regarding justification?

The third error is that man must meet part of the requirements of God's righteousness either by his own obedience, or by regarding faith as man's work and not God's gift, or by his own suffering as payment

---

6. Gangadean, *The Westminster Confession*. See Questions 53-57.

in part for sin. This attempts to add human works to the sufficiency of God's grace.

5. What is the fourth error regarding justification?

The fourth error is that justification is an infusion of grace through the sacraments that makes us actually righteous rather than an imputation through faith in Christ that accounts us righteous once and for all. Sin cancels infused righteousness, and righteousness infused cancels sin in an unending cycle in this life.

6. What is the fifth error regarding justification?

The fifth error is that being set free from having to obey the law in order to be justified, God's law no longer binds and guides the conduct of believers. This is the common error of antinomianism.

QUESTION 34

What is adoption?[7]

Adoption is an act of God's free grace, whereby we are received into the number, and have a right to all the privileges of, the sons of God.

1. What are the privileges of the sons of God?

The privileges of the sons of God are: being under God's fatherly care, being a member of the family of God, and being a joint heir with Christ in his inheritance.

2. In what does God's fatherly care consist?

God's fatherly care consists in his leading us by his Spirit sent into our hearts, in his chastening us in order that we might share in his holiness,

---

7. Gangadean, *The Westminster Confession.* See Question 58.

and in the access granted to us through prayer by which we approach him as our Father in heaven.

3. What is the family of God?

The family of God consists of all those who have been born of God, who hear the Word of God and do it. It consists of believers from all nations and all ages and is tied neither to common ancestry nor background. It is a fellowship of common interest and sharing in all the blessings of God by those who suffer and rejoice together.

4. What is the inheritance of God?

The inheritance of God consists in the new heavens and the new earth. It is the kingdom of God prepared for us from the foundation of the world and for which we labor and strive on earth. It is the City of God, the New Jerusalem, in which dwells righteousness. It is our heavenly reward, eternal life, the knowledge of God that will fill the earth as the waters cover the sea.

QUESTION 35

What is sanctification?[8]

Sanctification is the work of God's free grace, whereby we are renewed in the whole man after the image of God, and are enabled more and more to die unto sin, and live unto righteousness.

1. How are we sanctified?

The Holy Spirit illumines our minds to know God, through which truth we are sanctified. As we contemplate the glory of God, we are transformed into his likeness; we are set free from sin and made holy. Righteousness in conduct proceeds from this knowledge and holiness.

---

8. Gangadean, *The Westminster Confession*. See Questions 59-61.

2. What is the standard of sanctification?

Obedience to the law of God in all that it requires and forbids is the only standard for sanctification. Neither is there any other standard for sanctification, however zealous or sincere we may feel. Antinomianism is the rejection of God's law in favor of man's law, be it private or by tradition, as the measure of holiness of piety.

3. To what extent is sanctification possible?

Increase in holiness is possible to the extent that we hear the Word of God, pray, meditate on it, and put it into practice. But though there is diligence and growth throughout one's life, no mere man is ever free from all sin in this life.

QUESTION 36

What are the benefits which in this life do accompany or flow from justification, adoption, and sanctification?

The benefits which in this life do accompany or flow from justification, adoption, and sanctification, are, assurance of God's love, peace of conscience, joy in the Holy Ghost, increase of grace and perseverance therein to the end.

1. What is the assurance of God's love?[9]

The assurance of God's love is from knowing that he works all things together for good to those who love him and are called according to his purpose;[10] that nothing can separate us from the love of God;[11] that in all our trials and tribulations we are under his special loving care.

---

9. Gangadean, *The Westminster Confession*. See Questions 79-82.

10. *Romans 8:28.*

11. *Romans 8:38-39.*

2. What is the peace of conscience?

The peace of conscience is freedom from the torment of guilt through Christ in whom all our sins are pardoned; that we are accepted by God on the basis of Christ's perfect righteousness alone; that the sufferings of this life are not punishment for sin but, in God's grace, deliverance from its power.

3. What is the joy in the Holy Spirit?

From assurance of God's love and peace of conscience, there arises joy in all our expectations. The hope of the believer is steadfast and sure that God's purpose will be accomplished on the earth and that our labor in the Lord is not in vain.

4. What is the benefit of increase in grace and perseverance therein to the end?[12]

Because we are not left to ourselves in our struggle against sin, but are constantly enabled by the Holy Spirit, believers do overcome unbelief remaining in them and in the world, and so increase in grace. And by that same Spirit, they are kept in obedience so that they do not fall away, but persevere in grace to the end.

QUESTION 37

What benefits do believers receive from Christ at death?

The souls of believers are at their death made perfect in holiness, and do immediately pass into glory; and their bodies, being still united to Christ, do rest in their graves, till the resurrection.

---

12. Gangadean, *The Westminster Confession*. See Questions 76-78.

1. What is it to be made perfect in holiness?

The souls of believers at death are freed from all remaining errors in understanding so that there remains no hindrance to seeing God as he is and to growing in understanding God's revelation.

2. What is it to pass immediately into glory?

The souls of believers, when absent from the body at death, are immediately present with the Lord. There is no purgatory or any other intermediate state through which the souls of believers must pass before being present with the Lord.

3. What happens to the bodies of believers after death?[13]

Man, being created as a whole person in body and soul, is redeemed by Christ in both body and soul. The body of the believer is, therefore, not abandoned to the grave, but is raised up incorruptible at the completion of redemption at the last day.

QUESTION 38

What benefits do believers receive from Christ at the resurrection?

At the resurrection, believers, being raised up in glory, shall be openly acknowledged and acquitted in the day of judgment, and made perfectly blessed in the full enjoyment of God to all eternity.

1. What happens at the resurrection?[14]

At the resurrection, the bodies of both the just and the unjust are raised up incorruptible and united again with their souls, and all mankind appears before God to be judged according to their deeds.

---

13. Gangadean, *The Westminster Confession*. See Question 133.

14. Gangadean, *The Westminster Confession*. See Question 134.

2. What happens to believers at the judgment?[15]

Believers, at the judgment, are acknowledged by God as his children and are acquitted of sin on the basis of Christ's righteousness imputed to them.

3. What is the blessing of believers after the judgment?

Believers, after the judgment, inherit the kingdom of God in its fullness. They live in the new heavens and new earth in which dwells righteousness. They enjoy eternal life in knowing God, who reveals himself in all his works of creation and providence.

---

15. Gangadean, *The Westminster Confession.* See Questions 135-137.

Chapter 7

The Moral Law: The Rule of Our Obedience

QUESTION 39

What is the duty which God requires of man?

The duty which God requires of man, is obedience to his revealed will.

1. What is a duty?

A duty is an obligation we owe without conditions. It extends not only to words and deeds, but to the meditations of our hearts as well.

2. To whom is our duty?

Because God has made us, we are his and not our own.[1] Therefore, our duty is to God and not merely to ourselves or others, however much we benefit from our duty.

3. Do all men have a duty to God?

All men, being created by God, owe to God whatever duty God is pleased to require of man. Neither is one's duty set aside by unbelief, which itself is a failure in duty.

---

1. *Psalm 100:3.*

4. What is the relation of man's duty and his chief end?

The chief end of man, which is to glorify God, and his duty are one and the same.

QUESTION 40

What did God at first reveal to man for the rule of his obedience?

The rule which God at first revealed to man for his obedience, was the moral law.

1. When was the moral law first revealed to man?

The moral law was first revealed to man from the very beginning, from the time of his creation.

2. How is the moral law revealed to all men?

The moral law is written on the heart of man so that its requirements are clearly revealed to all men.[2]

3. Can the moral law be altered in any way?

The moral law, being a requirement of God's nature and the nature of man as made in the image of God, cannot be added to or changed in any way.

---

2. *Romans 2:14-15.*

QUESTION 41

Wherein is the moral law summarily comprehended?

*The moral law is summarily comprehended in the
Ten Commandments.*

1. What is the relation of the moral law and the Ten Commandments?

The moral law given to all men by general revelation and the Ten Commandments given to the people of God by special revelation are one and the same.

2. How is the moral law summarily comprehended in the Ten Commandments?

The Commandments are exceedingly broad in principle and application; by meditating on the law day and night, its meaning for all of life can be discerned.

3. Are there additional laws to the Ten Commandments?

The ceremonial laws concerning worship and holiness, and the civil laws concerning justice and discipline are not additional laws, but special applications of the law for the Church prior to the coming of the Messiah.

QUESTION 42

What is the sum of the Ten Commandments?

The sum of the Ten Commandments is, to love the Lord our God with all our heart, with all our soul, with all our strength, and with all our mind; and our neighbor as ourselves.

1. What is taught in the great commandment?

In the great commandment, which is, to love God with all our heart, we are taught that love and the law are one and the same, that the law cannot be set aside in the name of love, and that those who do so misunderstand both love and the law.

2. What does it mean to love God with all our heart?

Loving God with all our heart means that God claims for himself every part of our being and that there is no aspect of life, whether private or public, that is not to be governed by God's law.

3. What does it mean to love our neighbor as ourselves?

To love our neighbor as ourselves means that, all men being equally made in the image of God and that all being equally in need of grace and truth, we are to seek the good of others as we do for ourselves.

4. What is the goal of the law?

The goal of the law is eternal life, which is the knowledge of God.[3]

---

3. *John 17:3.*

Chapter 8

___

PREFACE AND COMMANDMENTS 1-4: OUR DUTY TO GOD

QUESTION 43

What is the preface to the Ten Commandments?

The preface to the Ten Commandments is in these words, I am the Lord thy God, which have brought you out of the land of Egypt, out of the house of bondage.

QUESTION 44

What doth the preface to the Ten Commandments teach us?

The preface of the Ten Commandments teacheth us, that because God is the Lord, and our God, and Redeemer, therefore we are bound to keep all his commandments.

1. What is meant by saying that God is the Lord?

That God is the Lord means that God is the Creator of heaven and earth and ruler over all that comes to pass; therefore, obedience is owed to him.

2. What is meant by saying that God is our God?

Although God is the Lord of all because he is the Creator, those who by covenant acknowledge God to be their God owe to him obedience by virtue of the covenant.

3. What is meant by saying that God is our redeemer?

Although we owe obedience to God as Creator and by covenant, we have sinned in failing to obey his commandments. God pardons and frees us from our sin by Christ's death on the cross. Therefore, we are further bound to obey all his commandments.

QUESTION 45

Which is the first commandment?[1]

The first commandment is, Thou shalt have no other gods before me.

---

1. Gangadean, *Philosophical Foundation*, 171-183.

QUESTION 46

What is required in the first commandment?

The first commandment requireth us to know and acknowledge God to be the only true God, and our God; and to worship and glorify him accordingly.

QUESTION 47

What is forbidden in the first commandment?

The first commandment forbiddeth the denying, or not worshipping and glorifying, the true God as God, and our God; and the giving of that worship and glory to any other, which is due to him alone.

QUESTION 48

What are we specially taught by these words *before me* in the first commandment?

*These words **before me** in the first commandment teach us, that God, who seeth all things, taketh notice of, and is much displeased with, the sin of having any other god.*

1. How can we be required to know God?

We can be required to know God because God has clearly revealed his eternal power and divine nature in the things that are made so that all unbelief is without excuse.[2]

2. In what way do we fail to know God?

All those who say we cannot know if there is a God who created heaven and earth fail to know God. This position is known as skepticism or agnosticism.

3. In what way is God denied?

God is denied by all those who say there is no God who created the heavens and the earth. There are many forms of this denial, including atheism, pantheism, polytheism, materialism, dualism, and shamanism.

4. How can we know that God exists?

We can know by reason from general revelation that there must be something eternal, and only God is eternal.[3]

5. Wherein consists the clarity of general revelation?

The clarity of general revelation is such that all who seek God can know that he is; that one has to shut one's eyes to avoid seeing this clear revelation; that one has to harden oneself to one's suffering to avoid considering God's self-revelation.

6. How is sin at its origin denied?

Sin at its origin is denied by those who say we cannot know that God exists, but we can believe that he is; and by those who say sin is not a failure to know, but a failure to acknowledge God. The former denies the clarity of general revelation and is known as fideism; the latter denies the primacy of the intellect and is known as mysticism and voluntarism.[4]

---

2. *Romans 1:18-20.*

3. Appendix 6; Gangadean, *Philosophical Foundation*, 71-161; Gangadean, *History of Philosophy*, 47-58; Gangadean, "Paper No. 3: The Principle of Clarity, Rational Presuppositionalism, and Proof," in *The Logos Papers*.

4. Gangadean, "Paper No. 120: Contra Voluntarism: The Will Is Not Independent of the Intellect," in *The Logos Papers*.

7. What are the consequences of denying clear general revelation?

The denial of clear general revelation requires the denial of reason which results in spiritual death.

8. What are the consequences of acknowledging clear general revelation?

The consequences of acknowledging the clarity of general revelation are the overcoming of all arguments that are raised up against the knowledge of God and the bringing of all mankind to confess God as Creator.

QUESTION 49

Which is the second commandment?[5]

The second commandment is, Thou shalt not make unto thee any graven image, or any likeness of anything that is in heaven above, or that is in the earth beneath, or that is in the water under the earth: thou shall not bow down thyself to them, nor serve them: for I the Lord thy God am a jealous God, visiting the iniquities of the fathers upon the children unto the third and fourth generation of them that hate me; and showing mercy unto thousands of them that love me and keep my commandments.

---

5. Gangadean, *Philosophical Foundation*, 185-198.

QUESTION 50

What is required in the second commandment?

The second commandment requireth the receiving, observing, and keeping pure and entire, all such religious worship and ordinances as God hath appointed in his Word.

QUESTION 51

What is forbidden in the second commandment?

The second commandment forbiddeth the worshipping of God by images, or any other way not appointed in his Word.

QUESTION 52

What are the reasons annexed to the second commandment?

The reasons annexed to the second commandment are, God's sovereignty over us, his propriety in us, and the zeal he hath to his own worship.

1. What is it to make a graven image?

To make a graven image is to liken the Creator to the creature; it is to think of the infinite in light of the finite; it is to deny the nature of God in any way.

2. What are some assumptions of this command?

This command assumes that thinking is presuppositional; that we are to think of the less basic in light of the more basic; that we are always to think of the finite, temporal, and changeable in light of the infinite, eternal, and unchanging; that we are to understand our experience in light of God rather than understand God in light of our experience.

3. What are some implications of this command?

This command implies that man is the image of God, that God is not to be made in the image of man; that man is the image of God, that man is not to be made in the image of the animal; that the distinction between God and man is never to be denied.

4. What is it to bow down to a graven image?

To bow down to a graven image is to worship God according to our own representation of him rather than according to his representation of himself in his Word. This regulative principle of worship is violated in corporate worship by singing songs of human composition rather than the inspired Psalms.[6]

5. How has God's nature been denied by those who profess belief in God?[7]

Those who profess belief in God the Creator deny the infinite justice of God by denying the need for forgiveness of sin through the atoning death of Jesus Christ.[8]

---

6. Appendix 9.

7. This question refers to those who hold to belief in God the Creator outside of Christianity.

8. Gangadean, "Paper No. 91: Christianity and Islam: The Difference," in *The Logos Papers*; "Paper No. 124: On Islam," in *The Logos Papers*; Gangadean, *Philosophical Foundation*, 190-194.

6. How has God's nature been denied in the Church?

The divisions in the Church are due to a failure to know and acknowledge the fullness of Jesus Christ who fills everything in every way.[9]

7. What are the consequences of denying God's nature?

The consequences of denying God's nature are divisions within the Church, the loss of effectiveness of its witness in the world, and the collapse of the culture by the accumulation of sin in three to four generations.[10]

8. What are the consequences of acknowledging God's nature?

The consequences of acknowledging God's nature are unity of faith within the Church, the world coming to believe that Jesus is the Messiah, and the earth being filled with the knowledge of God.[11]

QUESTION 53

Which is the third commandment?[12]

The third commandment is, Thou shalt not take the name of the Lord thy God in vain: for the Lord will not hold him guiltless that taketh his name in vain.

---

9. *Ephesians 1:22-23.*

10. Gangadean, "Paper No. 34: Globalism and Nationalism: A Biblical Perspective," in *The Logos Papers*; "Paper No. 58: The Spiritual War (Part I): On the State of the Church and the World," in *The Logos Papers.*

11. *Isaiah 11:9.*

12. Gangadean, *Philosophical Foundation,* 199-205.

QUESTION 54

What is required in the third commandment?

The third commandment requireth the holy and reverent use of God's names, titles, attributes, ordinances, Word, and works.

QUESTION 55

What is forbidden in the third commandment?

The third commandment forbiddeth all profaning or abusing of anything whereby God maketh himself known.

QUESTION 56

What is the reason annexed to the third commandment?

The reason annexed to the third commandment is, that however the breakers of this commandment may escape punishment from men, yet the Lord our God will not suffer them to escape his righteous judgment.

1. What is meant by the name of God?

By the name of God is meant all that by which God makes himself known. It is the revelation of God in his Word as well as in his works.

2. What is it to take the name of God in vain?

To take the name of God in vain is to fail to live our lives by the Word of God, which we profess, especially in our oaths and vows.[13] It is to lack integrity and to practice hypocrisy.

3. What is it to have integrity?

To have integrity is to have a concern for consistency in all our thoughts and deeds. It is to have a concern to know the truth and to practice it. It is manifested in the diligent use of ordinary means, especially in meditation and self-examination.

4. What is it to practice hypocrisy?

To practice hypocrisy is to profess one thing and to do another in a manner that conceals it from others and oneself. It is brought about by self-deception and self-justification, which comes from self-imposed blindness.

5. What is it to be held guiltless?

Although we may deceive ourselves and others by the appearance of righteousness, yet God does not excuse our disregard of his revelation. He brings to light the hidden things of darkness, thereby humbling our pride, or he gives us up to the hardening of our hearts and finally to removal from the privileges of his Word.

6. How is the evil of hypocrisy to be avoided?

The evil of hypocrisy is to be avoided by willing submission to the discipline of God, by personal discipline in thought and deed, by corporate discipline in the Church, and by avoiding foolish arguing which lacks integrity.

---

13. Gangadean, "Paper No. 2: Common Ground," in *The Logos Papers*; "Paper No. 51: Common Ground (Part II): Integrity," in *The Logos Papers*; "Paper No. 64: Aaron's Rod: God's Teaching Authority in the Church: A Call to Repentance," in *The Logos Papers*; "Paper No. 65: Aaron's Rod: A Permanent Witness Against Those Who Challenge God's Authority in the Church: Existential Hermeneutics Applied," in *The Logos Papers*.

7. What is the blessing of obeying this commandment?

Those who maintain integrity and endure discipline are brought by God, through holiness and purity of heart, to see God.

QUESTION 57

Which is the fourth commandment?[14]

The fourth commandment is, Remember the Sabbath day, to keep it holy, Six days shalt thou labor, and do all thy work; but the seventh day is the Sabbath of the Lord thy God; in it thou shalt not do any work, thou, nor thy son, nor thy daughter, thy manservant, nor thy maidservant, nor thy cattle, nor thy stranger that is within thy gates; for in six days the Lord made heaven and earth, the sea, and all that in them is, and rested the seventh day; wherefore the Lord blessed the Sabbath day, and hallowed it.

QUESTION 58

What is required in the fourth commandment?

The fourth commandment requireth the keeping holy to God such set times as he hath appointed in his Word; expressly one whole day in seven, to be a holy Sabbath to himself.

---

14. Gangadean, *Philosophical Foundation*, 207-219.

QUESTION 59

Which day of seven hath God appointed to be the weekly Sabbath?

From the beginning of the world to the resurrection of Christ, God appointed the seventh day of the week to be the weekly Sabbath; and the first day of the week ever since, to continue to the end of the world, which is the Christian Sabbath.

QUESTION 60

How is the Sabbath to be sanctified?

The Sabbath is to be sanctified by a holy resting all that day, even from such worldly employments and recreations as are lawful on other days; and spending the whole time in the public and private exercises of God's worship, except so much as is to be taken up in the works of necessity and mercy.

QUESTION 61

What is forbidden in the fourth commandment?

The fourth commandment forbiddeth the omission,
or careless performance, of the duties required and the
profaning the day by idleness, or doing that which is in itself
sinful, or by unnecessary thoughts, words, or works about our
worldly employments or recreations.

QUESTION 62

What are the reasons annexed to the
fourth commandment?

The reasons annexed to the fourth commandment are, God's
allowing us six days of the week for our own employments,
his challenging a special propriety in the seventh, his own
example, and his blessing the Sabbath day.

1. What is the Sabbath day?

The Sabbath day is the day of rest, signifying man's completion of his work even as God completed his work.[15]

2. What is it to keep the Sabbath day holy?

To keep the Sabbath day holy is to be devoted through all our work to complete the task God has given to man.

---

15. *Genesis 2:2.*

3. What is the work God has given to man?

God gave to man from the beginning the work of dominion through which man develops all the powers latent in himself and the creation.

4. What is the goal of dominion?

The goal of man's work of dominion is to fill the earth with the knowledge of God as the waters cover the sea,[16] which knowledge is eternal life.[17]

5. Is dominion necessary for the knowledge of God?

God, being Spirit, whom no man has seen nor can see, reveals himself in his work of creation and providence; neither is there any other revelation possible. Therefore, God can be known only through his work as man exercises dominion therein.

6. Will man complete the work God has given him?

The rest of the Sabbath day, being commanded by God, reaffirms the hope that the work will be completed. Because God is faithful as Creator and Redeemer, the Church will achieve unity in the faith, the nations will turn to the Lord, and the earth will be filled with the knowledge of God before Christ returns.[18]

7. How is the Sabbath day to be observed?

The Sabbath day is to be observed by corporate and private resting in hope, reflecting on our work, preparation for work through preaching, renewal of our commitment, and rejoicing in worship.

---

16. *Isaiah 11:9.*

17. *John 17:3.*

18. *1 Corinthians 15:24-28.*

Chapter 9

___

COMMANDMENTS 5-10: OUR DUTY TO MAN

QUESTION 63

Which is the fifth commandment?[1]

*The fifth commandment is, **Honor thy father and thy mother; that thy days may be long upon the land which the Lord thy God giveth thee.***

QUESTION 64

What is required in the fifth commandment?

The fifth commandment requireth the preserving the honor, and performing the duties, belonging to every one in their several place and relations, as superiors, inferiors, or equals.

---

1. Gangadean, *Philosophical Foundation*, 221-229.

QUESTION 65

What is forbidden in the fifth commandment?

The fifth commandment forbiddeth the neglecting of, or doing anything against, the honor and duty which belongeth to every one in their several places and relations.

QUESTION 66

What is the reason annexed to the fifth commandment?

The reason annexed to the fifth commandment is, a promise of long life and prosperity (as far as it shall serve for God's glory, and their own good) to all such as keep this commandment.

1. What is it to honor father and mother?

To honor father and mother is to recognize the legitimacy of their authority in the obedience we give to them.

2. What is the extent of authority?

All authority is of God. Authority is not exercised only by father and mother, but by all those who are over us in every area of life.

3. How is authority exercised?

Authority is exercised fundamentally through teaching and secondarily through deciding and directing. The authority of Christ is exercised through the Church in its teaching the nations to obey all he has commanded.[2]

4. Wherein consists the legitimacy of authority?

The legitimacy of authority consists in possessing insight into the good and the means to it; it is not based on might. The authority of insight is rational; it is not merely personal. Insight is historically cumulative; it is not merely individually originated.[3]

5. What is the order of authority within each person?

Man, being made in the image of God, reflects God's order of authority in the relation of knowledge, holiness, and righteousness. Though each aspect is equally in the image of God, there remains an order among them in which the intellect is primary in each person.

6. What is the order of authority within the Church?

Believers, being enabled by the Holy Spirit to carry out Christ's work, do show the unity there is in Christ by observing the order of his ministry as prophet, priest, and king, the work of the prophetic ministry being foundational to the priestly and kingly ministries.

7. What is the order of authority among institutions?

The corporate bodies of family, church, and state, being directly structured and instituted by God, are each, directly and immediately to be submitted to God according to his law. Neither is any institution in any of its forms to be placed under the authority of an institution of another kind.

8. How are we to give honor to whom honor is due?

We give honor to whom honor is due by submission to those who have understanding, by not submitting to those who lack understanding, and by seeking to put into positions of leadership those who, by talent and patience, have gained understanding.

---

2. *Matthew 28:18-20.*

3. Gangadean, *Philosophical Foundation*, 221-229.

9. What are the blessings of obedience?

As each person seeks to obey God's law in each institution, the joy and peace of righteousness abound. So that the nation is blessed whose God is the Lord.[4] But the people who do not honor God by his law will descend into the pit.

QUESTION 67

Which is the sixth commandment?[5]

The sixth commandment is, Thou shalt not kill.

QUESTION 68

What is required in the sixth commandment?

The sixth commandment requireth all lawful endeavors to preserve our own life, and the life of others.

QUESTION 69

What is forbidden in the sixth commandment?

The sixth commandment forbiddeth the taking away of our life, or the life of our neighbor, unjustly, or whatsoever tendeth thereunto.

---

4. *Psalm 33:12.*

5. Gangadean, *Philosophical Foundation*, 231-243.

1. What is it to kill?

To kill is to deny in any way the dignity of man as made in the image of God.

2. Wherein consists the dignity of man?

The dignity of man consists in his capacity to understand.

3. How is the dignity of man denied?

The dignity of man is denied when we do not acknowledge the capacity to understand in ourselves or others, when we do not address the unbelief that divides us, and when we use force in place of knowing the truth that sets us free.

4. What are the sanctions for denial of human dignity?

The denial of the dignity of others begins with the denial of one's own dignity, so that one becomes separated from human community in part or altogether.

5. Is separation a denial of one's dignity?

Separation of those who persist in the denial of the dignity of themselves and others, affirms their dignity by holding them accountable for unbelief.

QUESTION 70

Which is the seventh commandment?[6]

The seventh commandment is, Thou shalt not commit adultery.

---

6. Gangadean, *Philosophical Foundation*, 245-254.

QUESTION 71

What is required in the seventh commandment?

The seventh commandment requireth the preservation of our own and our neighbor's chastity, in heart, speech, and behavior.

QUESTION 72

What is forbidden in the seventh commandment?

The seventh commandment forbiddeth all unchaste thoughts, words, and actions.

1. What is the origin of adultery?

Adultery is based on lust, which is based on a false view of the good. It is first of all spiritual toward God, and only subsequently is it natural and outward in its expression.

2. What is the source of fidelity in marriage?

Fidelity in marriage is based on friendship, which is the effect of a mutual commitment to the good. The good is eternal life, which is the knowledge of God.[7]

3. Is commitment to the good necessary for friendship?

Although persons may for a time share a false view of the good, yet it is not the truth that lasts forever, which truth is necessary for friendship.

---

7. *John 17:3;* Gangadean, "Paper No. 4: The Cornerstone: Good & Evil – Life & Death: The Beginning of the Foundation," in *The Logos Papers*; Appendix 4.

4. Is commitment to the good sufficient for friendship?

Since the good is the source of unity within a person, between persons, and between groups of persons in every aspect of life, the good alone is sufficient for friendship.

5. What makes adultery wrong?

Adultery is wrong because it violates the order of unity established by God between body and soul, between the sign and the reality of sex and love, and between male and female becoming one flesh.

QUESTION 73

Which is the eighth commandment?[8]

The eighth commandment is, Thou shalt not steal.

QUESTION 74

What is required in the eighth commandment?

The eighth commandment requireth the lawful procuring and furthering the wealth and outward estate of ourselves and others.

---

8. Gangadean, *Philosophical Foundation*, 255-265.

QUESTION 75

What is forbidden in the eighth commandment?

The eighth commandment forbiddeth whatsoever doth, or may, unjustly hinder our own, or our neighbor's wealth or outward estate.

1. What is true wealth?

True wealth does not consist in earthly treasures that pass away, but in heavenly treasures that last forever.

2. What is the source of everlasting wealth?

What is of lasting value is derived from the use of one's ability in pursuit of the good, eternal life, the knowledge of God.

3. What is the source of our ability?

All ability is from God. Ability cannot, therefore, be owned absolutely by man, either individually or collectively.

4. For what purpose are we given diverse abilities?

We are given diverse abilities by God for the common good, to exercise dominion, to attain to the fullness of the knowledge of God.

5. What determines regard for ability?

Regard for ability, both in ourselves and in others, is determined by regard for the good.

6. What is stealing?

Stealing is a failure to develop one's ability in pursuit of the good.

QUESTION 76

Which is the ninth commandment?[9]

The ninth commandment is, Thou shalt not bear false witness against thy neighbor.

QUESTION 77

What is required in the ninth commandment?

The ninth commandment requireth the maintaining and promoting of truth between man and man, and our own and our neighbor's good name, especially in witness bearing.

QUESTION 78

What is forbidden in the ninth commandment?

The ninth commandment forbiddeth whatsoever is prejudicial to truth, or injurious to our own, or our neighbor's, good name.

---

9. Gangadean, *Philosophical Foundation*, 267-275.

1. Who is a false witness?

A false witness is anyone who fails to know and speak the truth regarding God and man.

2. How is falsehood injurious to my neighbor?

Truth is necessary for justice. Every falsehood, therefore, is injurious to justice for one's neighbor.

3. Who is a faithful witness?

A faithful witness is one who through understanding speaks the whole truth as an activity of the whole of life.

4. What are the consequences of failing to speak the truth?

The consequences of failing to speak the truth are to share in doing injustice and its consequences.

QUESTION 79

Which is the tenth commandment?[10]

The tenth commandment is, Thou shalt not covet thy neighbor's house, thou shalt not covet thy neighbor's wife, or his manservant or his maidservant, or his ox, or his ass, or anything that is thy neighbor's.

---

10. Gangadean, *Philosophical Foundation*, 277-283.

QUESTION 80

What is required in the tenth commandment?

The tenth commandment requireth full contentment with our own condition, with a right and charitable frame of spirit toward our neighbor, and all that is his.

QUESTION 81

What is forbidden in the tenth commandment?

The tenth commandment forbiddeth all discontentment with our own estate, envying or grieving at the good of our neighbor, and all inordinate motions and affections to anything that is his.

1. What is the origin of discontentment?

Discontentment arises from a failure to know what is good and God's providence by which the good is brought about. It was manifested in man's first disobedience in turning from the way of life.

2. Is contentment possible apart from the good?

Nothing less than the good can truly satisfy our hearts nor bring unity among men. In misconceiving the good, there arises continual restlessness, selfish ambition, and envy of every kind.

3. What is envy?

Envy is a desire to have for oneself what belongs to another as if it were the good or a mark of one's goodness. There is no envy of the true good.

4. Does suffering hinder our good?

The sufferings of this life, by God's grace, serve to restrain and recall us from and remove from us our sin of not knowing God. Our suffering, therefore, should not be disregarded by hardening, despised as worthless, nor discourage us from seeking God.

5. How is full contentment in God's providence manifested?

Knowing God is our Father and that all things work together for good, the believer, through joy and peace in the Holy Spirit, perseveres in doing good in all circumstances.

Chapter 10

_____

OUR FALLEN CONDITION AND THE CONSEQUENCE OF SIN

QUESTION 82

Is any man able perfectly to keep the commandments of God?

No mere man, since the Fall, is able in this life perfectly to keep the commandments of God, but doth daily break them, in thought, word, and deed.

Of what use is it to know we sin daily in thought, word, and deed?

True knowledge of our sin humbles our pride and magnifies the grace of God; it makes us more gentle and forgiving of others; it increases our understanding of the breadth of God's law and makes us more watchful against sin and diligent in the pursuit of God's kingdom and righteousness.

QUESTION 83

Are all transgressions of the law equally heinous?

Some sins in themselves, and by reason of several aggravations, are more heinous in the sight of God than others.

What makes some sins more heinous than others?

That some sins are more heinous than others depends on how directly one sins against the holiness of God, on the influence over others of the person who sins, and on the amount of light one has rejected in that sin.

QUESTION 84

What doth every sin deserve?

Every sin deserveth God's wrath and curse, both in this life, and that which is to come.

Why does every sin deserve God's wrath?

Every sin, being rooted in the original sin of not seeking God, deserves God's wrath of being given up to go one's own way.

Chapter 11

FAITH, REPENTANCE, AND
THE ORDINARY MEANS
OF SALVATION

QUESTION 85

What doth God require of us, that we may escape his wrath and curse, due to us for sin?

To escape the wrath and curse of God, due to us for sin, God requireth of us faith in Jesus Christ, repentance unto life, with diligent use of all the outward means whereby Christ communicateth to us the benefits or redemption.

What is the wrath of God?

The wrath of God is his infinite justice manifested in giving up the sinner to spiritual death and whatever is the inherent fruit of sin. It is neither imposed externally, nor is it merely future in the afterlife, but is manifested in all without Christ who now are dead in trespasses. It is also in some measure present where sin remains in the believer, manifesting itself in meaninglessness, boredom, and guilt, where the means of grace are not diligently used.

QUESTION 86

What is faith in Jesus Christ?

Faith in Jesus Christ is a saving grace, whereby we receive and rest upon him alone for salvation, as he is offered to us in the gospel.

Why must we receive and rest in Christ alone for salvation?

Because we need forgiveness and cleansing from sin both in root and in fruit, both imputed and personal, because Christ alone, by his life and death, has satisfied God's justice on our behalf, and because he has sent his Spirit to apply to us the benefits of his redemption, Christ's work alone is fully sufficient for our salvation. Nothing can in any way be added to it without denying it.

QUESTION 87

What is repentance unto life?[1]

Repentance unto life is a saving grace, whereby a sinner, out of a true sense of sin, and apprehension of the mercy of God in Christ, doth, with grief and hatred of his sin, turn from it unto God, with full purpose of, and endeavor after, new obedience.

---

1. Gangadean, *The Westminster Confession*. See Question 65.

1. Can we of ourselves repent?

Man, left to himself, always, in pride, resists repentance, through self-deception and self-justification. No man, therefore, can bring himself, or another, to true repentance, which depends wholly on the grace of God.

2. Is there only one repentance unto life?

Because no man in this life is ever free of all sin, repentance unto life must be throughout one's entire life, continually growing deeper as one grows in the knowledge of God.

3. How are we called by God unto repentance?

God calls us unto repentance not only through shame inwardly, and through the gospel outwardly, but also through all forms of natural evil imposed upon mankind since the Fall.

4. What are the marks of true repentance?

True repentance requires understanding of sin as truly evil, and God's mercy in Christ manifested in grief and hatred toward our sin and in the fruit of new obedience.

QUESTION 88

What are the outward and ordinary means wherein Christ communicateth to us the benefits of redemption?

The outward and ordinary means whereby Christ communicateth to us the benefits of redemption are, his ordinances, especially the Word, Sacraments, and prayer; all which are made effectual to the elect for salvation.

1. What are ordinary means?

Ordinary means are those means God has ordained to achieve his intended purpose. We cannot reasonably expect God's purpose to be achieved apart from the use of ordinary means.

2. How are outward means made effectual unto salvation?

To be made effectual, outward means require both our diligent use and the working of the Holy Spirit in and through them.

3. Are all ordinary means equally effectual unto salvation?

The ordinary means of the Word, sacraments, and prayer are so ordered by God that they are effectual unto salvation when used according to God's order.

Chapter 12

ORDINARY MEANS OF SALVATION: THE WORD OF GOD

QUESTION 89

How is the Word made effectual to salvation?

The Spirit of God maketh the reading, but especially the preaching, of the Word, an effectual means of convincing and converting sinners, and of building them up in holiness and comfort, through faith, unto salvation.

1. Why is the preaching of the Word especially effectual?

Preaching is especially effectual because, by preaching, the content of God's Word is made more manifest through the efforts of pastor-teachers, who have been prepared for and appointed unto this task by the Holy Spirit.

2. How does the Spirit make the Word of God effectual unto salvation?

The Word of God, as illuminated by the Spirit, is the sword of the Spirit. It brings piercing conviction of sin; it brings us to repentance and faith; it sets us free from sin; and it sanctifies us, making us devoted in holiness to God in all things.

QUESTION 90

How is the Word to be read and heard that it may become effectual to salvation?

That the Word may become effectual to salvation, we must attend thereunto with diligence, preparation, and prayer; receive it with faith and love, lay it up in our hearts, and practice it in our lives.

1. How is the Word attended to with diligence?

The Word of God is attended to with diligence when we set aside a due portion of time to hear it often and regularly.

2. How is the Word attended to with preparation?

The Word of God is attended to with preparation when we hear it without the distraction of the cares of this life and without the hindrances of the lack of learning.

3. How is the Word attended to through prayer?

Acknowledging that as creatures and fallen, we are dependent on God for all good, we earnestly pray that our minds would be illuminated to hear, with understanding, the Word of God.

4. How is the Word of God received in faith?

God's Word is received in faith when it is received as the Word of the infallible and all-wise God, when we seek to understand its meaning rather than question its truth.

5. How is the Word of God to be received in love?

God's Word is received in love when we have a love for the truth, when we love God who is the author of truth, and when we delight in God's love revealed in his Word.

6. What is it to lay up God's Word in our hearts?

We lay up God's Word in our hearts when we can at all times call it to mind and when we can meditate upon it day and night.

7. How does the practice of God's Word make it effectual unto salvation?

The practice of God's Word prevents us from being forgetful hearers and deceiving ourselves, brings us to fuller understanding, prepares us to receive more of God's Word, and bears fruit unto holiness and righteousness, pleasing to God and men.

Chapter 13

___

ORDINARY MEANS
OF SALVATION:
THE SACRAMENTS

QUESTION 91

How do the Sacraments become effectual means
of salvation?

*The Sacraments become effectual means of salvation, not
from any virtue in them, or in him that doth administer
them; but by the blessing of Christ, and the working of his
Spirit in them that by faith receive them.*

QUESTION 92

What is a Sacrament?[1]

*A Sacrament is a holy ordinance instituted by Christ;
wherein, by sensible signs, Christ and the benefits of the new
covenant, are represented, sealed, and applied to believers.*

---

1. Gangadean, *The Westminster Confession*. See Questions 116-118.

QUESTION 93

What are the Sacraments of the New Testament?

The Sacraments of the New Testament are, baptism, and the Lord's supper.

1. What are sacraments?

Sacraments are signs and seals of the covenant of grace.

2. How are the sacraments signs?

The sacraments are sensible signs which Christ has ordained to represent God's grace. The sign is not the reality of the grace which it signifies, nor is the grace signified always accompanied by the sign.

3. How are the sacraments seals?

The sacraments, when administered with godly discipline by those who are called to oversight, affirm to faithful recipients the benefits of Christ's redemption.

4. How do the sacramental signs become effectual?

The sacramental signs, administered by Christ's ordinance, become effectual only when they are received by faith, which faith apprehends the invisible grace represented visibly in the signs.

5. Are there more than two sacraments?

The sacraments, as signs and seals of the covenant of grace, are ordained by Christ and so limited. There is, therefore, no warrant for any more than two sacraments, which are, Baptism and the Lord's Supper.

6. Have the sacraments changed from the Old to the New Testament?

The Old and New Testaments, being but two administrations of the same covenant of grace, their sacraments have not changed in meaning, but only in outward form.

QUESTION 94

What is Baptism?[2]

Baptism is a Sacrament, wherein the washing with water in the name of the Father, and of the Son, and of the Holy Ghost, doth signify and seal our engrafting into Christ, and partaking of the benefits of the covenant of grace, and our engagement to be the Lord's.

1. Why are we baptized in the name of Christ?

Baptism in the name of Christ signifies our union with Christ in his death, burial, and resurrection. It thereby also signifies our union with God, Father, Son, and Holy Spirit.

2. What does the washing with water signify?

The washing with water signifies our cleansing by the putting off of the sinful nature. The grace of cleansing is realized in regeneration, in which we die unto sin and are raised unto new life in Christ.

3. How does baptism engage us to be the Lord's?

Baptism signifies our union with Christ. We are, therefore, no longer our own, but must glorify God in all our lives.

---

2. Gangadean, *The Westminster Confession.* See Questions 119-122.

QUESTION 95

To whom is Baptism to be administered?

Baptism is not to be administered to any that are out of the visible Church, till they profess their faith in Christ, and obedience to him; but infants of such as are members of the visible Church are to be baptized.

1. What is the visible Church?[3]

The visible Church consists of all those throughout the world that profess the true religion; and of their children; and is the kingdom of the Lord Jesus Christ, the house and family of God, out of which there is no ordinary possibility of salvation.

2. What are the marks of a true church?

The marks of a true church are: sound preaching of the Word, proper administration of the sacraments, and godly discipline. Churches differ in degree of purity according as these marks are present.

3. How does one become a member of the Church?

One becomes a member of the Church by a credible profession of faith, which consists in a saving understanding of the person and work of Christ along with obedience to his Word.

4. Why are infants of believers to be baptized?

Because the covenant of grace is one under the Old and New Testaments, and because the promise is to the believer and his household, and because circumcision and baptism signify the same reality of regeneration, the sign of baptism is to be applied to infants of believers.

---

3. Gangadean, *The Westminster Confession*. See Question 111.

QUESTION 96

What is the Lord's supper?[4]

The Lord's supper is a sacrament, wherein, by giving and receiving bread and wine, according to Christ's appointment, his death is showed forth; and the worthy receivers are, not after a corporal and carnal manner, but by faith, made partakers of his body and blood, with all his benefits, to their spiritual nourishment and growth in grace.

1. How is the death of Christ shown forth in the Lord's Supper?

In the Lord's Supper, we remember and proclaim, until the end of this age, that Christ our Passover was the Son of God who became flesh, that by his death, he might bear away our sins.

2. How do we discern the body of Christ in the Lord's Supper?

We discern the body of Christ by recognizing and putting away sin, which divides the body of Christ for which he died.

3. How do we partake of Christ in the Lord's Supper?

As Christ lived by every Word of God, so those who hear and obey his Word, which Word is spirit and life, feed on Christ after a spiritual manner.

---

4. Gangadean, *The Westminster Confession.* See Questions 123-128.

QUESTION 97

What is required to the worthy receiving of the Lord's supper?

It is required of them that would worthily partake of the Lord's supper, that they examine themselves of their knowledge to discern the Lord's body, of their faith to feed upon him, of their repentance, love, and new obedience; lest, coming unworthily, they eat and drink judgment to themselves.

1. Why is it necessary to examine oneself before partaking of the Lord's Supper?

Because the Lord's Supper is a sign and seal of our partaking of Christ, and because the deceitfulness of sin remains in us, worthy receivers must examine themselves so that they do not desecrate what the sacrament signifies.

2. For what must we examine ourselves?

We must examine ourselves for holding any doctrine or practice that divides the body of Christ, for our being teachable, and for the genuineness of our repentance in the fruit of new obedience.

3. Why are we judged for eating and drinking unworthily?

The Lord does not hold him guiltless that takes his name in vain,[5] but he chastens us that we should not be condemned with the world.[6]

---

5. *Exodus 20:7.*

6. *1 Corinthians 11:32.*

Chapter 14

_____

ORDINARY MEANS
OF SALVATION:
PRAYER

QUESTION 98

What is prayer?[1]

Prayer is an offering up our desires unto God, for things agreeable to his will, in the name of Christ, with confession of sin, and thankful acknowledgment of his mercies.

1. Why do we offer up our desires unto God?

In offering up our desires to God, we acknowledge every good we receive is a gift from God, and we trust him to give us what is good.

2. Why do we pray in the name of Christ?

We pray in the name of Christ because all our blessings are through his redemption and are sought not for ourselves, but for his kingdom and glory.

---

1. Gangadean, *The Westminster Confession*. See Question 95; Gangadean, "Paper No. 136: On Prayer," in *The Logos Papers*.

3. Why are confession of sins and thanksgiving part of prayer?

We confess our sins in prayer because sin hinders our fellowship with God and his hearing and answering our prayers. We give thanks in prayer to acknowledge that it is of his grace alone that we receive all that we have.

QUESTION 99

What rule has God given for our direction in prayer?

*The whole Word of God is of use to direct us in prayer;
but the special rule of direction is that form of prayer
which Christ taught his disciples, commonly called the
Lord's Prayer.*

1. Why do we need a rule to direct us in prayer?

Because prayer is part of the ordinary means whereby Christ communicates to us the benefits of his redemption, we are not left to the imaginations of our hearts; but we are directed by the Word of God on how we should pray so that we may know what we should pray for and what we should expect.

2. How does the Word of God direct us in prayer?

Prayer being offered for things agreeable to God's will, the whole Word of God instructs us in the will of God by precept and example.

3. How does the Lord's Prayer especially direct us in prayer?

The Lord's Prayer, being a form of prayer, summarily comprehends what we should pray for, and that in due order, if our prayers would be effectual.

QUESTION 100

What doth the preface of the Lord's Prayer teach us?

The preface of the Lord's Prayer, which is, **Our Father which art in heaven,** *teacheth us to draw near to God with all holy reverence and confidence, as children to a father, able and ready to help us; and that we should pray with and for others.*

1. How are we to draw near to God?

Because God is the sovereign Creator of heaven and earth, because he rules over all in majesty, and because he graciously condescends to receive us as his children, we approach God our Father with reverence and with all other child-like dispositions and with love.

2. What hope is there in approaching God as our Father?

Because God is our Father, we approach him in confidence, as children to a father, knowing he is able and ready to help us.

3. What are we taught in praying to God as our Father?

In praying to God as our Father, we are taught that we are to pray with and for others who are or will be children of God, that we all may be one as the Father and the Son are one.

QUESTION 101

What do we pray for in the first petition?

*In the first petition, which is, **Hallowed be thy name**, we pray that God would enable us, and others, to glorify him in all that whereby he maketh himself known; and that he would dispose all things to this own glory.*

1. What is it to glorify God?

We glorify God when we come to know his glory and make his glory known.

2. How does God make himself known?

God makes himself known in all his works of creation and providence. Man comes to know God as he, by God's grace, exercises dominion in the creation and over sin in himself.

3. Why is this the first petition of the Lord's Prayer?

Hallowed be thy name is the first petition of the Lord's Prayer because man's chief end is to glorify God and because eternal life is to know God.

4. Upon what promise can we hope for this petition?

God has promised in all ages that the earth will be filled with the knowledge of the glory of the Lord as the waters cover the sea.

QUESTION 102

What do we pray for in the second petition?

*In the second petition, which is, **Thy Kingdom come**, we pray that Satan's kingdom may be destroyed; and that the kingdom of grace may be advanced, ourselves and others brought into it, and kept in it; and that the kingdom of glory may be hastened.*

1. What is God's kingdom of power?

God's kingdom of power consists in his rule over all his works, and all the actions of men and angels, according to his sovereign purpose, for the praise of his glory.

2. What is the kingdom of Satan?

The kingdom of Satan consists in his rule in and through men, by the wisdom of this world, the desires of natural man, and all unjust use of power; which rule is signified as coming through the work of the false prophet, the harlot, and the beast.[2]

3. What is the kingdom of grace?

The kingdom of grace consists of Christ's present rule in and through his people, as prophet, priest, and king, to fill the earth with the knowledge of God.

4. What is the kingdom of glory?

The kingdom of glory is that kingdom of grace which, having grown to its fullness by overcoming the kingdom of darkness, is consummated by the return of Christ and the removal of all evil, forever.

---

2. Gangadean, "Paper No. 49: Eschatology: Summary and Response to FAQ," in *The Logos Papers*.

5. How does the kingdom of God come?

The kingdom of God is advanced and hastened as we take every thought captive that is raised up against the knowledge of God,[3] so that we may come into the unity of the faith,[4] and make disciples of all nations.[5]

QUESTION 103

What do we pray for in the third petition?

*In the third petition, which is, **Thy will be done on earth as it is in heaven**, we pray, that God, by his grace, would make us able and willing to know, obey, and submit to his will in all things, as the angels do in heaven.*

1. Where is the will of God revealed?

The will of God is summarily comprehended in the moral law, which law is written in the hearts of all men by creation and later given by special revelation in the Ten Commandments.

2. How are we made able to know and obey God's will?

The Spirit of God enables us to know and obey the will of God by bringing us to meditate on the law of God day and night, and to delight in the law of God as the way of life.

3. What is the fruit of obeying the law of God?

By obeying the law of God in its fullness, the kingdom of God is advanced in all the earth, and the name of God is hallowed in all that whereby God makes himself known.

---

3. *2 Corinthians 10:5.*

4. *Ephesians 4.*

5. *Matthew 28:19.*

QUESTION 104

What do we pray for in the fourth petition?

*In the fourth petition, which is, **Give us this day our daily bread**, we pray, that of God's free gift we may receive a competent portion of the good things of this life, and enjoy his blessing with them.*

1. What is our daily bread?

Our daily bread consists of a sufficiency of the outward blessings of life that we need each day to serve God's holy purpose.

2. Why do we ask God to give us what we need?

Because we cannot merit any of God's goodness nor enjoy it without his favor, we acknowledge, by asking, that all we have is by his free gift.

3. How are we given what we need?

God gives us what we need, not by the use of unlawful means, nor without the use of ordinary means, but by our waiting upon the providence of God in the use of lawful means.

QUESTION 105

What do we pray for in the fifth petition?

*In the fifth petition, which is, **And forgive us our debts, as
we forgive our debtors**, we pray, that God, for Christ's sake,
would freely pardon all our sins; which we are the rather
encouraged to ask, because by his grace we are enabled from
the heart to forgive others.*

1. For what must we seek forgiveness?

In this life, we still fail to know God as we ought, and must confess this
our sin, so that we may be forgiven and cleansed from it.

2. On what basis does God forgive us?

We are forgiven for Christ's sake only, who bore away our sin by his
death on the cross.

3. How can we know that God has forgiven us?

We can know God forgives us if we freely forgive others as we seek to
be forgiven by God.

QUESTION 106

What do we pray for in the sixth petition?

*In the sixth petition, which is, **And lead us not into
temptation, but deliver us from evil**, we pray that God
would either keep us from being tempted to sin, or support
and deliver us when we are tempted.*

1. What is it to be tempted?

In every trial of faith, our failure to understand what is good as we ought makes it possible to yield to sin.

2. How are we kept from temptation?

God, who is most wise and righteous, never tests us above what we are able to bear, but shows the way to escape to those who watch and pray.

3. How are we delivered from evil?

To those who by holiness endure the trial of their faith, God is pleased to further make himself known, which knowledge sanctifies us and sets us free from sin.

QUESTION 107

What doth the conclusion of the Lord's Prayer teach us?

*The conclusion of the Lord's Prayer, which is, **For thine is the kingdom, and the power, and the glory, forever, Amen,** teacheth us to take our encouragement in prayer from God only, and in our prayers to praise him, ascribing kingdom, power, and glory to him; and, in testimony of our desire, and assurance to be heard, we say Amen.*

1. How can we encourage ourselves in prayer?

We can encourage ourselves in prayer when we enforce our petitions with arguments, which are to be taken not from any worthiness in ourselves or in any other creature, but from God.

2. How is praise fitting to all our prayers?

As the desire of all our prayers is to the praise of God, so we ascribe to him alone eternal sovereignty, omnipotence, and glorious excellence, by which also we plead our requests and trust him to fulfill them.

3. How are we to end our prayers?

To testify to our desire for God's glory and our assurance that he hears us, we say Amen.

THE
LARGER
CATECHISM

Chapter 15

___

MAN'S CHIEF END AND THE WORD OF GOD

QUESTION 1

What is the chief and highest end of man?

Man's chief and highest end is to glorify God, and fully to enjoy him forever.

1. What is meant by chief end?

The chief end of man means that there is one ultimate purpose to human existence that gives meaning and unity to all of life. The chief end is the highest value (*Summum Bonum*), the end in itself.[1] In biblical revelation it is eternal life, which is knowing God.[2]

2. What is it to glorify God?

To glorify God is to know God in all that by which he makes himself known and to make his glory known to others.

---

1. Gangadean, *Philosophical Foundation*, 171-183.

2. *John 17:3.*

3. How does God make his glory known?[3]

God makes his glory known in all of his works of creation and providence. Man knows the glory of God through the work of dominion in God's creation.

4. What is the work of dominion?

In dominion, man is to name the creation, which reveals God's glory, and to rule over it, which is to develop the powers latent in man and the creation. Naming the natural world is the realm of science; ruling over it is the task of technology. Naming the human world is the task of humanities; ruling over it is the task of all forms of the arts of human culture.[4] The work of dominion requires the unity of all mankind in all aspects of man's diversity.

5. What does the work of dominion require to be completed?

The work of dominion requires all of mankind through all of history. It requires the unity of all mankind in all aspects of man's diversity.

6. What is the outcome of the work of dominion?

The outcome of the work of dominion is the establishment of the Kingdom of God, which is the City of God. The result is the earth filled with the knowledge of the LORD as the waters cover the sea.[5]

7. What is it to enjoy God?

To enjoy God is to behold the beauty of the LORD, which knowledge is eternal life. The lasting joy of eternal life comes from knowing God.[6]

8. What errors are here to be avoided?

We become divided rather than united if we do not seek man's ultimate end. We become man-centered rather than God-centered if we do not

---

3. Gangadean, "Paper No. 112: Why General Revelation Is Basic in the Christian Worldview," in *The Logos Papers*; "Paper No. 117: Knowing and Making God Known," in *The Logos Papers*.

4. Gangadean, "Paper No. 46: The Logos Curriculum: Foundational Principles," in *The Logos Papers*.

5. *Isaiah 11:9.*

6. *John 17:3;* Gangadean, *The Westminster Confession.* See Question 24; Gangadean, *Philosophical Foundation*, 208-211.

seek to glorify God. We become otherworldly or this worldly if we do not seek to know God through dominion.

QUESTION 2

How doth it appear that there is a God?

The very light of nature in man, and the works of God, declare plainly that there is a God; but his Word and Spirit only do sufficiently and effectually reveal him unto men for their salvation.

1. What is the light of nature in man?[7]

The light of nature is the Logos in man as reason. Reason is the first form of the Word of God that comes to man: the life of the Logos, the eternal Word of God, is in all men, made in the image of God. Reason is the self-attesting Word of God which makes thought possible. Reason is that by which we see, with the mind, that is, understand, both the book of nature/general revelation and the book of Scripture/ special revelation.

2. What is the plain revelation of God in creation?

The clear revelation of God in creation is known as general revelation.[8] General revelation consists of what may be known of God and man and good and evil by all men, everywhere, at all times. It manifests the power, wisdom, and goodness of God in its fullness—it is maximally

---

7. Gangadean, "Paper No.48: Reason and the Word of God: An Apologetic for Reason," in *The Logos Papers*.

8. Gangadean, "Paper No. 35: The Clarity of General Revelation," in *The Logos Papers*; "Paper No. 41: What is Clear About God: The Clarity of General Revelation," in *The Logos Papers*; Appendix 6.

clear.[9] It also includes the moral law, which is written on the hearts of all men.[10]

3. How is general revelation known?

General revelation is known inferentially by reason: it is deduced from the nature of things created. It is objectively clear and accessible to all who care to know by seeking diligently.

4. Why is man inexcusable before God?

Man is created in the image of God, fundamentally rational with the ability to know. Man must deny his own nature as rational to not see what is clear. One must neglect, avoid, resist, and deny reason in order not to see what is objectively clear. The shame and guilt of inexcusability are avoided by self-deception and resisted by self-justification. We are morally culpable before God for our failure to know him and to live according to our nature.

5. What is the Principle of Clarity?[11]

The Principle of Clarity affirms that the basic things about God and man and good and evil are clear to reason and that the failure to know what is clear to reason is inexcusable. Knowing what is clear requires that we can show (give proof of) what is clear. Proof consists of rational justification for one's belief.[12]

6. What is Scripture and why was it given?

Scripture is redemptive revelation. It assumes the rejection of the Word of God in man as reason and in the creation as clear general revelation. Scripture is the Word of God written. It reveals how God is both just and merciful to man in sin. Scripture focuses on the person and work of Christ, the Word of God incarnate, who restores mankind to life in the knowledge of God.

---

9. *Romans 1:20.*

10. *Romans 2:14-15.*

11. Gangadean, "Paper No. 53: Common Ground (Part IV): The Principle of Clarity," in *The Logos Papers*.

12. Gangadean, "Paper No. 72: What Is Knowledge? (Concise Version)," in *The Logos Papers*; Gangadean, *History of Philosophy*, 175-179; Gangadean, *Philosophical Foundation*, 49-50.

QUESTION 3

What is the Word of God?

The Holy Scriptures of the Old and New Testament are the Word of God, the only rule for faith and obedience.

1. What are the seven senses of the Word of God?

The Word of God (the Logos) 1) is eternal, 2) is in all men as reason, 3) is in creation as general revelation, 4) is in history as Scripture, 5) is incarnate in Jesus Christ, 6) by the Holy Spirit is in the Church as the Historic Christian Faith, and 7) in each believer by regeneration and sanctification.[13]

2. Explain "In the beginning was the Word."

The Logos is the Word of God in its fullness. The Word of God is eternal. The Word of God is God the Son who makes God known. The Son of God is the Creator by whom all things were made.

3. Explain "The life of the Logos was the light of men."

The Word of God is in all men made in the image of God. The life of the Word is the light of men. That light, by which we see and understand, is reason. The darkness of unbelief cannot withstand the light of reason.

4. Explain "The Logos was in the world."

The Word of God is revealed in all his works of creation and providence. The whole earth is full of his glory. Yet no one seeks, and no one understands what is clear about God.

---

13. Gangadean, "Paper No. 30: The Word of God: The Logos Is Truth," in *The Logos Papers.*

5. Explain "He came to His own."

The Word of God came to the covenant people of God in history through the prophets. The prophets were not received, but their Word became Scripture, the Word of God written.

6. Explain "And the Word was made flesh."

The Word of God became incarnate in Jesus Christ, full of grace and truth.[14] He is the Lamb of God who takes away the sin of the world.[15] He is the risen Lord who rules to make God known.

7. Explain "He will guide you into all truth."

Christ the Lord sends the Spirit to lead the Church into all Truth.[16] The historically cumulative insight summed up in the Church's creeds and confessions/councils is the holy, catholic, and apostolic faith, the basis of the unity of the faith for all who believe.

8. Explain "Sanctify them by thy truth."

The Word of God is in each believer by the work of the Holy Spirit. Each believer is born again by the living Word of God.[17] Each believer is sanctified by the Truth. The Word of God (the Logos) is Truth.[18]

9. What is the content of Scripture?[19]

The content of Scripture is consistent with clear general revelation. Scripture affirms that only God the Creator is eternal. Original creation is without natural evil. And it affirms covenant representation in that all are affected by the act of one. In Genesis 1–3 is given the foundation of Scripture in organic seed form. Scripture builds on, is to be understood by, and is the development of what is revealed in Genesis 1–3. Scripture consists of the 66 books of the Old Testament (39) and New Testament (27).

---

14. *John 1:14.*
15. *John 1:29.*
16. *John 16:13.*
17. *1 Peter 1:23.*
18. *John 17:17.*
19. Gangadean, *The Westminster Confession.* See Question 6.

QUESTION 4

How doth it appear that the Scriptures are the Word of God?

The Scriptures manifest themselves to be the Word of God, by their majesty and purity; by the consent of all the parts, and the scope of the whole, which is to give all glory to God; by their light and power to convince and convert sinners, to comfort and build up believers unto salvation: but the Spirit of God bearing witness by and with the Scriptures in the heart of man, is alone able fully to persuade it that they are the very Word of God.

1. Explain the objective aspects of the authority of Scripture.[20]

The objective authority of Scripture rests in that it is authored by God, given by God, and it is to be received because it is the Word of God. Scripture is self-evidently the Word of God through arguments.

2. What are the arguments that prove that the Scriptures are the Word of God?

1) The testimony of the Church, for it is the work of the Holy Spirit in Church history.

2) The heavenliness of the matter, for it answers how man is to be saved, which can only be known by special revelation.

3) The efficacy of the doctrine, for it is the rule for doctrine and life.

4) The majesty of the style, for it is a sublime expression of the truth.

5) The consent of all the parts, for the unity of the redemptive content is devoid of any contradiction.

---

20. Gangadean, *The Westminster Confession*. See Question 7.

6) The scope of the whole, which is the doxological focus—to give glory to God.

7) The full discovery it makes of the only way of man's salvation. It shows how God is both just and merciful to man in sin. Divine justice is satisfied through mercy. Christ, through vicarious atonement, fully pays for the requirements of divine justice.

3. Explain the subjective aspects of the authority of Scripture.

We subjectively come to know the objective truth of Scripture through the inward work of the Holy Spirit bearing witness by and with the Word in our hearts.

QUESTION 5

What do the Scriptures principally teach?

The Scriptures principally teach, what man is to believe concerning God, and what duty God requires of man.

1. For what purpose were the Scriptures given?[21]

The Scriptures, as redemptive revelation, show how God is both just and merciful to man in sin. The Scriptures were given to instruct and to correct us to prepare us for work through which God is glorified.

2. What work is given to man?

From the beginning, man was given the work of dominion,[22] the cultural mandate, through which God is glorified. In Christ, the work is continued in the mission mandate[23] to bring all men to know God.

---

21. Gangadean, "Paper No. 87: Scripture," in *The Logos Papers*; "Paper No. 112: Why General Revelation Is Basic in the Christian Worldview," in *The Logos Papers*.

22. *Genesis 1:26-28;* Appendix 4.

23. *Matthew 28:18-20.*

3. What is the relation between our knowledge of God and our duty?

Knowing God enables us to do our duty, and doing our duty, obeying God's law, enables us to increase in the knowledge of God.

QUESTION 6

What do the Scriptures make known of God?

The Scriptures make known what God is, the persons in the Godhead, his decrees, and the execution of his decrees.

1. Why do the Scriptures not give proof of God's existence?

The Scriptures affirm the clarity of general revelation and the inexcusability of unbelief. The Scriptures assume that God's eternal power and divine nature are clearly revealed in the things that are made.[24] The Scriptures are given as redemptive revelation for man's failure to use reason to see what is clear.

2. Is there an innate knowledge of God or *sensus divinitatis*?

Man has no innate knowledge of God, but has innate concepts bound with our rational nature. We have an innate sense of the qualities of infinite, eternal, and unchangeable, which can only, upon analysis, be applied to God.

---

24. *Romans 1:18-20.*

Chapter 16

GOD AND

HIS DECREES

QUESTION 7

What is God?

*God is a Spirit, in and of himself infinite in being,
glory, blessedness, and perfection; all-sufficient, eternal,
unchangeable, incomprehensible, everywhere present,
almighty, knowing all things, most wise, most holy, most just,
most merciful and gracious, long-suffering, and abundant in
goodness and truth.*

1. Explain what God is a Spirit means.

God is personal—with knowledge and will—and the source of all
personhood, the highest reality vs. impersonal (*advaita*; *dvaita*; Plato;
Aristotle; Plotinus; Spinoza; Hegel; Tao; Buddhism; not pure energy;
not pure will); Creator of all that is; in personal relationship with man;
without body, parts, and passions (vs. theophany and anthropomorphism).

2. What are the incommunicable attributes of God?[1]

The incommunicable attributes are attributes that God and only God has. These attributes are his being infinite, eternal, and unchangeable. Although distinguishable, they are inseparable; infinitude and unchangeability spring from eternality. Incommunicable implies the logical impossibility of communicating or giving them to another being—God cannot create (bring into being) an eternal being (uncreated being). It is logically impossible, for it implies a contradiction.

3. Explain what God is eternal means.

God is eternal means that God is without beginning and without end. God is timeless (outside of time; there is nothing before the beginning; time began with creation); God also acts in time, in providence (upholding, directing, disposing, and governing). God in timelessness cannot be known directly.

4. Explain what God is infinite means.

Infinitude cannot be increased or diminished; has all power over all that is; infinitude is an attribute of an attribute derived from eternality; God can do anything that is logically possible; God will always act according to his nature.

5. Explain what God is unchangeable means.

God cannot deny his nature, yet is free; God's "passions" do not change; expressed freely in the nature of things in creation and freely by grace and wisdom in all providence.

6. Explain how God is infinite, eternal, and unchangeable IEU in being.

God's essence is to be self-existent; his being is not abstract (a set of laws or qualities); he is the Creator (source) of all beings. His being is simple; it includes all perfections, distinct yet in unity, without any conflict or tension, so that the highest expression of the one is the highest expression of the other.

---

1. Gangadean, *The Westminster Confession*. See Question 13.

7. Explain how God is IEU in wisdom.

Wisdom knows the best way to achieve one's goal, all things considered; wisdom is seen in the fine-tuning of the natural world and in the general and particular providence under the moral law (including ordinary means, and miracles, which may work above, apart, and against ordinary means).

8. Explain how God is IEU in power.

Power expresses the divine goodness and purpose in creation and providence. God in creating man a body/soul unity, can (and must) create man without physical death, can impose death on all men, and can remove death from all men; freely, and not arbitrarily or necessarily.

9. Explain how God is IEU in holiness.

Holiness is devotion to the good, a zeal for excellence based on knowledge; it is spiritual beauty, manifest in splendor, majesty, and brilliance (and symbolized at times in precious stones). It is active, not passive, and prevails in good overcoming evil.

10. Explain how God is IEU in justice.

Justice is ultimately and fundamentally ontological, grounded in the nature of being. It is inherent in moral acts, and not arbitrarily imposed (both now and in the afterlife); the inherent consequence of moral evil (denying one's nature) is spiritual death (meaninglessness and its consequences).

11. Explain how God is IEU in goodness.

Goodness is love in all its aspects; kindness, gentleness, patience, forgiveness, compassion, mercy, grace in a way consistent with holiness (devotion to the good); yet it does not leave the guilty unpunished; mercy satisfies the divine justice, it does not set it aside; forgiveness is received only at the seat of mercy satisfying justice.

12. Explain how God is IEU in truth.

The Word of God (the *Logos*) is Truth in its fullness. The Logos is *that* light *by* which we know, and it is *that* which is known. The clarity of God's Word/Truth makes unbelief inexcusable. Understanding the

Truth increases in history, corporately and individually, in response to trials of faith.

13. Explain how God is incomprehensible.

Incomprehensible means that God cannot ever be known fully. It does not mean that he cannot be known, but that we can know now in part, and we will continue to grow in knowledge yet without ever exhausting the knowledge of the being of God.

QUESTION 8

Are there more Gods than one?

There is but one only, the living and true God.

1. What is affirmed in the unity of God?

There is no division within God, and all aspects of life are equally under God, in contrast to polytheism.

2. What is a false view of the unity of God?

Unity does not deny diversity within God or that God's being includes all being, in contrast to attributeless pantheism (*Nirguna Brahman*).

3. How are we to understand the oneness of God?

By the oneness of God,[2] we are to understand that both unity and diversity are ultimate in God and in his creation.

---

2. Gangadean, *History of Philosophy*, 40; Gangadean, *The Westminster Confession*. See Question 15.

QUESTION 9

How many persons are there in the Godhead?

There be three persons in the Godhead, the Father, the Son, and the Holy Ghost; and these three are one true, eternal God, the same in substance, equal in power and glory; although distinguished by their personal properties.

1. How is the doctrine of the Trinity known?

The Trinity is a revealed mystery; a mystery is communicated and known only by special revelation. A mystery is a revelation previously hidden but now revealed.[3] The Trinity is known by the great events of creation, the Incarnation, and Pentecost.

2. In what respect are Father, Son, and Holy Spirit ontologically equal?

The Father, Son, and Holy Spirit are united in substance and attributes. The three persons of the Trinity share one being in that each is of the same substance (spirit), and each has the same attributes.[4] This is set in contrast to various forms of subordination:

1) Modalism: one being expressed in three modes at different times.

2) Arianism: the Son is the first created being through whom God created all else.

3) Unitarianism: rejects the Trinity as a logical impossibility.

4) Deism: God is Creator but not ruler.

5) Islam: Allah's absolute oneness condemns any "partnership" as idolatry (*Shirk*).

---

3. *Colossians 1:25-27.*

4. Gangadean, *The Westminster Confession.* See Question 15.

3. In what respect are Father, Son, and Holy Spirit teleologically equal?

The Father, Son, and Holy Spirit are united in purpose. All of the works of creation and providence are for the manifestation of God's glory.

4. In what respects are the three persons different?

Each person of the Trinity has a different function, an economic trinitarianism. The economic Trinity refers to the three persons in terms of their relationship with one another. The Father eternally begets the Son, the Son is eternally begotten of the Father, and the Holy Spirit eternally proceeds from the Father and the Son. There is a distinct order within the Trinity. This is set in contrast to modalism.

5. In what respects are the three persons different in function in creation and redemption?

God the Father decrees in creation and elects in redemption. *God the Son* is the eternal Word of God who makes God known in creation and comes incarnate to satisfy the requirements of divine justice and redeem those the Father elects. *God the Holy Spirit,* upholds the creation and applies redemption to those the Father elects and for those whom the Son died.

6. Does the Trinity entail a logical contradiction?

The Trinity is not a contradiction. God is one in one sense and three in a different sense. God is one being and three persons. A contradiction would entail being one and three at the same time and in the same respect. The creedal formulation of the Trinity—through the process of much discussion—has formulated a theologically precise and nuanced understanding of the doctrine which avoids misunderstandings and logical contradictions.

7. Explain how the Trinity is expectational (what we should have expected):

The Trinity, being a mystery, is impossible to know apart from Scripture. Once revealed, we can and should understand it in part (like other Biblical mysteries). It is what we should have expected:

Being is a unity of diversity.

The highest being is a unity of the highest diversity.

The highest diversity is persons.

Therefore the highest unity would be of persons.

Therefore, God as the highest being is a unity of persons.

QUESTION 10

What are the personal properties of the three persons in the Godhead?

It is proper to the Father to beget the Son, and to the Son to be begotten of the Father, and to the Holy Ghost to proceed from the Father and the Son from all eternity.

How are we to understand the relationship between the Father and the Son?

The Son is of the Father, but the Father is not of the Son. Begotten is an eternal relationship. Father and Son are timeless relational terms, for one cannot be a father without there being a son. The Father makes himself known through the Son, and the Son makes God known.

QUESTION 11

How doth it appear that the Son and the Holy Ghost are God equal with the Father?

The Scriptures manifest that the Son and the Holy Ghost are God equal with the Father, ascribing unto them such names, attributes, works, and worship, as are proper to God only.

QUESTION 12

What are the decrees of God?[5]

God's decrees are the wise, free, and holy acts of the counsel of his will, whereby, from all eternity, he hath, for his own glory, unchangeably foreordained: Whatsoever comes to pass in time, especially concerning angels and men.

1. What did God decree?

God decreed whatsoever comes to pass. Everything in the universe that comes to pass is decreed by God.

2. What is the basis of God's sovereign rule over all?

God is Creator of all that exists and is self-existent and independent of the creation. The creature is not self-existent, but wholly dependent on God for its being and continued existence. Denial of God's sovereignty is rooted in denial of creaturely dependence.

---

5. Gangadean, *The Westminster Confession*. See Questions 16-21.

3. What are the common errors in denying God's sovereignty?

1) That ultimately things come about by chance or luck, that there is no plan of God, that if the will is free, it cannot be caused, e.g., in semi-Pelagian and Arminian Christianity, and in some philosophers (Kant, William James vs. Augustine, Luther, and Calvin).

2) That ultimately our lives are fated, that there is no freedom, and that the outcome is not affected by our beliefs and desires, e.g., the Greek fates, in Islam, karma, astrology, and in teachers of hard (vs. soft) determinism (Marx and Freud).

4. How are these errors to be avoided?

The guide for life is not the decree of God, but the revealed will of God summed up in the commandments. We are not to leave things to chance, nor are we to be resigned and fail to use ordinary means.

5. What is the extent and purpose of God's decrees?[6]

The decrees extend not only to salvation, but to all that comes to pass; their purpose is for the revelation of God's wisdom, power, justice, and goodness.

---

6. Gangadean, *The Westminster Confession*. See Question 16.

QUESTION 13

What hath God especially decreed concerning angels and men?[7]

God, by an eternal and immutable decree, out of his mere love, for the praise of his glorious grace, to be manifested in due time, hath elected some angels to glory; and in Christ hath chosen some men to eternal life, and the means thereof: and also, according to his sovereign power, and the unsearchable counsel of his own will (whereby he extendeth or withholdeth favor as he pleases), hath passed by and foreordained the rest to dishonor and wrath, to be for their sin inflicted, to the praise of the glory of his justice.

1. For what purpose did God decree concerning angels and men?

God, from all eternity, for the manifestation of his glory, out of his mere love predestinated some men and angels unto everlasting life; and for the praise of the glory of his justice, he foreordained others to everlasting death.

2. Upon what basis did God particularly choose some and not others?

God, in Christ, chose some particular men and the means thereof to everlasting life. The election is particular, not general. God deliberately chose some and not others, yet the choice lies solely in God in accordance with the unsearchable counsel of his own will.

---

7. Gangadean, *The Westminster Confession*. See Questions 17-18.

3. How is God's glorious grace praised in his eternal decree of election?

Grace is the deepest, richest level of mercy. In his decree of election, God's grace is being glorified, revealed, and magnified in his greatness. God is not obligated to extend grace; grace, by definition, is unmerited. It is a gift of God.

4. How is God's glorious justice praised in his eternal decree?

Justice requires that equals be treated equally. All fallen angels and men get what they deserve. In sin, left to themselves, fallen angels and sinful men turn their own way. God leaves them to go their own way. The Lord extends and withholds mercy as he pleases, yet fallen angels and men neither demand nor desire mercy. They get what they want.

QUESTION 14

How doth God execute his decrees?[8]

God executeth his decrees in the works of creation and providence, according to his infallible foreknowledge, and the free and immutable counsel of his own will.

1. How are God's decrees executed through his work of creation?

The decrees of God are not externally imposed upon the creature so as to nullify its nature, but come to expression through the nature of the creature. As God's nature is revealed in what he does, so what the creature does reveals its nature.

2. How are God's decrees executed through his work of providence?

God upholds, directs, disposes, and governs his creatures so that things come to pass according to their natures.

---

8. Gangadean, *The Westminster Confession.* See Questions 16-21.

3. Is God bound by the nature of the thing created?

God, in his ordinary providence, makes use of means, yet is free to work above, without, and against them at his pleasure, which is according to his own nature.

Chapter 17

CREATION AND
PROVIDENCE

QUESTION 15

What is the work of creation?

*The work of creation is that wherein God did in the
beginning, by the word of his power, make of nothing the
world, and all things therein, for himself, within the space of
six days, and all very good.*

1. What is creation *ex nihilo*?[1]

By the Word of God, the substance of the universe and all that is in it
came into being. This is set in contrast to contemporary naturalism,
which claims the universe is self-existing,[2] dualism, which claims matter eternally co-exists with spirit as in Platonic thought,[3] and spiritual
monism of Eastern mysticism, which claims the world is unreal or a
manifestation of God.[4]

---

1. Gangadean, *Philosophical Foundation*, 141-143; Gangadean, "Paper No. 142: The Biblical
   Worldview (Part II): Biblical Cosmology: Creation *Ex Nihilo*," in *The Logos Papers*; Gangadean, *The Westminster Confession*. See Question 22.

2. Gangadean, "Paper No. 78: Material Monism," in *The Logos Papers*; "Paper No. 90: Christianity and Secular Humanism: The Difference," in *The Logos Papers*.

3. Gangadean, "Paper No. 82: Dualism," in *The Logos Papers*.

4. Gangadean, "Paper No. 80: Spiritual Monism," in *The Logos Papers*.

2. What is special creation?

Special creation is the acts of God subsequent to creation *ex nihilo* by which God formed and filled the earth with creatures made each after its own kind.[5] Special creation ended with the Sabbath day in contrast to theistic evolution.[6]

3. What is meant in saying the world was created very good?

The goodness of the creation consists in it revealing God's glory as he intended in creating and in the absence of all evil, both moral and natural.

QUESTION 16

How did God create angels?

God created all the angels spirits, immortal, holy, excelling in knowledge, mighty in power, to execute his commandments, and to praise his name, yet subject to change.

What is the nature of angels?

Angels are finite, temporal, and changeable spirits endowed with ever-lasting souls, without a body yet able to take upon human form for a time, created as individual beings without procreation or covenant representation. Angels are changeable in themselves yet unchangeable when upheld by God.

---

5. Gangadean, *History of Philosophy*, 53; Gangadean, "Paper No. 143: The Biblical Worldview (Part III): Biblical Cosmology: Subsequent Creation by Forming and Filling," in *The Logos Papers*; Gangadean, *The Westminster Confession*. See Question 22.

6. Gangadean, "Paper No. 79: The Creation vs. Evolution Controversy," in *The Logos Papers*; "Paper No. 143: The Biblical Worldview (Part III): Biblical Cosmology: Subsequent Creation by Forming and Filling," in *The Logos Papers*.

QUESTION 17

How did God create man?

After God had made all other creatures, he created man male and female; formed the body of the man of the dust of the ground, and the woman of the rib of the man, endued them with living, reasonable, and immortal souls; made them after his own image, in knowledge, righteousness, and holiness; having the law of God written in their hearts, and power to fulfill it, and dominion over the creatures; yet subject to fall.

1. What are the various aspects of man as the image of God?

Man is created a body/soul unity, a male/female unity, with a formal or larger aspect of the image of God, with a triune personality, and with dominion.[7]

2. What is meant by body/soul unity?

Having a body is an essential part of being a human being. To be human is to be a body/soul unity. Physical death was not original, but imposed because of sin. Physical death is a natural evil imposed until the overcoming of moral evil (sin) by the rule of Christ. The rending of body and soul in death is removed in the resurrection—then we remain in the body in perpetuity. The visible body reveals the invisible soul and is the basis of analogous anthropomorphic language in speaking about God: "face to face," "walked with God," "I will stretch out my hand," "sitting at the right hand," etc.

---

7. Gangadean, "Paper No. 85: An Introduction to Christianity," in *The Logos Papers*; "Paper No. 87: Scripture," in *The Logos Papers*; Gangadean, *The Westminster Confession*. See Question 23.

3. What is meant by male/female unity?

Male and female are both aspects of the being of God. These characteristics are in God, spiritually, and originate from God. Both maleness
and femaleness equally reflect diverse aspects of what is united in God—
Creator and sustainer of the universe. Both are in God, and there is an
order (creation is prior). Maleness reflects God as Creator and ruler,
while femaleness reflects upholder and nurturer. Maleness is inferred
from God as Creator (origination, initiation, determination, planning,
bringing into being) and femaleness from providence (upholding,
directing, disposing, governing, and nurturing). Man was originally one
being (Adam), embodying two principles (male and female). Woman
was formed from man—a principle became a person. What became two
persons are to be united again in one flesh (by marriage in an economic
unity). The context of this unity is the pursuit of the good—the chief
end of man—which is the source of all unity.

4. What is meant by the larger aspect of the image of God?

God is a Spirit, infinite, eternal, and unchangeable in being, wisdom,
power, holiness, justice, goodness, and truth. Man, as made in the image
of God, shares in the same moral attributes (wisdom, power, holiness,
justice, goodness, and truth), but in a finite, temporal, and changeable
way. This is equally true of all human beings, always—pre-Fall, post-Fall,
regenerated, glorified, and resurrected. These are formal characteristics
that man never ceases to have, regardless of how their content may
change. Man will always be devoted (be holy) whether he is devoted
to God or to self. Man will always have beliefs about truth, whether
he believes God exists or believes there is no God. These attributes
exist as formal capacities only and structure human consciousness of
self and of God. We must recognize our similarities and our differences in thinking about ourselves and God. God's incommunicable
attributes (infinitude, eternality, and unchangeability) are different
in kind from our temporality, finitude, and changeability. We are to
think presuppositionally about God. We are to think about the finite
(man) in light of the infinite (God), not the infinite (God) in light of
the finite (man) or the finite (man) in light of the finite (nature). We
are to think of man as the image of God; we are not to think of God
as the image of man. The divine nature, which is infinite, eternal, and

unchangeable, is not to be likened to human nature, which is finite, temporal, and changeable.

5. What is meant by the triune personality of man?

Man is created in knowledge, holiness, and righteousness, called the narrower aspect of the image of God. This aspect has specific content; it was lost in the Fall and restored in regeneration. It reflects the structure of the human heart and is the basis of our diverse functions as prophet, priest, and king. Man as prophet is to understand God's revelation in creation, history, and Scripture so as to attain to the fullness of the knowledge of God. Man as priest is to teach God's revelation so as to bring all men to holiness—the sanctification that comes through knowing the truth. Man as king is to rule in God's creation so as to bring all men to righteousness through obeying God's law in all things. In Scripture, these offices are manifested in the person and work of Moses as prophet, Aaron as priest, and David as king, and in those who continued these offices. The three offices are united doxologically in the work of the kingdom. The order in the Trinity (Father, Son, and Holy Ghost) is reflected in the order of these functions within each person (intellect, emotion, and will—also described as mind, soul, and strength), and the order should be maintained between persons in any group (prophetic, priestly, and kingly).

6. What is the dominion that man is to exercise?

Man is created with dominion over the creatures: man's work of dominion reflects God's dominion in creation; man is to name (grasp the essence of things) and rule (develop all the powers latent in himself and the created order). Man is to name the creation so as to know God, who reveals his glory in creation and providence. Man is to fill everything in every way as the rule of God's kingdom over all. The task of dominion is for the entire race throughout history. The work will be completed when the earth is filled with the knowledge of God as the waters cover the sea.[8] The Sabbath given to man signifies the goal and completion of this work. Just as God completed his work and then rested,[9] so man as made in the image of God will complete his work and then rest.

---

8. *Isaiah 11:9.*

9. *Genesis 2:2.*

QUESTION 18

What are God's works of providence?

God's works of providence are his most holy, wise, and powerful preserving and governing all his creatures; ordering them, and all their actions, to his own glory.

1. What is the general providence of God?[10]

In general providence, God upholds everything by the word of his power and rules over all by the natural laws of creation.

2. What is the particular providence of God?[11]

In particular providence, God rules over men and nations by his moral law, withholding grace and permitting sin and death, and giving grace that brings righteousness and life as he pleases.

3. What is the end of God's holy rule?

God works all things to the praise of his glory.

4. How can it be shown that God has acted since original creation?

Natural evil is not original in creation. Since God is all good and all-powerful, then he could, would, must have, and therefore did make a world that was good, that is, without natural evil/physical death. Natural evil/physical death is not inherent in moral evil; spiritual death is inherent in moral evil. Natural evil, therefore, is imposed by an act of God.

5. How is deism inconsistent with clear general revelation?[12]

Deism is the belief that the world was created by God, but not actively ruled by God; God did not act after creation to bring about natural

---

10. Gangadean, *The Westminster Confession*. See Questions 24-25.

11. Gangadean, *The Westminster Confession*. See Questions 26-29.

12. Gangadean, "Paper No. 127: God Is Creator and Ruler vs. Deism," in *The Logos Papers*.

evil in the world or to give any redemptive revelation to mankind. It is clear from general revelation that God both creates and actively rules in the creation.

QUESTION 19

What is God's providence towards the angels?

God by his providence permitted some of the angels, wilfully and irrecoverably, to fall into sin and damnation, limiting and ordering that, and all their sins, to his own glory; and established the rest in holiness and happiness; employing them all, at his pleasure, in the administrations of his power, mercy, and justice.

What purpose does God's providence for angels and men share in common?

God's providence towards angels and men is doxological in purpose. God permitted some angels to fall for the praise of God's glorious justice, and God established the rest of the angels for the praise of his goodness and mercy. God's providence for both has the same goal of deepening the revelation of his glory.

QUESTION 20

What was the providence of God toward man in the estate in which he was created?

The providence of God toward man in the estate in which he was created, was the placing him in paradise, appointing him to dress it, giving him liberty to eat of the fruit of the earth; putting the creatures under his dominion, and ordaining marriage for his help; affording him communion with himself; instituting the Sabbath; entering into a covenant of life with him, upon condition of personal, perfect, and perpetual obedience, of which the tree of life was a pledge; and forbidding to eat of the tree of the knowledge of good and evil, upon the pain of death.

1. What was God's purpose in the covenant?[13]

God's purpose in the covenant was to establish mankind in life on the basis of obedience. By keeping this covenant, man would be changed by God from a condition in which it was possible to sin to one in which it would not be possible to sin.

2. What was signified by the two trees?

The two trees outwardly represented the two ways that are always before all men: the way of life and the way of death, good and evil, the knowledge of God and the knowledge of good and evil.

---

13. Gangadean, *The Westminster Confession.* See Questions 35-38; Gangadean, "Paper No. 145: The Biblical Worldview (Part V): The Fall: The Covenant of Creation and the Temptation," in *The Logos Papers.*

3. Did the covenant forbid mankind to have the knowledge of good and evil?

Only God determines what is good for a being based upon the nature of the being he creates. Good for man as a rational being is the use of reason to the fullest to understand the meaning of the world, which reveals the glory of God; thus, the good for man is to possess the knowledge of God. What is forbidden as evil is man's self-determination of good and evil apart from his nature as a being made in the image of God.

Chapter 18

THE FALL OF MAN

QUESTION 21

Did man continue in that estate wherein God at first created him?

Our first parents being left to the freedom of their own will, through the temptation of Satan, transgressed the commandment of God in eating the forbidden fruit; and thereby fell from the estate of innocency wherein they were created.

1. What does it mean to be left to the freedom of their own will?

It means that God is not the cause of man's sin but permits it; that God could have prevented their sin by upholding them in his grace.

2. What is the state of man that made it possible to sin?

Man is created changeable in knowledge, holiness, and righteousness, which changeable condition would have been altered by obedience through the covenant.

3. Why did God permit sin?[1]

God permitted sin, not by a bare permission merely, but according to his eternal plan, having purposed to deepen the revelation of his glory by his rule over sin.

QUESTION 22

Did all mankind fall in that first transgression?

The covenant being made with Adam as a public person, not for himself only, but for his posterity, all mankind descending from him by ordinary generation, sinned in him, and fell with him in that first transgression.

1. What is original sin?

Original sin is the origin of all sin, historically and logically.[2]

2. How is Adam's sin the historical origin of all sin?

The guilt of Adam's sin is imputed to all those united to him by ordinary generation by virtue of the covenant of life. By this guilt, the effect of his sin on his nature is passed on so that all men are born spiritually dead and must be regenerated to have life.

3. How is Adam's sin the logical origin of all sin?

The logical origin of all sin is the denial of God in the denial of clear general revelation, which was the sin of Adam.

---

1. Gangadean, "Paper No. 146: The Biblical Worldview (Part VI): The Fall: Sin," in *The Logos Papers*; "Paper No. 147: The Biblical Worldview (Part VII): The Fall: Death and Theodicy," in *The Logos Papers*; Gangadean, *The Westminster Confession*. See Question 30.

2. Gangadean, *The Westminster Confession*. See Questions 30-34; Appendix 7.

4. Is there any injustice in imputing the sin of Adam?

No, but where sin abounded grace did much more abound in imputing the righteousness of the last Adam.[3]

QUESTION 23

Into what estate did the Fall bring mankind?[4]

The Fall brought mankind into an estate of sin and misery.

1. What is to be distinguished in man's estate of sin?

In sin, there is to be distinguished the change in the condition of man's entire heart, the narrower aspect of his nature, commonly called the depravity of our nature, and actual transgressions that proceed from this nature, whether by omission or by commission.

2. What is to be distinguished in man's estate of misery?

In human misery, there is to be distinguished spiritual death, which is the inherent consequence of sin, and the miseries of this life which are imposed upon man as a call to repentance from sin.

---

3. *Romans 5.*

4. Gangadean, "Paper No. 146: The Biblical Worldview (Part VI): The Fall: Sin," in *The Logos Papers*; "Paper No. 147: The Biblical Worldview (Part VII): The Fall: Death and Theodicy," in *The Logos Papers*; "Paper No. 148: The Biblical Worldview (Part VIII): Redemption: The First and Second Calls to Repentance," in *The Logos Papers*; "Paper No. 149: The Biblical Worldview (Part IX): Redemption: The Third Call to Repentance," in *The Logos Papers*; Gangadean, *The Westminster Confession.* See Questions 30-34.

QUESTION 24

What is sin?[5]

Sin is any want of conformity unto, or transgression of, any law of God, given as a rule to the reasonable creature.

1. Are any of the commands of God arbitrary?

The commands of God are based on his nature and the nature of man who is made in the image of God. No command of God is arbitrary, nor can God deny himself. Sin as moral evil always involves a denial of God's nature and a violation of our nature.

2. What generally is denied in sin?

In sin, there is generally a denial of who God is and what is good for man. This can be seen in the account of the Fall of man in the Garden of Eden, in what man must believe in coming to God, and in understanding what the Scriptures principally teach.

3. How is sin revealed in the temptation?

1) The temptation of man reveals the state of man in the pursuit of good or evil.

2) Sin as unbelief and not understanding is revealed in man's rejection of God's Word.

3) Sin as unholiness is revealed in man not seeking the knowledge of God.

4) Sin as unrighteousness is revealed in man's eating of the tree of the knowledge of good and evil.

5) Sin as autonomy is revealed in man's choosing to determine good and evil for himself.

---

5. Gangadean, *The Westminster Confession.* See Questions 30-34; Appendix 7.

6) Sin at root is revealed as the denial of God as infinite, eternal, and unchanging Creator.

7) Sin at root is revealed as man's denial of being a finite, temporal, and changeable creature.

8) Sin is revealed as the denial of the clear difference between the finite and the infinite.

9) Sin is revealed as the denial of human nature in denying reason to avoid what is clear.

10) The consequence inherent in sin is spiritual death: meaninglessness, boredom, and guilt.

4. How else is sin described in Scripture?

Sin is described as denial of clear general revelation; as not seeking God, not understanding God, not doing righteousness; as shutting one's eyes and closing one's ears, and hardening one's heart.

5. What common errors show misunderstanding of sin?

Antinomianism denies the universal and perpetual nature of the law as the way of life. Legalism denies the spiritual and total nature of the law as the way of life. Both reduce the purpose of the law to that of justification, but differ over its continued necessity.

6. What are the two aspects of sin?

Sin is either by omission, what we fail to do, or by commission, what we do.

QUESTION 25

Wherein consists the sinfulness of that estate whereinto man fell?

The sinfulness of that estate whereinto man fell, consisteth in the guilt of Adam's first sin, the want of that righteousness wherein he was created, and the corruption of his nature, whereby he is utterly indisposed, disabled, and made opposite unto all that is spiritually good, and wholly inclined to all evil, and that continually; which is commonly called original sin, and from which do proceed all actual transgressions.

1. What is meant by our whole nature?

God created man finite, temporal, and changeable in knowledge, holiness, and righteousness, which is the narrower aspect of man's nature, also called the heart of man. The whole heart is affected by the Fall of man, not merely one or two aspects. The Fall does not affect the larger, formal aspect of man's nature, which is the essence of his humanness.

2. How is each aspect of the heart corrupted or changed by the Fall?

Man changed in knowledge from understanding the nature of God and believing that he exists to misunderstanding that nature and to unbelief. Man changed in holiness from desiring the knowledge of God as the good to desiring what pleases him in unbelief. Man is changed in righteousness from doing what God commanded to doing what is pleasing in his own eyes.

3. How do actual transgressions proceed from this corrupt nature?

Having shut his eyes to the contradictoriness of his unbelief, and hardening himself to natural evil, which calls to repentance, man, in self-deception and in self-justification, acts upon his unbelief and his unholy desires.

4. How does original sin affect foundational teachings of the entire Christian worldview?

Evil is not seen as the failure to understand what is clear about God. It is seen as a willful act of disobedience of a command of God.[6] Faith is not seen as based on understanding and evidence.[7] It is a choice to believe above, apart from, or against evidence. The wages of sin is not seen as spiritual death, present and inherent in sin. The wages of sin is seen as hell, which is future and imposed. Eternal life is not seen as the knowledge of God. It is seen as the absence of the curse in heaven.

QUESTION 26

How is original sin conveyed from our first parents unto their posterity?

Original sin is conveyed from our first parents unto their posterity by natural generation, so as all that proceed from them in that way are conceived and born in sin.

1. What are the objective and subjective effects of original sin?

The objective effect is the imputation of original sin (root sin) through Adam—our covenant representative. The subjective effect of original sin is twofold: negatively, we are utterly indisposed to all good, and positively we are wholly inclined to all evil. It does not mean we do all evil, but that we are wholly inclined towards all evil. All actual sin proceeds from original sin.[8] Original sin is to be distinguished from actual sin. Original sin is root sin, and out of it proceeds fruit sin. Actual sin accepts of degrees, and the consequence of sin accepts of degrees as well.

---

6. Gangadean, "Paper No. 120: Contra Voluntarism: The Will Is Not Independent of the Intellect," in *The Logos Papers*.

7. Gangadean, "Paper No. 21: Faith and Reason in Christianity," in *The Logos Papers*; "Paper No. 28: Prepare the Way of the Lord: By Faith We Understand," in *The Logos Papers*; "Paper No. 98: Faith and the Word of God: The Object of Faith," in *The Logos Papers*.

8. Appendix 7.

2. How is original sin passed down?

Original sin is passed down through the male descendants of our covenant representative.

3. How was Christ born without sin?

The sin of Adam was not imputed to Christ, for Christ was not born of man, but of the Holy Spirit. Mary, on the contrary, was born of natural descent and therefore had original sin by imputation (vs. the immaculate conception of Mary).

QUESTION 27

What misery did the Fall bring upon mankind?

The Fall brought upon mankind the loss of communion with God, his displeasure and curse; so as we are by nature children of wrath, bond slaves to Satan, and justly liable to all punishments in this world, and that which is to come.

1. What was the loss of communion with God?

The loss of communion with God was having his Word remain in us and our obeying that Word.

2. What is the curse?[9]

The curse is natural evil. Natural evil encompasses the miseries of this life, imposed upon man after the Fall by God in light of man's self-deception and self-justification. The curse is God's call to man to repentance. It consists of toil and strife, and old age, sickness, and physical death in all their manifestations—increased in war, famine, and plague.

---

9. Gangadean, "Paper No. 149: The Biblical Worldview (Part IX): Redemption: The Third Call to Repentance," in *The Logos Papers*.

QUESTION 28

What are the punishments of sin in this world?

*The punishments of sin in this world are either inward,
as blindness of mind, a reprobate sense, strong delusions,
hardness of heart, horror of conscience, and vile affections; or
outward, as the curse of God upon the creatures for our sakes,
and all other evils that befall us in our bodies, names, estates,
relations, and employments; together with death itself.*

1. What is spiritual death?

Spiritual death is the wages of sin;[10] the inherent effect of the destruction of our nature in the denial of God; the effect of being given up to sin by God's wrath. It consists of meaninglessness, boredom, and the shame of guilt in all their manifestations. It is present now in this life, continuing in the next life, and is the essence of what hell is.[11]

2. What purpose does the curse serve in relation to sin?

The curse serves to restrain all from sin, to recall all from sin, and to remove the sin remaining in believers. In all the suffering of the curse, there is a call to stop and think deeply about good and evil, about the meaning and purpose of life. It is a call to know God. The curse is intensified in history in war, famine, and plague. At death, there is no further call back. A person continues in the condition in which they died. The curse is fully removed, not at death, but at the end of this age in the resurrection, when all things have been subdued to Christ.[12] The last enemy to be destroyed is death.[13]

---

10. *Genesis 2:17; Romans 6:23; Ephesians 2:1.*
11. Gangadean, *Philosophical Foundation*, 195-197; Gangadean, *The Westminster Confession.* See Questions 31-32.
12. *1 Corinthians 15:28.*
13. *1 Corinthians 15:26.*

3. Is the curse punishment for sin?

Although the curse is sometimes referred to as punishment and some-times as chastening, it is not punishment in the strict or absolute sense of the term. Physical death cannot (in the strict sense) be considered punishment for sin in this life or the next. If physical death were punishment for the believer, then Christ did not bear the full penalty of sin. If physical death were punishment for the non-believer, there would be no resurrection for the bodies of non-believers. If the curse were punishment for both believers and non-believers, there would be some proportionality in its manifestation. But the most righteous, for example, Job, often suffer more than others, and the wicked often prosper more than the righteous.[14]

QUESTION 29

What are the punishments of sin in the world to come?

The punishments of sin in the world to come, are everlasting separation from the comfortable presence of God, and most grievous torments in soul and body, without intermission, in hell-fire forever.

1. How is spiritual death different from hell as commonly conceived?

The wages of sin is death.[15] Spiritual death is present and inherent in sin, whereas hell, as a literal lake of fire, is future and imposed. Hell, in biblical language, is a symbolic representation of spiritual death. It is called the second death.[16] Taken literally, hell, as a lake of fire, is without meaning. Spirits are not affected by physical fire. To appeal to

---

14. *Psalm 75.*

15. *Romans 6:23; Genesis 2:17; Ephesians 2:1.*

16. *Revelation 20:14.*

a continual miracle in order to make a literal hell possible is to deny God's justice and to invite blasphemy.[17]

2. How is spiritual death spoken of in Scripture?

Spiritual death is spoken of as the second death. The second death is spiritual death continuing on after physical death is removed by the resurrection of the body. It is spiritual death that is affirmed as the wages of sin,[18] inherently connected with sin ("in the day you eat you will surely die"[19]) and present in this life ("you that were dead in your trespasses. . ."[20]). The soul destroys itself by acting contrary to its nature. Fire is the apt symbol of destruction. The destruction is not the annihilation of being or cessation of activity, but futility and waste, in the self-contradictoriness of sin. To be given up to the futility of one's choice reveals the divine justice: a man reaps what he sows.

3. How is the fear of God different from the fear of hell?

The fear of hell (avoiding natural evil) is not the fear of God (avoiding moral evil). There is a necessary connection between sin (not seeking and not understanding) and death (meaninglessness, boredom, and guilt). Understanding the connection between sin and death brings the fear of the Lord, which moves us to diligently seek him. Thus, the fear of the Lord is the beginning of wisdom.[21]

4. Why do the Westminster Divines advocate grievous bodily torments without intermission, in hell fire forever?

The pastor-teachers respond to the most prominent unaddressed challenges of their time through the process of much discussion. Some ideas in the Reformation were extensively discussed (e.g., the five *Solas*, the *ordo salutis*, TULIP, the priesthood of all believers, the sovereignty of God over all of life, the purity of worship, and church government) and some have not yet risen to awareness of the Church at large (faith vs. reason, otherworldliness, and secularism vs. knowledge of God,

---

17. *Romans 2:24.*
18. *Romans 6:23.*
19. *Genesis 2:17.*
20. *Ephesians 2:1.*
21. *Proverbs 1:7; 9:10; Psalm 111:10.*

continuing divisions within theism vs. unity of the faith). This question serves as an illustration of the role of creeds and councils in history. What was extensively discussed was settled and therefore serves as a high-water mark from which to build. What eluded much discussion is yet to undergo the ordinary process of settling disputes. We eagerly await for the pastor-teachers in our time to answer the challenges since the Westminster Assembly (1648).

Chapter 19

THE COVENANT OF GRACE AND THE PERSON AND WORK OF CHRIST

QUESTION 30

Doth God leave all mankind to perish in the estate of sin and misery?

*God doth not leave all men to perish in the estate of sin and misery, into which they fell by the breach of the first covenant, commonly called the **covenant of works**; but of his mere love and mercy delivereth his elect out of it, and bringeth them into an estate of salvation by the second covenant, commonly called the **covenant of grace**.*

1. Are there constraints on God's mercy?

God is not required to have mercy by anything outside of himself, but being infinite in goodness, he is pleased to have mercy. Yet his mercy is not arbitrary but according to his eternal plan, which is to the praise of his glory. His mercy is sovereign, having elected some to life, according as God has mercy on whom he will have mercy.[1]

---

1. *Romans 9:16-18.*

2. How is man redeemed by the covenant of grace?[2]

Those who are fallen according to the covenant of works made with Adam must be redeemed by the terms of that covenant. The redeemer must perfectly obey in place of Adam and must pay the penalty of sin due to that covenant. The grace of God does not negate but satisfies the justice of God. Yet the covenant is gracious in that God himself fulfills the terms of the covenant in place of man. And there are not two covenants by which man is redeemed but one covenant of grace, differently administered under the Old and New Testaments.

3. How is man brought into the estate of salvation?

Through union with the new covenant head, man's sins are pardoned. The power of sin and its misery is progressively removed, and man is thereby enabled to fulfill his task of dominion through which he achieves the goal of the knowledge of God, which is eternal life.[3]

QUESTION 31

With whom was the covenant of grace made?

The covenant of grace was made with Christ as the second Adam, and in him with all the elect as his seed.

1. Why is Christ called "the second Adam"?

Christ stood in place of Adam to fulfill the requirements of the covenant of works by perfect and personal obedience. Christ superseded and replaced Adam as a covenant representative to those who are united to him.

---

2. Gangadean, "Paper No. 114: The Gospel: For Everyone," in *The Logos Papers*; "Paper No. 148: The Biblical Worldview (Part VIII): Redemption: The First and Second Calls to Repentance," in *The Logos Papers*; "Paper No. 149: The Biblical Worldview (Part IX): Redemption: The Third Call to Repentance," in *The Logos Papers*; "Paper No. 150: The Biblical Worldview (Part X): Redemption: Justification and Sanctification," in *The Logos Papers*.

3. *John 17:3.*

2. How does Christ relate to Adam?

Christ, as the second Adam, is to *undo* what Adam did (paying the penalty of sin) and to *do* what Adam failed to do (fill the earth with the knowledge of God).

3. Where do believers and unbelievers stand in relation to Christ and Adam?

All not united to Christ in the covenant of grace are united to Adam in the covenant of works. Believers are united to Christ by faith and all those outside of Christ stand condemned under the covenant of works.

QUESTION 32

How is the grace of God manifested in the second covenant?

The grace of God is manifested in the second covenant, in that he freely provideth and offereth to sinners a Mediator, and life and salvation by him; and requiring faith as the condition to interest them in him, promiseth and giveth his Holy Spirit to all his elect, to work in them that faith, with all other saving graces; and to enable them unto all holy obedience, as the evidence of the truth of their faith and thankfulness to God, and as the way which he hath appointed them to salvation.

1. What is the relation between the covenant of works and the covenant of grace?[4]

The covenant of grace must be understood in relation to the covenant of works. It is the same covenant made with a new representative who will undo Adam's failure and complete the work that Adam failed to do.

---

4. Gangadean, *The Westminster Confession.* See Question 36.

2. Why is the covenant of grace called so?

By God's grace, God himself fulfills the requirements of the covenant of works through a second representative, Christ. In Christ, salvation is by grace alone, from beginning to end, without any admixture of human works, and solely by the atoning work of Christ.

3. What does the second covenant entail?

The second covenant entails the incarnation and atoning work of Christ to fulfill the law and pay the punishment for sin on our behalf; the application of the benefits of Christ to the elect as summarized in the *ordo salutis*; and the sending of the Holy Spirit to lead the Church into all truth[5] so as to fill the earth with the knowledge of God.[6]

QUESTION 33

Was the covenant of grace always administered after one and the same manner?

The covenant of grace was not always administered after the same manner, but the administrations of it under the Old Testament were different from those under the New.

How do the administration and the substance of the covenant relate?

There is one covenant of grace from the Garden[7] until Christ. There is a unity and continuity of the covenant of grace in both testaments. The administrations differ in the testaments, but the covenant of grace is in substance one and the same in both.

---

5. *John 16:13.*

6. *Isaiah 11:9.*

7. *Genesis 3:15.*

QUESTION 34

How was the covenant of grace administered under the Old Testament?[8]

The covenant of grace was administered under the Old Testament, by promises, prophecies, sacrifices, circumcision, the Passover, and other types and ordinances, which did all fore-signify Christ then to come, and were for that time sufficient to build up the elect in faith in the promised Messiah, by whom they then had full remission of sin, and eternal salvation.

1. What is the content of the Old Testament?

The Old Testament points forward to the person and work of the Messiah to come. Christ is the testator who dies on our behalf and blesses us with his inheritance.

2. Explain the sevenfold description of the Messiah in the testaments:

1) Second Adam (another in place of Adam to *undo* what Adam did and *do* what Adam failed to do).[9]

2) The seed of the woman (redemptive line of the promise).[10]

3) Prophet, Priest, and King (perfectly fulfills the three offices).[11]

4) Incarnation (God and man).[12]

---

8. Gangadean, *The Westminster Confession.* See Question 37.

9. *Genesis 3:15; Romans 5:12-19; I Corinthians 15:45-47; Genesis 1:28; Matthew 28:16-20.*

10. *Genesis 11:10-32; Matthew 1:1-16.*

11. *Deuteronomy 18:15-19; John 6:14-15; Mark 6:4; Psalm 110:4; Hebrews 3:1, 7:23-25; Psalm 2; Matthew 21:5, 27:11; Revelation 19:11-16.*

12. *Matthew 1:23; Psalm 110:1; Matt. 22:41-42.*

5) Vicarious atonement (the Lamb of God).[13]

6) Resurrection (overcomes sin and the curse).[14]

7) Session (rules until all things are subdued to him).[15]

3. How does the administration of the covenant of grace become effectual?

The Holy Spirit worked in the hearts of believers under the Old Testament (Adam's heart, Abel's heart, Noah's heart, etc.) to help them see that these sacrifices were foresignifying Christ, the promised Messiah, the seed of the woman who was to come.

QUESTION 35

How is the covenant of grace administered under the New Testament?[16]

Under the New Testament, when Christ the substance was exhibited, the same covenant of grace was and still is to be administered in the preaching of the Word, and the administration of the sacraments of Baptism and the Lord's supper; in which grace and salvation are held forth in more fulness, evidence, and efficacy, to all nations.

How is the covenant of grace differently administered under the New Testament in contrast to the Old Testament?

What was foretold and foresignified under the Old Testament is fulfilled in Christ. The ceremonial law was fulfilled in Christ. The covenant of grace under the New Testament is administered through the ordinances

---

13. *Isaiah 53; John 1:29.*

14. *Numbers 17; Jonah 1:17; Luke 11:29-32; Psalm 16:10; Acts 2:22-35.*

15. *I Corinthians 15:20-28; Psalm 110.*

16. Gangadean, *The Westminster Confession.* See Question 38.

of the preaching of the Word and the sacraments, fewer in number than the Old Testament, yet with greater fullness of meaning, efficacy, and applicability.

QUESTION 36

Who is the Mediator of the covenant of grace?[17]

The only Mediator of the covenant of grace is the Lord Jesus Christ, who, being the eternal Son of God, of one substance and equal with the Father, in the fulness of time became man, and so was and continues to be God and man, in two entire distinct natures, and one person, forever.

1. Is there any salvation apart from Christ?

Since all have sinned and come short of the glory of God in failing to acknowledge God's clear general revelation,[18] and since the wages of sin is death,[19] all men need salvation. There is no other name under heaven given to men by which we must be saved.[20] Only he has perfectly obeyed God's will in all things, and only he has borne the penalty of sin by his death on the cross. There is only one mediator between God and men. There are not, therefore, many paths to God, nor can any person by his own works save himself.

2. Who is the Lord Jesus Christ?

The Lord Jesus Christ is the eternal Son of God who became man, so that he is both the Son of God and the Son of Man. In contrast to Eastern mysticism, he is not one of many incarnations of the divine, but the only incarnation of God. In contrast to Western humanism, he

---

17. Gangadean, *The Westminster Confession*. See Question 39-43.

18. *Romans 3:23.*

19. *Romans 6:23.*

20. *Acts 4:12.*

is not merely a wise human teacher, but God incarnate. In contrast to ancient Gnosticism, he is not merely a higher spiritual being appearing in the form of man, but God incarnate.

3. How can there be one person in two natures?

In Christ, two whole, perfect, and distinct natures, the Godhead and the manhood were inseparably joined together in one person, without *conversion* (one nature does not change and become the other—God does not change into man or man into God), without *composition* (Christ is not partly God and partly man), or *confusion* (each nature acts distinctly according to its own essence). Which person is very God, and very man, yet one Christ, the only mediator between God and man.

QUESTION 37

How did Christ, being the Son of God, become man?

Christ the Son of God became man, by taking to himself a true body, and a reasonable soul, being conceived by the power of the Holy Ghost in the womb of the virgin Mary, of her substance, and born of her, yet without sin.

1. How can God become man?

God being infinite can take to himself the finite, but man being finite cannot take to himself the infinite. The infinite is not opposed to but is inclusive of the finite; the finite, however, is not inclusive of the infinite.

2. How is Christ truly man?

Christ has both a body and soul: he was conceived of the virgin Mary, of her substance; he grew in wisdom and stature; he was, as man, anointed by the Holy Spirit; he was tempted in all points as we are, yet without sin; he suffered under Pontius Pilate; he was crucified, dead, and buried.[21]

3. How is Christ man, yet without sin?[22]

Christ was conceived by the power of the Holy Spirit in the womb of the virgin Mary. Only Christ, of those born of women, was not conceived by a human father, so the sin of Adam was not imputed to him. Only Christ, as sinless in nature, is able to undertake man's redemption.

QUESTION 38

Why was it requisite that the Mediator should be God?

It was requisite that the Mediator should be God, that he might sustain and keep the human nature from sinking under the infinite wrath of God, and the power of death; give worth and efficacy to his sufferings, obedience, and intercession; and to satisfy God's justice, procure his favor, purchase a peculiar people, give his Spirit to them, conquer all their enemies, and bring them to everlasting salvation.

1. What is the office of the mediator?[23]

The office of the mediator brings reconciliation between God and humanity. It cannot be a man merely, and it cannot be God merely. A mediator is to take upon both divine and human nature.

---

21. See *The Apostles' Creed.*

22. Gangadean, *The Westminster Confession.* See Question 40.

23. Gangadean, *The Westminster Confession.* See Question 39.

2. What does the full satisfaction of God's justice require?[24]

Only a divine person can satisfy God's divine justice to fully cover the sins of many. The substitutionary work of Christ as mediator extends to the total number of the elect.

3. What does the application of redemption require?[25]

Only the Holy Spirit can make effectual the salvation purchased by Christ. The Holy Spirit can only be sent by God and not a mere man. Therefore, the mediator must be God.

QUESTION 39

Why was it requisite that the Mediator should be man?

It was requisite that the Mediator should be man, that he might advance our nature, perform obedience to the law, suffer and make intercession for us in our nature, have a fellow-feeling of our infirmities; that we might receive the adoption of sons, and have comfort and access with boldness unto the throne of grace.

Why does mediation require representation?

Mediation as a reconciliation requires that the demands of justice be fulfilled. Justice requires payment in kind. The second Adam is to stand in the place of the first. Only a human can represent mankind.

---

24. Gangadean, *The Westminster Confession*. See Question 43.
25. Gangadean, *The Westminster Confession*. See Question 42.

QUESTION 40

Why was it requisite that the Mediator should be God and man in one person?

It was requisite that the Mediator, who was to reconcile God and man, should himself be both God and man, and this in one person, that the proper works of each nature might be accepted of God for us, and relied on by us, as the works of the whole person.

QUESTION 41

Why was our mediator called Jesus?

Our Mediator was called Jesus, because he saveth his people from their sins.

QUESTION 42

Why was our Mediator called Christ?

Our Mediator was called Christ, because he was anointed with the Holy Ghost above measure; and so set apart, and fully furnished with all authority and ability, to execute the offices of prophet, priest, and king of his church, in the estate both of his humiliation and exaltation.

1. What is the origin of these offices?

Man, made in the image of God, in knowledge, holiness, and righteousness, was to function as prophet, priest, and king in God's creation. Man is to love God with his whole heart: with all his mind, his soul, and his strength.[26]

2. What is the function of each office?

Man as prophet is to understand God's revelation, in creation, history, and in the Scriptures, so as to attain to the fullness of the knowledge of God. Man as priest is to teach God's revelation, so as to bring all men to holiness, the sanctification that comes through knowing the truth. Man as king is to rule in God's creation, so as to bring all men to righteousness through obeying God's law in all things.

3. How does Christ execute these offices in humiliation and exaltation?

In his humiliation, Christ, by his perfect obedience, both active and passive, fulfills the law and accomplishes the redemption of those who are given to him. In his exaltation, Christ, seated at the right hand of God, rules over men and nations by his Word and Spirit to apply his redemption to those who are given to him.

4. Where in Scripture are these offices manifested?

These offices are manifested in the person and work of Moses as prophet, Aaron as priest, and David as king, and in those who continued these offices. They are also manifested in the various gifts Christ gives to every believer for the building up of his body, the Church.

---

26. *Deuteronomy 6:5; Mark 12:30.*

QUESTION 43

How doth Christ execute the office of a prophet?

*Christ executeth the office of a prophet, in his revealing to
the church, in all ages, by his Spirit and Word, in divers
ways of administration, the whole will of God, in all things
concerning their edification and salvation.*

1. What is the goal of Christ's work as prophet?

Christ, as prophet, brings his people to the knowledge of God, which
is eternal life.[27]

2. How does Christ bring us to the knowledge of God?

God is a Spirit whom no man has seen nor can see.[28] Christ, the eternal
Word of God, reveals God through his work as Creator, Ruler, and
Redeemer. As the Word of God incarnate, Christ rules in history to
bring his people, by his Spirit, to understand this revelation.

3. What does Christ reveal as the will of God for our salvation?

Christ, in the Scriptures, reveals our need for deliverance from the
penalty and the power of sin by his work, by which also he brings us
to understand God's law, so that by obeying it in all things, we may
know God in all that by which he makes himself known.

---

27. *John 17:3.*
28. *1 Timothy 6:16.*

QUESTION 44

How doth Christ execute the office of a priest?

Christ executeth the office of a priest, in his once offering himself a sacrifice without spot to God, to be a reconciliation for the sins of his people; and in making continual intercession for them.

1. What is the goal of Christ's priestly work?

Christ's priestly work brings his people to holiness, in which we are devoted to God in all of life.

2. How does Christ as priest bring us to holiness?

Christ brings us to holiness by removing the penalty of sin through the sacrifice of himself on the cross and by removing the power of sin through the daily sanctifying work of his Word and Spirit, for which also he ever lives to make intercession for us.[29]

3. What is the goal of holiness?

The goal of holiness is the knowledge of God. God is the rewarder of those who diligently seek him.[30] Without holiness, no one shall see God.[31]

---

29. *Hebrews 7:25.*
30. *Hebrews 11:6.*
31. *Hebrews 12:14.*

QUESTION 45

How doth Christ execute the office of a king?

Christ executeth the office of a king, in calling out of the world a people to himself, and giving them officers, laws, and censures, by which he visibly governs them; in bestowing saving grace upon his elect, rewarding their obedience, and correcting them for their sins, preserving and supporting them under all their temptations and sufferings, restraining and overcoming all their enemies, and powerfully ordering all things for his own glory, and their good; and also in taking vengeance on the rest, who know not God, and obey not the gospel.

1. What is the goal of Christ's work as king?

Christ as king brings his people to righteousness, to do justice in the earth, to exercise dominion over the creation and over sin.

2. How does Christ subdue us to himself?

Christ subdues us to himself by removing the enmity in our hearts by regenerating and sanctifying us by his Word and Spirit.

3. How does Christ rule and defend us?

Christ rules us by bringing us to know and to do his will revealed in the law of God. He defends us by his name, which is a strong tower for the righteous.[32]

4. How does Christ restrain and conquer all his and our enemies?

The enemy of Christ is sin, dwelling in the world, in our flesh, and in the devil. He restrains sin by his judgments on the earth. He conquers

---

32. *Proverbs 18:10.*

sin by the proclamation of the Word of God, which is the sword of the Spirit.

QUESTION 46

What was the estate of Christ's humiliation?

The estate of Christ's humiliation was that low condition, wherein he for our sakes, emptying himself of his glory, took upon him the form of a servant, in his conception and birth, life, death, and after his death, until his resurrection.

1. How is Christ humiliated in every condition of his life?

In every condition of his life, Christ identifies more and more with man as a creature in his need and with man as sinner in his misery.

2. Why did God become man?

Christ came as a substitutionary atonement for our sins, according to the Scriptures. All we, like sheep, have gone astray; we have turned everyone to his own way, and the Lord has laid on him the iniquity of us all.[33] He is the Lamb of God who takes away the sin of the world.[34]

3. How does Christ represent us in atonement?

Christ represents us in place of Adam in the covenant of grace. As in Adam all die, even so in Christ shall all be made alive. Since by man came death, by man came also the resurrection of the dead.[35]

---

33. *Isaiah 53:6.*
34. *John 1:29.*
35. *1 Corinthians 15:20-22.*

QUESTION 47

How did Christ humble himself in his conception and birth?

Christ humbled himself in his conception and birth, in that, being from all eternity the Son of God, in the bosom of the Father, he was pleased in the fulness of time to become the son of man, made of a woman of low estate, and to be born of her; with divers circumstances of more than ordinary abasement.

QUESTION 48

How did Christ humble himself in his life?

Christ humbled himself in his life, by subjecting himself to the law, which he perfectly fulfilled; and by conflicting with the indignities of the world, temptations of Satan, and infirmities in his flesh, whether common to the nature of man, or particularly accompanying that his low condition.

QUESTION 49

How did Christ humble himself in his death?

Christ humbled himself in his death, in that having been betrayed by Judas, forsaken by his disciples, scorned and rejected by the world, condemned by Pilate, and tormented by his persecutors; having also conflicted with the terrors of death, and the powers of darkness, felt and borne the weight of God's wrath, he laid down his life an offering for sin, enduring the painful, shameful, and cursed death of the cross.

QUESTION 50

Wherein consisted Christ's humiliation after his death?

*Christ's humiliation after his death consisted in his being buried, and continuing in the state of the dead, and under the power of death till the third day; which hath been otherwise expressed in these words, **He descended into hell**.*

QUESTION 51

What was the estate of Christ's exaltation?

The estate of Christ's exaltation comprehendeth his resurrection, ascension, sitting at the right hand of the Father, and his coming again to judge the world.

1. What does Christ's rising from the dead signify?

Christ's rising from the dead shows that he has triumphed over sin and death by the perfect righteousness of his sinless life and by the full payment of the penalty of sin by his atoning death.

2. What is signified by Christ's ascending into heaven and his sitting at the right hand of the Father?

Christ's ascension and session show that he has been given all authority in heaven and earth and that he now exercises that authority in making disciples of all nations.

3. When does Christ come to judge the world?

Christ comes to judge individual men, nations, and churches suddenly; at any moment throughout history; but his final coming to judge all men will occur after he has overcome all opposition to his rule through the preaching of the gospel.

QUESTION 52

How was Christ exalted in his resurrection?

Christ was exalted in his resurrection, in that, not having seen corruption in death (of which it was not possible for him to be held), and having the very same body in which he suffered, with the essential properties thereof (but without mortality, and other common infirmities belonging to this life), really united to his soul, he rose again from the dead the third day by his own power; whereby he declared himself to be the Son of God, to have satisfied divine justice, to have vanquished death, and him that had the power of it, and to be Lord of quick and dead: all which he did as a public person, the head of his church, for their justification, quickening in grace, support against enemies, and to assure them of their resurrection from the dead at the last day.

1. What is the relation between natural and moral evil?

Natural evil is imposed because of moral evil. Natural evil is a call back from moral evil; it is a call to stop and think. Physical death is a call back from spiritual death. Physical death is mercy, while spiritual death is justice.

2. Why did Christ not see corruption?

Since natural evil is a call back from moral evil, Christ being sinless, had no need for natural evil to be imposed upon him. Corruption is part of the curse, and Christ had no need for the curse.

3. To what does the resurrection point?

The resurrection points to the resurrection life, which is God's seal of approval of the one in authority. The resurrection affirms that this is the one with whom God is well pleased.[36] He has been granted authority to rule in heaven and on earth.

QUESTION 53

How was Christ exalted in his ascension?

Christ was exalted in his ascension, in that having after his resurrection often appeared unto and conversed with his apostles, speaking to them of the things pertaining to the kingdom of God, and giving them commission to preach the gospel to all nations, forty days after his resurrection, he, in our nature, and as our head, triumphing over enemies, visibly went up into the highest heavens, there to receive gifts for men, to raise up our affections thither, and to prepare a place for us, where himself is, and shall continue till his second coming at the end of the world.

1. What did Christ teach regarding the kingdom of God?

Entrance into the kingdom is by being born again.[37] The kingdom is governed by the moral law, under the rule of Christ. It began its expansion at Pentecost with the outpouring of the Holy Spirit and it will expand through the witness of the Church until all unbelief has been taken captive. The spiritual war of belief and unbelief will be present in the Church until its consummation. The work of the kingdom will be completed when the whole earth is filled with the knowledge of the glory of God as the waters cover the sea.[38]

---

36. *Matthew 3:17.*

37. *John 3:3-8.*

38. *Habbakuk 2:14.*

2. What does the Great Commission entail?

The Great Commission entails discipling the nations by teaching them to obey all that Christ has commanded.[39] Discipling the nations requires taking every thought captive and making them subject to Christ.[40]

3. What is the relation between the dominion/cultural mandate and the Great Commission?

The dominion mandate entails naming the creation and ruling over it, developing the potential latent in man and the creation. The Great Commission presupposes the dominion mandate and adds the rule over sin and the teaching of redemption. The Great Commission (the mission mandate) builds upon the dominion mandate and completes the work by bringing all of life and all of history under the lordship of Christ, who fills everything in every way.

QUESTION 54

How is Christ exalted in his sitting at the right hand of God?

Christ is exalted in his sitting at the right hand of God, in that as God-man he is advanced to the highest favor with God the Father, with all fullness of joy, glory, and power over all things in heaven and earth; and doth gather and defend his church, and subdue their enemies; furnisheth his ministers and people with gifts and graces, and maketh intercession for them.

39. *Matthew 28:18-20.*
40. *2 Corinthians 10:4-5.*

1. How does Christ rule at the right hand of the Father through the curse?

Christ uses the curse to restrain, recall from, and remove moral evil. The curse is a merciful call back that intensifies as sin intensifies. Christ uses the curse to call back individuals, churches, and nations, that we may seek after him.

2. How does Christ rule at the right hand of the Father through the Church?

Christ has sent the Holy Spirit to lead the Church into all truth.[41] Believers are enabled by the Spirit to make disciples of all the nations,[42] to engage in the spiritual war by taking thoughts captive and making them subject unto Christ,[43] and by building upon the cumulative work of the Historic Christian Faith, i.e., the work of the pastor-teachers summed up in creeds and councils in Church history.

3. How do believers take thoughts captive?

Believers take thoughts captive, positively and negatively; negatively by testing ideas for meaning through the critical use of reason and showing their incoherence through reason and argument; positively by providing a coherent response in light of clear general revelation and the Biblical worldview. Negatively, we demolish pretensions, and positively, we build up by bringing falsehood and unbelief under the lordship of Christ.

4. What is a pretention to knowledge?

A pretention to knowledge is any claim to knowledge that is contrary to the revelation of God in general revelation, special revelation, and the Historic Christian Faith. It is any claim contrary to the nature of reality as God has made himself known in all his works of creation and providence.

---

41. *John 16:13.*

42. *Matthew 28:20.*

43. *2 Corinthians 10:4-5.*

5. How does the Apostle Paul attest to Christ's rule?

Paul taught that where sin increased, grace increased all the more.[44] He taught that God placed all things under Christ who, through his body the Church, is to fill everything in every way,[45] that through the work of the Spirit in the ministry of pastor-teachers, the Church is to attain to the unity of the faith, to the whole measure of the fullness of Christ.[46] He taught that all Israel will be saved when the fullness of the Gentiles has come in;[47] that Christ will reign until he has put all his enemies under his feet, the last enemy to be destroyed, at his second coming, is death.[48]

6. How does the Apostle Peter attest to Christ's rule?

Peter exhorts his readers to be patient in suffering for the cause of Christ; that although false teachers are bold and arrogant, God rules, as in the days of Noah, when he brought that world to a sudden end. So too now the world of wickedness will be destroyed. Believers are to speed the coming of that day by their witness. The rule of spiritual forces of evil in the heavenly realms (the heavens) will be destroyed, and the fundamental principles (the elements/*stoicheia*) of the world will be destroyed suddenly. In the place of the old, believers look for a new heaven and a new earth in which the will of God is done.

7. How does the Apostle John attest to Christ's rule in the Book of Revelation?

John's Revelation brings the blessing of hope to all who read it and take it to heart. The time is near to readers in every age. After a seven-fold description of the state of the Church in John's age, the rule of God through the curse and the promise, in an age-long spiritual war, is unveiled in a seven-fold vision: the seven seals, the seven trumpets, the woman and the dragon, the seven bowls, the woman on the beast, the age-long spiritual war (Armageddon—fought with the sword coming out of the mouth), the thousand-year rule of believers (the millennium,

---

44. *Romans 5.*
45. *Ephesians 1.*
46. *Ephesians 4.*
47. *Romans 11.*
48. *1 Corinthians 15.*

in which all rule, who are raised from the dead spiritually—the first resurrection). Each vision covers the entire period of Christ's rule, from the first to the second coming. Each vision depicts the spiritual war between believers and non-believers under different aspects. Each vision shows the conquest of the kingdom of God over the kingdom of darkness. John's Revelation ends with the consummation of the kingdom of God. The work given to mankind in the Garden of Eden is completed by Christ through the Church. The City of God, perfected in beauty, comes down from heaven to earth. The river of life flows through the middle of the city, bringing blessing to all nations, life in its fullness. The hope of the Sabbath, of work and rest, is fully realized. The earth is filled with the knowledge of God as the waters cover the sea.[49]

QUESTION 55

How doth Christ make intercession?

Christ maketh intercession, by his appearing in our nature continually before the Father in heaven, in the merit of his obedience and sacrifice on earth, declaring his will to have it applied to all believers; answering all accusations against them, and procuring for them quiet of conscience, notwithstanding daily failings, access with boldness to the throne of grace, and acceptance of their persons and services.

Upon what basis does Christ make intercession for believers?

Christ fulfilled the covenant of works, suffered the penalty for sin, and ascended to the Father. Christ fulfilled the requirements of God's justice and imputes his righteousness to believers. We are counted righteous by being clothed with his righteousness. Christ is our high priest who intercedes on our behalf before the Father.

---

49. *Isaiah 11:9; Habakkuk 2:14.*

QUESTION 56

How is Christ to be exalted in his coming again to judge the world?

Christ is to be exalted in his coming again to judge the world, in that he, who was unjustly judged and condemned by wicked men, shall come again at the last day in great power, and in the full manifestation of his own glory, and of his Father's, with all his holy angels, with a shout, with the voice of the archangel, and with the trumpet of God, to judge the world in righteousness.

1. What is the Last Judgment?

God has appointed a day, wherein he will judge the world, in righteousness, by Jesus Christ, to whom all power and judgment are given of the Father. In which day, not only the apostate angels shall be judged, but likewise all persons that have lived upon earth shall appear before the tribunal of Christ, to give an account of their thoughts, words, and deeds; and to receive according to what they have done in the body, whether good or evil.

2. Why is Christ given the honor to preside over the Last Judgment?

Christ, the Son of God incarnate, who represents man, is able, and has been appointed to judge. In him, the fullness of the Father dwells. Christ rules in history to subdue all his enemies.[50] Christ has been given all authority in heaven and on earth; this includes judging.

---

50. *Psalm 110.*

Chapter 20

___

THE BENEFITS OF
CHRIST'S WORK

QUESTION 57

What benefits hath Christ procured by his mediation?

*Christ, by his mediation, hath procured redemption, with all
other benefits of the covenant of grace.*

1. What are the benefits derived from the covenant of grace?

The benefits for believers encompass this life, at death, and at the resurrection.

2. What benefits do they that are effectually called partake in this life?

They that are effectually called do in this life partake of justification,
adoption, sanctification, and the several benefits, which in this life, do
either accompany or flow from them.

3. What is the order of salvation?

The order of salvation or *ordo salutis*, is the order of the application of
the redemption accomplished by Christ and applied by the Holy Spirit
to those who are elect in Christ.

4. What is the sequence of the order of salvation?

The sequence of the *ordo salutis* is first regeneration, then conversion, which is repentance and faith, then justification, adoption, sanctification, and finally, glorification at death.

5. How is the order of salvation to be understood?

While each benefit is inseparable in experience, yet each is to be distinguished from the other, and each is to be understood on the basis of the preceding benefit.

6. What common errors occur in understanding the *ordo salutis*?

Some common errors in the *ordo salutis* are the reversal of regeneration and conversion (confessional regeneration), omitting the necessity of repentance (Arminianism), reducing justification to sanctification through infused grace (sacramentalism), and denial of glorification at death by the continuation of the curse beyond this life (purgatory).

7. What are the benefits which in this life do accompany or flow from justification, adoption, and sanctification?

The benefits which in this life do accompany or flow from justification, adoption, and sanctification are assurance of God's love, peace of conscience, joy in the Holy Ghost, increase of grace, and perseverance therein to the end.

8. What is the assurance of God's love?

The assurance of God's love is from knowing that he works all things together for good to those who love him and are called according to his purpose; that nothing can separate us from the love of God; that in all our trials and tribulations we are under his special loving care.

9. What is the peace of conscience?

The peace of conscience is freedom from the torment of guilt through Christ in whom all our sins are pardoned; that we are accepted by God on the basis of Christ's perfect righteousness alone; that the sufferings of this life are not punishment for sin, but in God's grace, deliverance from its power.

10. What is the joy in the Holy Spirit?

From assurance of God's love and peace of conscience, there arises joy in all our expectations. The hope of the believer is steadfast and sure that God's purpose will be accomplished on the earth and that our labor in the Lord is not in vain.

11. What is the benefit of increase in grace and perseverance therein to the end?

Because we are not left to ourselves in our struggle against sin, but are constantly enabled by the Holy Spirit, believers do overcome unbelief remaining in them and in the world, and so increase in grace. And by that same Spirit, they are kept in obedience so that they do not fall away, but persevere in grace to the end.

12. What benefits do believers receive from Christ at death?

The souls of believers are at their death made perfect in holiness and do immediately pass into glory, and their bodies being still united to Christ, do rest in their graves until the resurrection.

13. What is it to be made perfect in holiness?

The souls of believers at death are freed from all remaining errors in understanding so that there remains no hindrance to seeing God as he is and to growing in understanding God's revelation.

14. What is it to pass immediately into glory?

The souls of believers, when absent from the body at death, are immediately present with the Lord. There is no purgatory or any other intermediate state through which the souls of believers must pass before being present with the Lord.

15. What happens to the bodies of believers after death?

Man, being created as a whole person in body and soul, is redeemed by Christ in both body and soul. The body of the believer is, therefore, not abandoned to the grave, but is raised up incorruptible at the completion of redemption on the last day.

16. What benefits do believers receive from Christ at the resurrection?

At the resurrection, believers being raised up in glory shall be openly acknowledged and acquitted on the day of judgment and made perfectly blessed in the full enjoyment of God to all eternity.

17. What happens at the resurrection?

At the resurrection, the bodies of both the just and the unjust are raised up incorruptible and united again with their souls, and all mankind appears before God to be judged according to their deeds.

18. What happens to believers at the judgment?

Believers, at the judgment, are acknowledged by God as his children and are acquitted of sin on the basis of Christ's righteousness imputed to them.

19. What is the blessing of believers after the judgment?

Believers, after the judgment, inherit the kingdom of God in its fullness. They live in the new heavens and new earth in which dwells righteousness. They enjoy eternal life in knowing God, who reveals himself in all his works of creation and providence.

QUESTION 58

How do we come to be made partakers of the benefits which Christ hath procured?

We are made partakers of the benefits which Christ hath procured, by the application of them unto us, which is the work especially of God the Holy Ghost.

1. Who is the Holy Spirit?

The Holy Spirit is the third person of the Trinity. He is a person, not a force. He is God, not lesser in power or glory. He is third in the work of the Trinity in that he proceeds from the Father and the Son.

2. What is the work of the Holy Spirit?

The Holy Spirit, as the Lord and giver of life, makes the work of Christ effectual by regenerating the elect and by dwelling in and with them to illumine their minds to understand God's Word, thereby enabling them to carry out the work of Christ in discipling the nations.

3. What are some common misunderstandings of the person and work of the Holy Spirit?

In deism, the reality of the Holy Spirit is denied; in Arminianism, the priority of the work of the Holy Spirit is denied; in sacramentalism, the immediateness of the work of the Holy Spirit is denied; in Pentecostalism, the ordinary means used by the Holy Spirit is denied.

QUESTION 59

Who are made partakers of redemption through Christ?

Redemption is certainly applied, and effectually communicated, to all those for whom Christ hath purchased it; who are in time by the Holy Ghost enabled to believe in Christ according to the gospel.

1. What is faith?

Faith is a conviction based upon understanding. Faith rests on reason as truth rests on meaning. Faith grows as understanding grows; faith is tested as understanding is tested.[1]

2. What is the object and act of faith?

The object of faith is fundamentally concerned with the existence and nature of God and all that is derived from this. The act of faith is trusting in God according to his nature and the promises of Scripture which are grounded in his nature.[2]

3. How does the Holy Spirit work faith in us?

The Holy Spirit works faith in us by regenerating and sanctifying us. In regeneration, the life of God is restored in us, by which life we are brought to the conviction that God is, that we have sinned, and that we are redeemed by Christ. In sanctification, we are brought to know the truth by the illuminating work of the Spirit, by which truth we are set free.

---

1. Gangadean, "Paper No. 8: Belief and Unbelief—The Spiritual War: Introductory Remarks," in *The Logos Papers*; "Paper No. 21: Faith and Reason in Christianity," in *The Logos Papers*; "Paper No. 98: Faith and the Word of God: The Object of Faith," in *The Logos Papers*; "Paper No. 128: Abraham's Faith: The Elements of Abraham's Faith in Offering up Isaac," in *The Logos Papers;* "Paper No. 129: Faith and Reason in the Life of Abraham," in *The Logos Papers*; Gangadean, *The Westminster Confession*. See Questions 62-64.

2. Gangadean, *Philosophical Foundation*, 124-127; Gangadean, "Paper No. 128: Abraham's Faith: The Elements of Abraham's Faith in Offering up Isaac," in *The Logos Papers*; "Paper No. 129: Faith and Reason in the Life of Abraham," in *The Logos Papers*.

QUESTION 60

Can they who have never heard the gospel, and so know not Jesus Christ, nor believe in him, be saved by their living according to the light of nature?

They who, having never heard the gospel, know not Jesus Christ, and believe not in him, cannot be saved, be they never so diligent to frame their lives according to the light of nature, or the laws of that religion which they profess; neither is there salvation in any other, but in Christ alone, who is the Savior only of his body the church.

1. By what standard are all humans held to account?

All humans, after the age of accountability, are inexcusable for their unbelief in light of clear general revelation in creation and in providence.

2. What is the doctrine of total depravity?

Sin affects the whole (total) heart of man so that no one seeks God, no one understands, and no one is righteous.[3] Sin (moral evil) has become rooted in self-deception and self-justification so that the curse was imposed by God to restrain, recall from, and remove moral evil in man.[4] While sin is total in extent, sin varies in degrees (men are more or less conscious and consistent in their unbelief), and it may increase to ever-deeper depravity. The sin of not seeking results in culpable ignorance of what is clear about God and the moral law.

3. Can fallen men frame their lives according to the light of nature?

No fallen man can come to see apart from the grace of God. In regeneration, the light of reason is restored to us. Those who are regenerated

---

3. *Romans 3:10-11.*

4. *Genesis 3.*

come to see the need for Christ. General revelation shows the need for special revelation, and special revelation shows the elect how salvation comes through the imputed righteousness of Christ's vicarious atonement.

4. Is there salvation outside of the true religion?

All religions outside of the only true religion are the result of unbelief; they are the failure to know and acknowledge God as he has revealed himself in creation and providence. To believe in any other religion is proof of our guilt and, therefore, cannot serve as the basis for salvation.

5. Does the doctrine of common grace deny the exclusivity of salvation through Christ?

God, in his abundant grace, bestows grace upon both believer and unbeliever. Man, as made in the image of God, partakes in common grace, which extends natural and moral dominion, yet lacks any redemptive merit. Salvation comes only through the perfect satisfaction of the divine law attained by Christ alone. Common grace shows that apart from life in Christ, the human aspiration for excellence falls short of the fullness to be attained in Christ, who fills everything in every way.

QUESTION 61

Are all they saved who hear the gospel, and live in the church?

All that hear the gospel, and live in the visible church, are not saved; but they only who are true members of the church invisible.

1. Who are true members of the invisible Church?

All those who have been effectually called, justified, and adopted are members of the invisible Church.

2. What is the relation between the outward and inward call?

The non-elect may or may not have the outward call. The non-elect without the outward call perishes in their sin for their culpable ignorance. The non-elect, although called outwardly by the ministry of the Word, yet without inward regeneration, is not saved—regardless of how diligently they frame their lives according to the light of nature. The outward call without the inward call increases one's responsibility, given the increase of light.

QUESTION 62

What is the visible church?[5]

The visible church is a society made up of all such as in all ages and places of the world do profess the true religion, and of their children.

1. What is the visible Church?

The visible Church consists of all those throughout the world that profess the true religion; and of their children; and is the kingdom of the Lord Jesus Christ, the house and family of God, out of which there is no ordinary possibility of salvation.

2. What are the marks of a true church?

The marks of a true church are: sound preaching of the Word, proper administration of the sacraments, and godly discipline. Churches differ in degree of purity according as these marks are present.

3. How does one become a member of the Church?

One becomes a member of the Church by a credible profession of faith, which consists in a saving understanding of the person and work of Christ along with obedience to his Word.

---

5. Gangadean, *The Westminster Confession*. See Question 111.

QUESTION 63

What are the special privileges of the visible church?

The visible church hath the privilege of being under God's special care and government; of being protected and preserved in all ages, notwithstanding the opposition of all enemies; and of enjoying the communion of saints, the ordinary means of salvation, and offers of grace by Christ to all the members of it in the ministry of the gospel, testifying, that whosoever believes in him shall be saved, and excluding none that will come unto him.

1. What constitutes the privilege of being under God's special care and government?

The Church is the pillar and ground of the truth,[6] led by the Holy Spirit,[7] cleansed and built up through the curse and the promise. The Church is to grow from the Garden to the City of God.[8] God builds up the Church through the locus of the magisterium (creeds and councils) and the three marks of the Church: doctrine (Truth), sacraments (signs and seals of the Truth), and discipline through its oversight (upholding the practice of Truth in the Church).

2. How is the Church preserved and protected in all ages?

The Church under the Old and New Testaments has undergone many cycles of apostasy and captivity. The Lord rules through the curse and the promise—never leaving the Church without a remnant to carry on

---

6. *1 Timothy 3:15;* Gangadean, "Paper No. 40: The Church: The Pillar and Ground of the Truth," in *The Logos Papers.*

7. *John 16:13.*

8. Gangadean, "Paper No. 54: From Foundation to Fullness: A Biblical Worldview for Maturity, Fruitfulness, Unity, and Fullness," in *The Logos Papers.*

the work. "The gates of hell will not prevail against it."[9] The Church will become the City of God, subdue all nations, and attain to the fullness that there is in Christ.

QUESTION 64

What is the invisible Church?[10]

The invisible Church is the whole number of the elect, that have been, are, or shall be gathered into one under Christ the head.

Why is the Church said to be invisible?

The total number of the elect in every age (have been, are, and shall be) is known to God alone. The invisible Church accepts no membership, yet all who consider themselves believers must be members of a visible church.

QUESTION 65

What special benefits do the members of the invisible Church enjoy by Christ?

The members of the invisible Church by Christ enjoy union and communion with him in grace and glory.

---

9. *Matthew 16:18.*

10. Gangadean, *The Westminster Confession.* See Question 111.

What does the enjoyment of union and communion with Christ entail?

The full description of the enjoyment of union and communion with Christ is explained in questions 66-90.

QUESTION 66

What is that union which the elect have with Christ?

The union which the elect have with Christ is the work of God's grace, whereby they are spiritually and mystically, yet really and inseparably, joined to Christ as their head and husband; which is done in their effectual calling.

What is meant by "spiritually and mystically, yet really and inseparably"?

Believers are united to Christ through representation in the covenant of grace, in purpose by fulfilling the Cultural Mandate and the Great Commission, in adoption by becoming part of the family of God, in communion through the Lord's Supper, and in fellowship through the sanctifying work of the Holy Spirit.

QUESTION 67

What is effectual calling?[11]

Effectual calling is the work of God's almighty power and grace, whereby (out of his free and special love to his elect, and from nothing in them moving him thereunto) he doth, in his accepted time, invite and draw them to Jesus Christ, by his Word and Spirit; savingly enlightening their minds, renewing and powerfully determining their wills, so as they (although in themselves dead in sin) are hereby made willing and able freely to answer his call, and to accept and embrace the grace offered and conveyed therein.

1. What is to be distinguished in effectual calling?

The two parts of effectual calling are the inward work of the Holy Spirit called regeneration, and the outward effect of this work called conversion.

2. What is regeneration?

Regeneration is an act of the Holy Spirit in which a person is changed from a state of spiritual death to life.

3. What is conversion?[12]

Conversion is the outward effect of regeneration in which a person is convicted of sin, has repentance toward God, and faith in Jesus as Lord.

4. How does the Holy Spirit bring us to the conviction of sin?

The Holy Spirit brings us to see that there is no life apart from God and that the misery of spiritual death is due to our unbelief.

---

11. Gangadean, *The Westminster Confession*. See Question 41.

12. Gangadean, *The Westminster Confession*. See Questions 65-69.

QUESTION 68

Are the elect only effectually called?

All the elect, and they only, are effectually called; although others may be, and often are, outwardly called by the ministry of the Word, and have some common operations of the Spirit; who, for their wilful neglect and contempt of the grace offered to them, being justly left in their unbelief, do never truly come to Jesus Christ.

QUESTION 69

What is the communion in grace which the members of the invisible church have with Christ?

The communion in grace which the members of the invisible church have with Christ, is their partaking of the virtue of his mediation, in their justification, adoption, sanctification, and whatever else, in this life, manifests their union with him.

QUESTION 70

What is justification?[13]

Justification is an act of God's free grace unto sinners, in which he pardoneth all their sins, accepteth and accounteth their persons righteous in his sight; not for any thing wrought in them, or done by them, but only for the perfect obedience and full satisfaction of Christ, by God imputed to them, and received by faith alone.

1. What is revealed in the need for justification?

The need for justification shows that God has so made us that we are required to give an account for all our behavior.

2. What is the first error regarding justification?

The first error is that man can justify himself in his unbelief, either by seeking to deny the clarity of general revelation and the inexcusability of unbelief or by blaming another for his conduct.

3. What is the second error regarding justification?

The second error (Pelagianism) is that we can, by our own conduct, live up to the righteousness required by God's law. Legalism is the religious practice that reduces the requirements of the law to a set of outward rules and religious observances in order to achieve righteousness.

4. What is the third error regarding justification?

The third error is that man must meet part of the requirements of God's righteousness either by his own obedience, or by regarding faith as man's work and not God's gift, or by his own suffering as payment

---

13. Gangadean, *The Westminster Confession.* See Questions 53-57.

in part for sin. This attempts to add human works to the sufficiency of God's grace.

5. What is the fourth error regarding justification?

The fourth error (sacramentalism) is that justification is an infusion of grace through the sacraments that makes us actually righteous rather than an imputation through faith in Christ that accounts us righteous once and for all. Sin cancels infused righteousness, and righteousness infused cancels sin in an unending cycle in this life.

6. What is the fifth error regarding justification?

The fifth error (antinomianism) is that by being set free from having to obey the law in order to be justified, God's law no longer binds and guides the conduct of believers.

QUESTION 71

How is justification an act of God's free grace?

Although Christ, by his obedience and death, did make a proper, real, and full satisfaction to God's justice in the behalf of them that are justified; yet inasmuch as God accepteth the satisfaction from a surety, which he might have demanded of them, and did provide this surety, his own only Son, imputing his righteousness to them, and requiring nothing of them for their justification but faith, which also is his gift, their justification is to them of free grace.

1. How does the doctrine of justification show God as both just and merciful?

The atoning work of Christ and the faith by which we believe are both by God's mercy. God's justice required a perfect and full satisfaction of the demands of justice. The doctrine of justification reconciles the demands of justice through mercy for we are made righteous by Christ's righteousness.

2. How is justification a gift of God?

Justification is by unmerited free grace. God, out of his infinite mercy, provided payment for sin (vicarious atonement) and the faith to understand and obey. Faith is the work of the Holy Spirit in renewing our minds through knowledge of the truth (*the Logos* in its fullness).

QUESTION 72

What is justifying faith?

Justifying faith is a saving grace, wrought in the heart of a sinner by the Spirit and Word of God, whereby he, being convinced of his sin and misery, and of the disability in himself and all other creatures to recover him out of his lost condition, not only assenteth to the truth of the promise of the gospel, but receiveth and resteth upon Christ and his righteousness, therein held forth, for pardon of sin, and for the accepting and accounting of his person righteous in the sight of God for salvation.

1. What is the content of justifying faith?

The content of justifying faith is the understanding of our fallen condition, our inexcusability before God in light of the clarity of general revelation, and our natural inability to satisfy the demands of the moral law. Justifying faith brings us to understand the need for Christ (vicarious atonement), his full and real satisfaction of the divine justice, and mediation before God.

2. What doctrines are presupposed in the need for justifying faith?

The doctrines presupposed in the need for justifying faith include:

1) Understanding the clarity of general revelation and the inexcusability of unbelief.

2) Total depravity in light of root sin. The noetic effect as a result of root sin misunderstands sin, spiritual death, natural evil, and eternal life.[14]

3) The hardening of the heart in self-deception and self-justification added to root sin.

4) The shutting of one's eyes and covering of one's ears in light of the merciful call back through the curse.

5) Apart from the resurrection power of being restored to the life of the Logos, there is no possibility of understanding the truth of God.

3. What do we become persuaded of through justifying faith?

Through justifying faith, we become persuaded of our sinful condition, our state of misery due to sin, our helplessness—for we are dead in our trespasses and sins—and the need for God to atone for our sin and justify us to himself.

QUESTION 73

How doth faith justify a sinner in the sight of God?

Faith justifies a sinner in the sight of God, not because of those other graces which do always accompany it, or of good works that are the fruits of it, nor as if the grace of faith, or any act thereof, were imputed to him for his justification; but only as it is an instrument by which he receiveth and applies Christ and his righteousness.

---

14. Appendix 7.

How does the doctrine of salvation by faith alone relate to salvation by Christ alone?

Justification is based on a person having righteousness. This righteousness is from Christ, whose righteousness is perfect and complete and not from oneself. Christ's righteousness is imputed to the believer. This act of imputation assumes that Adam's sin is imputed to all men and that man's sin is imputed to Christ. The righteousness of Christ is received by faith alone which is a gift of God. Justification is not sanctification; imputation of righteousness is not infusion of righteousness; forgiveness of sin is not cleansing from sin, but cleansing flows from forgiveness.

QUESTION 74

What is adoption?[15]

Adoption is an act of the free grace of God, in and for his only Son Jesus Christ, whereby all those that are justified are received into the number of his children, have his name put upon them, the Spirit of his Son given to them, are under his fatherly care and dispensations, admitted to all the liberties and privileges of the sons of God, made heirs of all the promises, and fellow-heirs with Christ in glory.

1. What are the privileges of the sons of God?

The privileges of the sons of God are: being under God's fatherly care, being a member of the family of God, and being a joint heir with Christ in his inheritance.

2. In what does God's fatherly care consist?

God's fatherly care consists in his leading us by his Spirit sent into our hearts, in his chastening us in order that we might share in his holiness,

---

15. Gangadean, *The Westminster Confession*. See Question 58.

and in the access granted to us through prayer by which we approach him as our Father in heaven.

3. What is the family of God?

The family of God consists of all those who have been born of God, who hear the Word of God and do it. It consists of believers from all nations and all ages and is tied neither to common ancestry nor background. It is a fellowship of common interest and sharing in all the blessings of God by those who suffer and rejoice together.

4. What is the inheritance of God?

The inheritance of God consists of the new heavens and the new earth. It is the kingdom of God prepared for us from the foundation of the world and for which we labor and strive on earth. It is the City of God, the New Jerusalem, in which dwells righteousness. It is our heavenly reward, eternal life, and the knowledge of God that will fill the earth as the waters cover the sea.[16]

QUESTION 75

What is sanctification?[17]

Sanctification is a work of God's grace, whereby they whom God hath, before the foundation of the world, chosen to be holy, are in time, through the powerful operation of his Spirit applying the death and resurrection of Christ unto them, renewed in their whole man after the image of God; having the seeds of repentance unto life, and all other saving graces, put into their hearts, and those graces so stirred up, increased, and strengthened, as that they more and more die unto sin, and rise unto newness of life.

---

16. *Isaiah 11:9.*

17. Gangadean, *The Westminster Confession.* See Questions 59-61.

1. What is the basis for our sanctification?

By virtue of Christ's death and resurrection, the elect are set apart by justification.

2. How are we sanctified?

The Holy Spirit illumines our minds to know God, through which truth we are sanctified. As we contemplate the glory of God, we are transformed into his likeness; we are set free from sin and made holy. Righteousness in conduct proceeds from this knowledge and holiness.

3. What are the ordinary means established for our sanctification?

Ordinary means are the God-ordained means to exercise dominion over an area of life or discipline. It entails making use of the means provided by God to proceed in wisdom: Word, Worship, Witness (WWW) after the pattern of the priesthood in the Old Testament; hearing and reading of the Word, prayer, and witness by knowing, speaking, and living faithfully; and seeking diligently to understand general revelation, special revelation, and Historic Christianity and the relation among each and their application.

4. What is the standard of sanctification?

Obedience to the law of God in all that it requires and forbids is the only standard for sanctification. Neither is there any other standard for sanctification, however zealous or sincere we may feel. Antinomianism is the rejection of God's law in favor of man's law, be it private or by tradition, as the measure of holiness of piety.

5. To what extent is sanctification possible?

Increase in holiness is possible to the extent that we hear the Word of God, pray, meditate on it, and put it into practice. But though there is diligence and growth throughout one's life, no mere man is ever free from all sin in this life.

6. What is the relation between sanctification and suffering?

In our fallen state, there is a foolish complacency that makes us resistant to correction and instruction. Apart from the grace of God, we harden against God. We neglect, avoid, resist, and deny what is clear, coupled with self-deception and self-justification. No one apart from suffering is diligent in seeking. Only through much suffering do we enter more fully into the knowledge of the truth.

7. What is the end of sanctification?

In sanctification, we become more holy; through holiness, one comes to the knowledge of God, which is eternal life. Apart from holiness, no one shall see God.[18]

QUESTION 76

What is repentance unto life?[19]

Repentance unto life is a saving grace, wrought in the heart of a sinner by the Spirit and Word of God, whereby, out of the sight and sense, not only of the danger, but also of the filthiness and odiousness of his sins, and upon the apprehension of God's mercy in Christ to such as are penitent, he so grieves for and hates his sins, as that he turns from them all to God, purposing and endeavoring constantly to walk with him in all the ways of new obedience.

1. Can we of ourselves repent?

Man, left to himself, always, in pride, resists repentance through self-deception and self-justification. No man, therefore, can bring himself, or another, to true repentance, which depends wholly on the grace of God.

2. Is there only one repentance unto life?

Because no man in this life is ever free of all sin, repentance unto life must be throughout one's entire life, continually growing deeper as one grows in the knowledge of God.

---

18. *Hebrews 12:14.*

19. Gangadean, *The Westminster Confession.* See Questions 65-69.

3. How are we called by God unto repentance?

God calls us unto repentance not only through shame inwardly, and through the gospel outwardly, but also through all forms of natural evil imposed upon mankind since the Fall.

4. What are the marks of true repentance?

True repentance requires first, understanding of sin as truly evil, and of God's mercy in Christ, and is manifested in grief and hatred toward our sin and in the fruit of new obedience.

QUESTION 77

Wherein do justification and sanctification differ?

Although sanctification be inseparably joined with justification, yet they differ, in that God in justification imputeth the righteousness of Christ; in sanctification his Spirit infuseth grace, and enableth to the exercise thereof; in the former, sin is pardoned; in the other, it is subdued: the one doth equally free all believers from the revenging wrath of God, and that perfectly in this life, that they never fall into condemnation; the other is neither equal in all, nor in this life perfect in any, but growing up to perfection.

1. How are justification and sanctification inseparably joined together?

Both justification and sanctification share their origin in God. God pardons our sins (declares us righteous) and cleanses us from the sin that remains. One cannot be sanctified without first being justified, nor can one be justified without being cleansed from sin. They can be conceptually distinguished, but are existentially inseparable.

2. How are justification and sanctification conceptually distinguished?

Justification entails pardoning of sin through the imputed righteousness of Christ, it is a judicial act equally administered to all, and it is complete—a finished work in need of no further judicial action. Sanctification is a cleansing from sin that remains in this life through God's infused grace to subdue sin, it is administered in different degrees to each person, and it is ongoing throughout the whole of one's life.

3. What common errors are there between justification and sanctification?

In sacramentalism, justification is reduced to sanctification; one's righteous actions make one righteous before God through human effort. In antinomianism, justification denies the need for sanctification; one's salvation sets aside conformity to the law of God.

QUESTION 78

Whence ariseth the imperfection of sanctification in believers?

The imperfection of sanctification in believers ariseth from the remnants of sin abiding in every part of them, and the perpetual lustings of the flesh against the spirit; whereby they are often foiled with temptations, and fall into many sins, are hindered in all their spiritual services, and their best works are imperfect and defiled in the sight of God.

1. How do justification and remaining sin relate?

In justification, one is declared righteous before God, yet one's sin remains to be ruled over and overcome by the grace of God. Justification does not remove actual sin nor cleanse us from it.

2. How is sanctification part of the spiritual war?

In sanctification, the believer is brought to understand the depth of sin in one's life and the need to vanquish sin for the sake of knowing God. The spiritual war begins in oneself, between belief and unbelief.[20] Overcoming sin is connected with having dominion over oneself (moral dominion) and over the natural world (natural dominion).

3. How does sanctification relate to the larger and narrower aspects of our nature?

We are created finite, temporal, and changeable. By nature, we grow. In sanctification, the larger aspect of our nature remains, and it is guided through the narrower aspect, which has content (knowledge, holiness, and righteousness). Through knowledge of the truth, by the grace of God, we grow in our understanding, devotion, and obedience.

4. Why do we have to work out our salvation with fear and trembling?

Knowledge of the human condition and God's justice and mercy cannot be gained vicariously. Only by undergoing sanctification in this life does one come to understand the fear of the Lord, spiritual death, the odiousness of sin, and the fullness of spiritual life found in the knowledge of God and obedience to the moral law.

---

20. Gangadean, "Paper No. 8: Belief and Unbelief—The Spiritual War: Introductory Remarks," in *The Logos Papers*; "Paper No. 109: The Spiritual War: Its Many Dimensions," in *The Logos Papers*.

QUESTION 79

May not true believers, by reason of their imperfections, and the many temptations and sins they are overtaken with, fall away from the state of grace?

True believers, by reason of the unchangeable love of God, and his decree and covenant to give them perseverance, their inseparable union with Christ, his continual intercession for them, and the Spirit and seed of God abiding in them, can neither totally nor finally fall away from the state of grace, but are kept by the power of God through faith unto salvation.

1. How does remaining in the state of grace depend on God and not the creature?

Remaining in the state of grace depends on the unchangeable love of God, God's decree and covenant to give believers perseverance, believers' inseparable union with Christ, Christ's continual intercession for believers, and the Spirit and seed of God abiding in believers.

2. How does the doctrine of justification bring us peace in our sanctification?

In justification, we are declared righteous through the perfect obedience of Christ. It is by his merits that we are reconciled to God. It is not a work of our own, we did not earn it, and we cannot lose it. In sanctification, we fully rely upon the vicarious work of Christ—which brought us peace with God.

QUESTION 80

Can true believers be infallibly assured that they are in the estate of grace, and that they shall persevere therein unto salvation?

Such as truly believe in Christ, and endeavor to walk in all good conscience before him, may, without extraordinary revelation, by faith grounded upon the truth of God's promises, and by the Spirit enabling them to discern in themselves those graces to which the promises of life are made, and bearing witness with their spirits that they are the children of God, be infallibly assured that they are in the estate of grace, and shall persevere therein unto salvation.

1. What is the basis for the perseverance of the saints?

Election is a sovereign work of God depending on God alone—not for anything in man or done by man. Once the work of salvation is done, it cannot be undone. The elect can neither totally nor finally fall away from the state of grace, but shall certainly persevere in the state of grace until the end, to be eternally saved.

2. What is the basis for assurance of salvation?

Assurance of salvation rests on the perseverance of the saints. Assurance of salvation comes by obedience to God's Word and his commandments. Assurance of salvation apart from ordinary means is mere presumption. If we love God, we will obey his commandments.

3. How does assurance relate to good works?

By good works, believers manifest their thankfulness, strengthen their assurance, edify their brethren, adorn the profession of the gospel, stop the mouths of adversaries, and glorify God by acting for the good.

QUESTION 81

Are all true believers at all times assured of their present being in the estate of grace, and that they shall be saved?

Assurance of grace and salvation not being of the essence of faith, true believers may wait long before they obtain it; and, after the enjoyment thereof, may have it weakened and intermitted, through manifold distempers, sins, temptations, and desertions; yet are they never left without such a presence and support of the Spirit of God as keeps them from sinking into utter despair.

1. What is the necessity, means, obligation, and effects of assurance?[21]

1) Necessity: one can be a believer and not have an awareness of assurance of salvation.

2) Means: the right use of ordinary means as opposed to extraordinary means.

3) Obligation: to give all diligence to the use of ordinary means as to attain assurance subjectively.

4) Effects: peace and joy in the Holy Spirit, love and thankfulness of God, and cheerfulness in obedience and good works, which are the fruits of assurance.

2. How and to what extent can assurance be shaken?

Assurance of salvation can be shaken, diminished, and intermitted by negligence, grievous sin, or God withdrawing the light of his countenance (e.g., Job, David, Elijah, and Peter). Assurance may be shaken

---

21. Gangadean, *The Westminster Confession*. See Question 81.

to the point of perplexity, yet not utter despair—to outwardly curse and renounce Christ.

QUESTION 82

What is the communion in glory which the members of the invisible church have with Christ?

The communion in glory which the members of the invisible church have with Christ, is in this life, immediately after death, and at last perfected at the resurrection and day of judgment.

QUESTION 83

What is the communion in glory with Christ which the members of the invisible church enjoy in this life?

The members of the invisible Church have communicated to them in this life the firstfruits of glory with Christ, as they are members of him their head, and so in him are interested in that glory which he is fully possessed of; and, as an earnest thereof, enjoy the sense of God's love, peace of conscience, joy in the Holy Ghost, and hope of glory; as, on the contrary, sense of God's revenging wrath, horror of conscience, and a fearful expectation of judgment, are to the wicked the beginning of their torments which they shall endure after death.

QUESTION 84

Shall all men die?

Death being threatened as the wages of sin, it is appointed unto all men once to die; for that all have sinned.

1. What are the two kinds of death?

There are two kinds of death: physical and spiritual.[22] The wages of sin is spiritual (not physical) death, which is present and inherent in sin,[23] not future and imposed. The lake of fire is figuratively the second (or spiritual) death.[24]

2. How is spiritual death figuratively described in Scripture?

The spiritual death inherent in the sin of not seeking and not understanding is meaninglessness (the darkened mind, pictured as outer darkness), boredom (burning desire without satisfaction, pictured as the fire that is not quenched), and guilt (the torment of conscience, pictured as the gnawing worm that does not die)—all of which is unending, pictured as the bottomless pit.

3. How is physical death to be understood in light of the promise of redemption?

All have sinned in that all die physically. All are under the curse of toil and strife, and old age, sickness and (physical) death. The curse is imposed by God to restrain, recall from, and remove moral evil (the sin of not seeking and not understanding). It is God's third and final call back from not only sin, but self-deception and self-justification. This call back is mercy and is always (to be) given with the promise of redemption.

---

22. *John 11:25-26;* Gangadean, "Paper No. 147: The Biblical Worldview (Part VII): The Fall: Death and Theodicy," in *The Logos Papers.*

23. *Ephesians 2:1.*

24. *Revelation 20:6, 14.*

QUESTION 85

Death, being the wages of sin, why are not the righteous delivered from death, seeing all their sins are forgiven in Christ?

The righteous shall be delivered from death itself at the last day, and even in death are delivered from the sting and curse of it; so that, although they die, yet it is out of God's love, to free them perfectly from sin and misery, and to make them capable of further communion with Christ in glory, which they then enter upon.

QUESTION 86

What is the communion in glory with Christ, which the members of the invisible Church enjoy immediately after death?

The communion in glory with Christ, which the members of the invisible Church enjoy immediately after death, is, in that their souls are then made perfect in holiness, and received into the highest heavens, where they behold the face of God in light and glory, waiting for the full redemption of their bodies, which even in death continue united to Christ, and rest in their graves as in their beds, till at the last day they be again united to their souls. Whereas the souls of the wicked are at their death cast into hell, where they remain in torments and utter darkness, and their bodies kept in their graves, as in their prisons, till the resurrection and judgment of the great day.

1. What is meant by the souls of the righteous are made perfect at death?

Sanctification, while partial in this life, is complete at death by a sovereign act of God. All sin and unbelief are removed, yet all knowledge attained in this life is preserved free from any admixture with unbelief.

2. Why did God not make our sanctification perfect in this life?

In this life, evil is removed gradually by overcoming unbelief in ourselves and the world to deepen the revelation of God's glory.

3. What is meant by beholding the face of God?

Beholding the face of God is a figurative or metaphorical expression describing seeing the essence of God—the very nature of God—as he reveals himself in his works of creation and providence. Believers behold the unfolding of providence, the advancement of the promise, without hindrance from sin, as they behold the face of God.

QUESTION 87

What are we to believe concerning the resurrection?[25]

We are to believe, that at the last day there shall be a general resurrection of the dead, both of the just and unjust: when they that are then found alive shall in a moment be changed; and the selfsame bodies of the dead which were laid in the grave, being then again united to their souls forever, shall be raised up by the power of Christ. The bodies of the just, by the Spirit of Christ, and by virtue of his resurrection as their head, shall be raised in power, spiritual, incorruptible, and made like to his glorious body; and the bodies of the wicked shall be raised up in dishonor by him, as an offended judge.

---

25. Gangadean, *The Westminster Confession.* See Questions 133-134.

1. How should one argue for the resurrection?

Evidentialists have argued from the *actuality* of the resurrection to belief in God; one should argue from belief in God to the *necessity* of the resurrection. The necessity of the resurrection is to be established before the actuality of it.

2. What is the argument from necessity to actuality?

1) Clear general revelation shows that God exists, and original creation was very good (without natural evil—*could-would-must-did* argument[26]).

2) Natural evil is imposed subsequent to the creation, after the occurrence of moral evil.

3) Natural evil—culminating in physical death—is imposed, not as punishment, since it is not inherent in moral evil. It is imposed as a merciful call back from moral evil.

4) If physical death is imposed as a call back, then when moral evil is removed, natural evil will also be removed.

5) The removal of physical death requires the resurrection.

6) The argument for the resurrection is based, therefore, on the existence and nature of natural evil.

3. From the argument from necessity to actuality, what follows regarding the relationship between the general resurrection and Christ's resurrection?

Christ's resurrection is to be understood in light of the necessity for the general resurrection. *If there is no resurrection of the dead, then not even Christ has been raised.*[27] *For since death came through a man, the resurrection of the dead comes also through a man. For as in Adam all die, so in Christ all will be made alive.*[28] Christ's resurrection is the first fruits in restoring mankind to life in the knowledge of God.

---

26. See LCQ. 18, Commentary Q. 4.

27. *1 Corinthians 15:13.*

28. *1 Corinthians 15:21-22.*

4. Why is the resurrection considered a foundational doctrine? If there is no resurrection, then what follows?

If there is no resurrection, then not even Christ has been raised.[29]

And if Christ has not been raised, our preaching is useless and so is your faith.[30]

More than that, we are then found to be false witnesses about God, for we have testified about God that he raised Christ from the dead. But he did not raise him if in fact the dead are not raised.[31]

And if Christ has not been raised, your faith is futile; you are still in your sins.[32] For, *He was delivered over to death for our sins and was raised to life for our justification.*[33]

But God raised him from the dead, freeing him from the agony of death, because it was impossible for death to keep its hold on him.[34] Christ has the seal of approval to rule.

Now if there is no resurrection, what will those do who are baptized for the dead?[35]

If only for this life we have hope in Christ, we are of all people most to be pitied.[36]

---

29. *1 Corinthians 15:13.*

30. *1 Corinthians 15:14.*

31. *1 Corinthians 15:15-16.*

32. *1 Corinthians 15:18.*

33. *Romans 4:25.*

34. *Acts 2:24.*

35. *1 Corinthians 15:29.* Baptized for the dead is to be understood as the continuation of the work of those who came before us, i.e., being named after a faithful person whose work we should continue (e.g., Daniel, David, Paul, etc.).

36. *1 Corinthians 15:19.*

QUESTION 88

What shall immediately follow after the resurrection?

Immediately after the resurrection shall follow the general and final judgment of angels and men; the day and hour whereof no man knows, that all may watch and pray, and be ever ready for the coming of the Lord.

QUESTION 89

What shall be done to the wicked at the day of judgment?

At the day of judgment, the wicked shall be set on Christ's left hand, and, upon clear evidence, and full conviction of their own consciences, shall have the fearful but just sentence of condemnation pronounced against them; and thereupon shall be cast out from the favorable presence of God, and the glorious fellowship with Christ, his saints, and all his holy angels, into hell, to be punished with unspeakable torments, both of body and soul, with the devil and his angels forever.

How is punishment for sin to be understood?

1) The wages of sin is *spiritual* death, present and inherent in sin, not future and imposed.[37] In a person, it is meaninglessness, boredom, and guilt; in a relation, it is alienation; in a culture, it is decay and collapse; in general, it is destruction (according to its kind).

---

37. *Genesis 2:17; Ephesians 2:1.*

2) The lake of fire *is* the second death, present and inherent in sin. There is, therefore, no literal lake of fire which is future and imposed. What *is* future is full manifestation of God's glory in the Last Judgment and final separation of good and evil.[38]

QUESTION 90

What shall be done to the righteous at the day of judgment?

At the day of judgment, the righteous, being caught up to Christ in the clouds, shall be set on his right hand, and there openly acknowledged and acquitted, shall join with him in the judging of reprobate angels and men, and shall be received into heaven, where they shall be fully and forever freed from all sin and misery; filled with inconceivable joys, made perfectly holy and happy both in body and soul, in the company of innumerable saints and holy angels, but especially in the immediate vision and fruition of God the Father, of our Lord Jesus Christ, and of the Holy Spirit, to all eternity. And this is the perfect and full communion, which the members of the invisible Church shall enjoy with Christ in glory, at the resurrection and day of judgment.

---

38. *Revelation 19:20; 20:6, 10, 14-15; 21:8.*

Chapter 21

THE MORAL LAW:
THE RULE OF OUR OBEDIENCE

QUESTION 91

What is the duty which God requireth of man?

The duty which God requireth of man, is obedience to his revealed will.

1. What is a duty?

A duty is an obligation we owe without conditions. It extends not only to words and deeds, but to the meditations of our hearts as well.

2. To whom is our duty?

Because God has made us, we are his and not our own.[1] Therefore, our duty is to God, and not merely ourselves or others, however much we benefit from our duty.

3. Do all men have a duty to God?

All men, being created by God, owe to God whatever duty God is pleased to require of man. Neither is one's duty set aside by unbelief, which is itself a failure in duty.

---

1. *Psalm 100:3.*

4. What is the relation of man's duty and his chief end?

The chief end of man, which is to glorify God, and his duty are one and the same.

QUESTION 92

What did God at first reveal unto man as the rule of his obedience?

The rule of obedience revealed to Adam in the estate of innocence, and to all mankind in him, besides a special command not to eat of the fruit of the tree of the knowledge of good and evil, was the moral law.

1. When was the moral law first revealed to man?

The moral law was first revealed to man from the very beginning, from the time of his creation.

2. How is the moral law revealed to all men?

The moral law is written on the heart of man[2] so that its requirements are clearly revealed to all men.

3. Can the moral law be altered in any way?

The moral law, being a requirement of God's nature and the nature of man as made in the image of God, cannot be added to or changed in any way.

---

2. *Romans 2:14-15.*

QUESTION 93

What is the moral law?

The moral law is the declaration of the will of God to mankind, directing and binding everyone to personal, perfect, and perpetual conformity and obedience thereunto, in the frame and disposition of the whole man, soul and body, and in performance of all those duties of holiness and righteousness which he oweth to God and man: promising life upon the fulfilling, and threatening death upon the breach of it.

What are the characteristics of the moral law?

1) The moral law is clear; it is grounded in human nature, which is easily knowable by all human beings.

2) The moral law is comprehensive; it guides all choices that express all aspects of human nature.

3) The moral law is spiritual; it has inherent consequences of spiritual life or death.

4) The moral law is absolute, central to all moral concerns; it assumes choices and the highest value; "good" is understood in relation to the good.

5) The moral law is universal, for all men, everywhere, at all times.

6) The moral law is personal, relating to God as a person.

7) The moral law is exact; it has specific implications for every thought, word, and deed.

8) The moral law is the source of unity in each person and among all persons.

9) The moral law is teleological, aimed at the good, the end in itself, which is the knowledge of God.

10) The moral law is perpetual; it is forever, for no higher standard exceeds it nor supersedes it, for the law is the same as love.

11) The moral law from general revelation is the same in content as the moral law given in special revelation (the Decalogue).

12) The moral law is doxological, for it gives all glory to God.

QUESTION 94

Is there any use of the moral law since the Fall?

Although no man, since the Fall, can attain to righteousness
and life by the moral law; yet there is great use thereof,
as well common to all men, as peculiar either to the
unregenerate, or the regenerate.

What are the three uses of the law?

1) For all men, it serves a common grace purpose of informing the conscience of man, restraining sin, and promoting righteousness.[3]

2) For the unregenerate, it brings man under conviction of sin and makes us conscious of our inability to meet the demands of the law.[4]

3) For the regenerate, the moral law is the rule of life.[5]

---

3. Further explained in Question 95.

4. Further explained in Question 96.

5. Further explained in Question 97.

QUESTION 95

Of what use is the moral law to all men?

The moral law is of use to all men, to inform them of the holy nature and will of God, and of their duty, binding them to walk accordingly; to convince them of their disability to keep it, and of the sinful pollution of their nature, hearts, and lives; to humble them in the sense of their sin and misery, and thereby help them to a clearer sight of the need they have of Christ, and of the perfection of his obedience.

QUESTION 96

What particular use is there of the moral law to unregenerate men?

The moral law is of use to unregenerate men, to awaken their consciences to flee from wrath to come, and to drive them to Christ; or, upon their continuance in the estate and way of sin, to leave them inexcusable, and under the curse thereof.

QUESTION 97

What special use is there of the moral law to the regenerate?

Although they that are regenerate, and believe in Christ, be delivered from the moral law as a covenant of works, so as thereby they are neither justified nor condemned; yet, besides the general uses thereof common to them with all men, it is of special use, to show them how much they are bound to Christ for his fulfilling it, and enduring the curse thereof in their stead, and for their good; and thereby to provoke them to more thankfulness, and to express the same in their greater care to conform themselves thereunto as the rule of their obedience.

QUESTION 98

Where is the moral law summarily comprehended?

The moral law is summarily comprehended in the Ten Commandments, which were delivered by the voice of God upon Mount Sinai, and written by him in two tables of stone; and are recorded in the twentieth chapter of Exodus. The four first commandments containing our duty to God, and the other six our duty to man.

1. What is the relation between the moral law and the Ten Commandments?

The moral law is given to all men by general revelation and the Ten Commandments given to the people of God by special revelation are one and the same.[6]

2. How is the moral law summarily comprehended in the Ten Commandments?

The commandments are exceedingly broad in principle and application; by meditating on the law day and night, its meaning for all of life can be discerned.

3. Are there additional laws to the Ten Commandments?

The ceremonial laws (concerning worship and holiness) and the civil laws (concerning justice and discipline) are not additional laws, but special applications of the law for the Church prior to the coming of the Messiah.

4. What is the sum of the Ten Commandments?

The sum of the Ten Commandments is to love the Lord our God with all our heart, with all our soul, with all our strength, and with all our mind; and our neighbor as ourselves.

5. What is taught in the great commandment?

In the great commandment, we are taught that love and the law are one and the same, that the law cannot be set aside in the name of love, and that those who do so misunderstand both love and the law.

6. What does it mean to love God with all our heart?

Loving God with all our heart means that God claims for himself every part of our being and that there is no aspect of life, whether private or public, that is not to be governed by God's law.

---

6. *Deuteronomy 30:11-14; Romans 2:14-15.*

7. What does it mean to love our neighbor as ourselves?

To love our neighbor as ourselves means that, all men being made equally in the image of God, and that all being equally in need of grace and truth, we are to seek the good of others as we do for ourselves.

8. What is the goal of the law?

The goal of the law is eternal life, which is the knowledge of God.[7]

QUESTION 99

What rules are to be observed for the right understanding of the Ten Commandments?[8]

For the right understanding of the Ten Commandments, these rules are to be observed:

1. That the law is perfect, and bindeth everyone to full conformity in the whole man unto the righteousness thereof, and unto entire obedience forever; so as to require the utmost perfection of every duty, and to forbid the least degree of every sin.

1. How is the law perfect?

The law contains the will of God for man. God as Creator determined human nature for man. The law is derived from and is a fulfillment of God's intended purpose for man and his creation. It binds man to full conformity in perpetuity. The law is perfect in that nothing can be added nor taken away without distorting it.

---

7. *John 17:3.*

8. Gangadean, "Paper No. 25: Moral Law and Culture: The City with Foundations," in *The Logos Papers*.

2. That it is spiritual, and so reaches the understanding, will, affections, and all other powers of the soul; as well as words, works, and gestures.

2. How is the law spiritual?

Man is constituted as a triune personality (intellect, emotions, and will). There is an order from intellect (understanding, beliefs, ideas) to emotions (feelings, passions, affections) to will (words, works, and gestures). The law encompasses all aspects of our nature, and it is expressed thereby.

3. That one and the same thing, in divers respects, is required or forbidden in several commandments.

3. How is the law a unity?

The law is systematically arranged (from the more basic to less basic), all subsequent commandments presuppose the prior commandments. To comply with the latter commandments requires obedience to the earlier; breaking the latter entails breaking the earlier. Breaking the earlier will result in breaking the latter. What is required or forbidden in the earlier commandments is expressed in the latter commandments.

4. Where a duty is commanded, the contrary sin is forbidden; and, where a sin is forbidden, the contrary duty is commanded: so, where a promise is annexed, the contrary threatening is included; and, where a threatening is annexed, the contrary promise is included.

4. How are the blessings and curses connected with the commandments?

The promises and threats are connected necessarily in light of the nature of God and man. The consequences of obedience and disobedience to the commandments can be derived by understanding their implications.

5. That what God forbids, is at no time to be done; What he commands, is always our duty; and yet every particular duty is not to be done at all times.

5. How are God's commands related to our duties?

God's commands and prohibitions are part of the revealed will of God. We are morally obligated to understand and do the revealed will of God, yet wisdom is required to discern what duties are required in light of the teleological context.

6. That under one sin or duty, all of the same kind are forbidden or commanded; together with all the causes, means, occasions, and appearances thereof, and provocations thereunto.

6. How does one understand the sins or duties under each commandment?

The use of good and necessary consequences is to be exercised in understanding human nature, the basic concepts contained in the law, and their implications in human life.

7. That what is forbidden or commanded to ourselves, we are bound, according to our places, to endeavor that it may be avoided or performed by others, according to the duty of their places.

7. How does one's moral responsibility extend to those under our care?

The law being synonymous with love is an extension of our moral responsibility. The love of self and the love of neighbor are connected with the love of God. In love, we seek the good for those under our care and stewardship.

*8. That in what is commanded to others, we are bound,
according to our places and callings, to be helpful to them;
and to take heed of partaking with others in what is
forbidden them.*

8. How do the responsibilities of others extend to us?

The good is corporate, for it requires others to achieve; communal, for it is increased by sharing; and cumulative, for it increases from generation to generation. There is a shared responsibility in working with others to either help in what is commanded or not contribute to what is forbidden.

QUESTION 100

What special things are we to consider in the Ten Commandments?

We are to consider, in the Ten Commandments, the preface, the substance of the commandments themselves, and several reasons annexed to some of them, the more to enforce them.

Chapter 22

PREFACE AND COMMANDMENTS 1-4: OUR DUTY TO GOD

QUESTION 101

What is the preface to the Ten Commandments?

The preface to the Ten Commandments is contained in these words, **I am the Lord thy God, which have brought thee out of the land of Egypt, out of the house of bondage.** *Wherein God manifesteth his sovereignty, as being JEHOVAH, the eternal, immutable, and almighty God; having his being in and of himself, and giving being to all his words and works: and that he is a God in covenant, as with Israel of old, so with all his people; who, as he brought them out of their bondage in Egypt, so he delivers us from our spiritual thraldom; and that therefore we are bound to take him for our God alone, and to keep all his commandments.*

1. What is meant by saying that God is the Lord?

That God is the Lord means that God is the Creator of heaven and earth and ruler over all that comes to pass; therefore, obedience is owed to him.

2. What is meant by saying that God is our God?

Although God is the Lord of all because he is the Creator, those who by covenant acknowledge God to be their God owe to him obedience by virtue of the covenant.

3. What is meant by saying that God is our redeemer?

Although we owe obedience to God as Creator and by covenant, we have sinned in failing to obey his commandments. God pardons and frees us from our sin by Christ's death on the cross. Therefore, we are further bound to obey all his commandments.

QUESTION 102

What is the sum of the four commandments which contain our duty to God?

The sum of the four commandments containing our duty to God is, to love the Lord our God with all our heart, and with all our soul, and with all our strength, and with all our mind.

QUESTION 103

Which is the first commandment?[1]

The first commandment is, Thou shall have no other gods before me.

QUESTION 104

What are the duties required in the first commandment?

The duties required in the first commandment are, the knowing and acknowledging of God to be the only true God, and our God; and to worship and glorify him accordingly, by thinking, meditating, remembering, highly esteeming, honoring, adoring, choosing, loving, desiring, fearing of him; believing him; trusting, hoping, delighting, rejoicing in him; being zealous for him; calling upon him, giving all praise and thanks, and yielding all obedience and submission to him with the whole man; being careful in all things to please him, and sorrowful when in anything he is offended; and walking humbly with him.

---

1. Gangadean, *Philosophical Foundation*, 171-183; Gangadean, "Paper No. 9: The Moral Law: Derived from Human Nature," in *The Logos Papers*; Gangadean, "Paper No. 10: The Moral Law: The Origin, Nature, Law, Application, and Consequences of the Moral Laws," in *The Logos Papers*.

QUESTION 105

What are the sins forbidden in the first commandment?

The sins forbidden in the first commandment are, atheism, in denying or not having a God; Idolatry, in having or worshiping more gods than one, or any with or instead of the true God; the not having and avouching him for God, and our God; the omission or neglect of anything due to him, required in this commandment; ignorance, forgetfulness, misapprehensions, false opinions, unworthy and wicked thoughts of him; bold and curious searching into his secrets; all profaneness, hatred of God; self-love, self-seeking, and all other inordinate and immoderate setting of our mind, will, or affections upon other things, and taking them off from him in whole or in part; vain credulity, unbelief, heresy, misbelief, distrust, despair, incorrigibleness, and insensibleness under judgments, hardness of heart, pride, presumption, carnal security, tempting of God; using unlawful means, and trusting in lawful means; carnal delights and joys; corrupt, blind, and indiscreet zeal; lukewarmness, and deadness in the things of God; estranging ourselves, and apostatizing from God; praying, or giving any religious worship, to saints, angels, or any other creatures; all compacts and consulting with the devil, and hearkening to his suggestions; making men the lords of our faith and conscience; slighting and despising God and his commands; resisting and grieving of his Spirit, discontent and impatience at his dispensations, charging him foolishly for the evils he inflicts on us; and ascribing the praise of any good we either are, have, or can do, to fortune, idols, ourselves, or any other creature.

QUESTION 106

What are we specially taught by these words, *before me*, in the first commandment?

*These words, **before me**, or before my face, in the first commandment, teach us, that God, who seeth all things, taketh special notice of, and is much displeased with, the sin of having any other God: that so it may be an argument to dissuade from it, and to aggravate it as a most impudent provocation: as also to persuade us to do as in his sight, whatever we do in his service.*

1. How can we be required to know God?

We can be required to know God because God has clearly revealed his eternal power and divine nature in the things that are made so that all unbelief is without excuse.[2]

2. In what way do we fail to know God?

All those who say we cannot know if there is a God who created heaven and earth fail to know God. This position is known as skepticism and agnosticism.

3. In what way is God denied?

God is denied by all those who say there is no God who created the heavens and the earth. There are many forms of this denial including atheism, pantheism, polytheism, materialism, dualism, and shamanism.

4. How can we know that God exists?

We can know by reason from general revelation that there must be something eternal, and only God is eternal.

---

2. *Romans 1:18-20.*

5. Wherein consists the clarity of general revelation?[3]

The clarity of general revelation is such that all who seek God can know that he is; that one has to shut one's eyes to avoid seeing this clear revelation; that one has to harden oneself to one's suffering to avoid considering God's self-revelation.

6. How is sin at its origin denied?

Sin at its origin is denied by those who say we cannot know that God exists, but we can believe that he is, and by those who say sin is not a failure to know, but a failure to acknowledge God. The former denies the clarity of general revelation and is known as fideism; the latter denies the primacy of the intellect and is known as mysticism and voluntarism.[4]

7. What are the consequences of denying clear general revelation?

The denial of clear general revelation requires the denial of reason which results in spiritual death.

8. What are the consequences of acknowledging clear general revelation?

The consequences of acknowledging the clarity of general revelation are the overcoming of all arguments that are raised up against the knowledge of God and the bringing of all mankind to confess God as Creator.

---

3. Appendix 6; Gangadean, *Philosophical Foundation*, 71-161; Gangadean, *History of Philosophy*, 47-58; Gangadean, "Paper No. 3: The Principle of Clarity, Rational Presuppositionalism, and Proof," in *The Logos Papers*.

4. Gangadean, "Paper No. 120: Contra Voluntarism: The Will Is Not Independent of the Intellect," in *The Logos Papers*.

QUESTION 107

Which is the second commandment?[5]

The second commandment is, Thou shalt not make unto thee any graven image, or any likeness of anything that is in heaven above, or that is in the earth beneath, or that is in the water under the earth: Thou shalt not bow down thyself to them, nor serve them: for I the Lord thy God am a jealous God, visiting the iniquity of the fathers upon the children unto the third and fourth generation of them that hate me; and shewing mercy unto thousands of them that love me, and keep my commandments.

QUESTION 108

What are the duties required in the second commandment?

The duties required in the second commandment are, the receiving, observing, and keeping pure and entire, all such religious worship and ordinances as God hath instituted in his Word; particularly prayer and thanksgiving in the name of Christ; the reading, preaching, and hearing of the Word; the administration and receiving of the sacraments; church government and discipline; the ministry and maintenance thereof; religious fasting; swearing by the name of God, and vowing unto him: as also the disapproving, detesting, opposing, all false worship; and, according to each one's place and calling, removing it, and all monuments of idolatry.

5. Gangadean, *Philosophical Foundation*, 185-198.

QUESTION 109

What are the sins forbidden in the second commandment?

The sins forbidden in the second commandment are, all devising, counseling, commanding, using, and anywise approving, any religious worship not instituted by God himself; tolerating a false religion; the making any representation of God, of all or of any of the three persons, either inwardly in our mind, or outwardly in any kind of image or likeness of any creature whatsoever; all worshiping of it, or God in it or by it; the making of any representation of feigned deities, and all worship of them, or service belonging to them; all superstitious devices, corrupting the worship of God, adding to it, or taking from it, whether invented and taken up of ourselves, or received by tradition from others, though under the title of antiquity, custom, devotion, good intent, or any other pretense whatsoever; simony; sacrilege; all neglect, contempt, hindering, and opposing the worship and ordinances which God hath appointed.

QUESTION 110

What are the reasons annexed to the second commandment, the more to enforce it?

*The reasons annexed to the second commandment, the more to enforce it, contained in these words, **For I the Lord thy God am a jealous God, visiting the iniquity of the fathers upon the children unto the third and fourth generation of them that hate me; and showing mercy unto thousands of them that love me, and keep my commandments;** are, besides God's sovereignty over us, and propriety in us, his fervent zeal for his own worship, and his revengeful indignation against all false worship, as being a spiritual whoredom; accounting the breakers of this commandment such as hate him, and threatening to punish them unto divers generations; and esteeming the observers of it such as love him and keep his commandments, and promising mercy to them unto many generations.*

1. What is it to make a graven image?

To make a graven image is to liken the Creator to the creature; it is to think of the infinite in light of the finite; it is to deny the nature of God in any way.

2. What are some assumptions of this command?

This command assumes that thinking is presuppositional; that we are to think of the less basic in light of the more basic; that we are always to think of the finite, temporal, and changeable in light of the infinite, eternal, and unchanging; that we are to understand our experience in light of God rather than understanding God in light of our experience.

3. What are some implications of this command?

This command implies that man is made in the image of God, that God is not to be made in the image of man; that man is the image bearer and not to be made in the image of the animal; that the distinction between God and man is never to be denied.

4. What is it to bow down to a graven image?

To bow down to a graven image is to worship God according to our own representation of him rather than according to his representation of himself. We represent God to ourselves when we worship him in any way that he has not prescribed in his Word. This regulative principle of worship is violated in corporate worship by singing songs of human composition rather than the inspired Psalms.[6]

5. How has God's nature been denied by those who profess belief in God?[7]

Those who profess belief in God the Creator deny the infinite justice of God by denying the need for forgiveness of sin through the atoning death of Jesus Christ.[8]

6. How has God's nature been denied in the Church?

The divisions in the Church are due to a failure to know and acknowledge the fullness of Jesus Christ who fills everything in every way.[9]

7. What are the consequences of denying God's nature?

The consequences of denying God's nature are divisions within the Church, the loss of effectiveness of its witness in the world, and the

---

6. Appendix 9.

7. This question refers to those who hold to belief in God the Creator outside of Christianity.

8. Gangadean, "Paper No. 91: Christianity and Islam: The Difference," in *The Logos Papers*; "Paper No. 124: On Islam," in *The Logos Papers*; Gangadean, *Philosophical Foundation*, 190-194.

9. *Ephesians 1:22-23*; Gangadean, "Paper No. 31: Divisions Among Theists: Sources and Response," in *The Logos Papers*; "Paper No. 60: The Spiritual War (Part II): Church Councils and Settling Current Divisions in the Church," in *The Logos Papers*; Paper No. 61: The Present and Future State of the Church: To and For the Church," in *The Logos Papers*; Paper No. 62: The Next Reformation: Prepare the Way of the Lord," in *The Logos Papers*.

collapse of the culture by the accumulation of sin in three to four generations.[10]

8. What are the consequences of acknowledging God's nature?

The consequences of acknowledging God's nature are unity of the faith within the Church, the world coming to believe that Jesus is the Messiah, and the earth being filled with the knowledge of God.[11]

QUESTION 111

Which is the third commandment?[12]

The third commandment is, Thou shalt not take the name of the Lord thy God in vain: for the Lord will not hold him guiltless that taketh his name in vain.

QUESTION 112

What is required in the third commandment?

The third commandment requires, that the name of God, his titles, attributes, ordinances, the Word, sacraments, prayer, oaths, vows, lots, his works, and whatsoever else there is whereby he makes himself known, be holily and reverently used in thought, meditation, word, and writing; by an holy profession, and answerable conversation, to the glory of God, and the good of ourselves, and others.

10. Gangadean, "Paper No. 34: Globalism and Nationalism: A Biblical Perspective," in *The Logos Papers*; "Paper No. 58: The Spiritual War (Part I): On the State of the Church and the World," in *The Logos Papers*.

11. *Isaiah 11:9.*

12. Gangadean, *Philosophical Foundation*, 199-205.

QUESTION 113

What are the sins forbidden in the third commandment?

The sins forbidden in the third commandment are, the not using of God's name as is required; and the abuse of it in an ignorant, vain, irreverent, profane, superstitious, or wicked mentioning, or otherwise using his titles, attributes, ordinances, or works, by blasphemy, perjury; all sinful cursings, oaths, vows, and lots; violating of our oaths and vows, if lawful; and fulfilling them, if of things unlawful; murmuring and quarreling at, curious prying into, and misapplying of God's decrees and providences; misinterpreting, misapplying, or any way perverting the Word, or any part of it, to profane jests, curious or unprofitable questions, vain janglings, or the maintaining of false doctrines; abusing it, the creatures, or anything contained under the name of God, to charms, or sinful lusts and practices; the maligning, scorning, reviling, or any wise opposing of God's truth, grace, and ways; making profession of religion in hypocrisy, or for sinister ends; being ashamed of it, or a shame to it, by unconformable, unwise, unfruitful, and offensive walking, or backsliding from it.

QUESTION 114

What reasons are annexed to the third commandment?

*The reasons annexed to the third commandment, in these words, **The Lord thy God**, and, For the Lord will not hold him guiltless that taketh his name in vain, are, because he is the Lord and our God, therefore his name is not to be profaned, or any way abused by us; especially because he will be so far from acquitting and sparing the transgressors of this commandment, as that he will not suffer them to escape his righteous judgment, albeit many such escape the censures and punishments of men.*

1. What is meant by the name of God?

By the name of God is meant all that by which God makes himself known; all of his works of creation and providence. It is the revelation of God in his Word as well as in his works.

2. What is it to take the name of God in vain?

To take the name of God in vain is to fail to live our lives by the Word of God, which we profess, especially in our oaths and vows.[13] It is to lack integrity and to practice hypocrisy.

3. What is it to have integrity?

To have integrity is to have a concern for consistency in all our thoughts and deeds. It is to have a concern to know the truth and to practice

---

13. Gangadean, "Paper No. 2: Common Ground," in *The Logos Papers*; "Paper No. 51: Common Ground (Part II): Integrity," in *The Logos Papers*; "Paper No. 64: Aaron's Rod: God's Teaching Authority in the Church: A Call to Repentance," in *The Logos Papers*; "Paper No. 65: Aaron's Rod: A Permanent Witness Against Those Who Challenge God's Authority in the Church: Existential Hermeneutics Applied," in *The Logos Papers*.

it. It is manifested in the diligent use of ordinary means, especially in meditation and self-examination.

4. What is it to practice hypocrisy?

To practice hypocrisy is to profess one thing and to do another in a manner that conceals it from others and oneself. It is brought about by self-deception and self-justification, which comes from self-imposed blindness.

5. What is it to be held guiltless?

Although we may deceive ourselves and others by the appearance of righteousness, yet God does not excuse our disregard of his revelation. He brings to light the hidden things of darkness, thereby humbling our pride, or he gives us up to the hardening of our hearts and, finally, removal from the privileges of his Word.

6. How is the evil of hypocrisy to be avoided?

The evil of hypocrisy is to be avoided by willing submission to the discipline of God, by personal discipline in thought and deed, by corporate discipline in the Church, and by avoiding foolish arguing which lacks integrity.

7. What is the blessing of obeying this commandment?

Those who maintain integrity and endure discipline are brought by God, through holiness and purity of heart, to see God.

QUESTION 115

Which is the fourth commandment?[14]

The fourth commandment is, Remember the Sabbath day, to keep it holy. Six days shalt thou labor, and do all thy work: but the seventh day is the Sabbath of the Lord thy God: in it thou shalt not do any work, thou, nor thy son, nor thy daughter, thy manservant, nor thy maidservant, nor thy cattle, nor thy stranger that is within thy gates: For in six days the Lord made heaven and earth, the sea, and all that in them is, and rested the seventh day: wherefore the Lord blessed the Sabbath day, and hallowed it.

QUESTION 116

What is required in the fourth commandment?

*The fourth commandment requires of all men the sanctifying or keeping holy to God such set times as he hath appointed in his Word, expressly one whole day in seven; which was the seventh from the beginning of the world to the resurrection of Christ, and the first day of the week ever since, and so to continue to the end of the world; which is the Christian Sabbath, and in the New Testament called **The Lord's day.***

---

14. Gangadean, *Philosophical Foundation*, 207-219.

QUESTION 117

How is the Sabbath or the Lord's day to be sanctified?

The Sabbath or Lord's day is to be sanctified by an holy resting all the day, not only from such works as are at all times sinful, but even from such worldly employments and recreations as are on other days lawful; and making it our delight to spend the whole time (except so much of it as is to be taken up in works of necessity and mercy) in the public and private exercises of God's worship: and, to that end, we are to prepare our hearts, and with such foresight, diligence, and moderation, to dispose and seasonably dispatch our worldly business, that we may be the more free and fit for the duties of that day.

QUESTION 118

Why is the charge of keeping the Sabbath more specially directed to governors of families, and other superiors?

The charge of keeping the Sabbath is more specially directed to governors of families, and other superiors, because they are bound not only to keep it themselves, but to see that it be observed by all those that are under their charge; and because they are prone ofttimes to hinder them by employments of their own.

QUESTION 119

What are the sins forbidden in the fourth commandment?

The sins forbidden in the fourth commandment are, all omissions of the duties required, all careless, negligent, and unprofitable performing of them, and being weary of them; all profaning the day by idleness, and doing that which is in itself sinful; and by all needless works, words, and thoughts, about our worldly employments and recreations.

QUESTION 120

What are the reasons annexed to the fourth commandment, the more to enforce it?

The reasons annexed to the fourth commandment, the more to enforce it, are taken from the equity of it, God allowing us six days of seven for our own affairs, and reserving but one for himself, in these words, Six days shalt thou labor, and do all thy work: from God's challenging a special propriety in that day, The seventh day is the Sabbath of the Lord thy God: from the example of God, who in six days made heaven and earth, the sea, and all that in them is, and rested the seventh day: and from that blessing which God put upon that day, not only in sanctifying it to be a day for his service, but in ordaining it to be a means of blessing to us in our sanctifying it; Wherefore the Lord blessed the Sabbath day, and hallowed it.

1. What is the Sabbath day?

The Sabbath day is the day of rest, signifying man's completion of his work even as God completed his work.[15]

2. What is it to keep the Sabbath day holy?

To keep the Sabbath day holy is to be devoted through all our work to complete the task God has given to man.

3. What is the work God has given to man?

God gave to man from the beginning the work of dominion through which man develops all the powers latent in himself and the creation.

4. What is the goal of dominion?

The goal of man's work of dominion is to fill the earth with the knowledge of God as the waters cover the sea,[16] which knowledge is eternal life.[17]

5. Is dominion necessary for the knowledge of God?

God, being spirit, whom no man has seen nor can see, reveals himself in his work of creation and providence; neither is there any other revelation possible. Therefore, God can be known only through his work as man exercises dominion therein.

6. Will man complete the work God has given him?

The rest of the Sabbath day, being commanded by God, reaffirms the hope that the work will be completed. Because God is faithful as Creator and Redeemer, the Church will achieve unity in the faith, the nations will turn to the Lord, and the earth will be filled with the knowledge of God before Christ returns.[18]

---

15. *Genesis 2:2.*
16. *Isaiah 11:9.*
17. *John 17:3.*
18. *1 Corinthians 15:24-28.*

7. How is the Sabbath day to be observed?

The Sabbath day is to be observed by corporate and private resting in hope, reflecting on our work, preparation for work through preaching, renewal of our commitment, and rejoicing in worship.

QUESTION 121

Why is the word *Remember* set in the beginning of the fourth commandment?

*The word **Remember** is set in the beginning of the fourth commandment, partly, because of the great benefit of remembering it, we being thereby helped in our preparation to keep it, and, in keeping it, better to keep all the rest of the commandments, and to continue a thankful remembrance of the two great benefits of creation and redemption, which contain a short abridgment of religion; and partly, because we are very ready to forget it, for that there is less light of nature for it, and yet it restraineth our natural liberty in things at other times lawful; that it cometh but once in seven days, and many worldly businesses come between, and too often take off our minds from thinking of it, either to prepare for it, or to sanctify it; and that Satan with his instruments much labor to blot out the glory, and even the memory of it, to bring in all irreligion and impiety.*

Chapter 23

COMMANDMENTS 5-10: OUR DUTY TO MAN

QUESTION 122

What is the sum of the six commandments which contain our duty to man?

The sum of the six commandments which contain our duty to man is, to love our neighbor as ourselves, and to do to others what we would have them to do to us.

QUESTION 123

Which is the fifth commandment?[1]

*The fifth commandment is, **Honor thy father and thy mother; that thy days may be long upon the land which the Lord thy God giveth thee.***

---

1. Gangadean, *Philosophical Foundation*, 221-229.

QUESTION 124

Who are meant by father and mother in the fifth commandment?

*By **father** and **mother**, in the fifth commandment, are meant, not only natural parents, but all superiors in age and gifts; and especially such as, by God's ordinance, are over us in place of authority, whether in family, church, or commonwealth.*

QUESTION 125

Why are superiors styled father and mother?

*Superiors are styled **father** and **mother**, both to teach them in all duties toward their inferiors, like natural parents, to express love and tenderness to them, according to their several relations; and to work inferiors to a greater willingness and cheerfulness in performing their duties to their superiors, as to their parents.*

QUESTION 126

What is the general scope of the fifth commandment?

The general scope of the fifth commandment is, the performance of those duties which we mutually owe in our several relations, as inferiors, superiors, or equals.

QUESTION 127

What is the honor that inferiors owe to their superiors?

The honor which inferiors owe to their superiors is, all due reverence in heart, word, and behavior; prayer and thanksgiving for them; imitation of their virtues and graces; willing obedience to their lawful commands and counsels; due submission to their corrections; fidelity to, defense and maintenance of their persons and authority, according to their several ranks, and the nature of their places; bearing with their infirmities, and covering them in love, that so they may be an honor to them and to their government.

QUESTION 128

What are the sins of inferiors against their superiors?

The sins of inferiors against their superiors are, all neglect of the duties required toward them; envying at, contempt of, and rebellion against, their persons and places, in their lawful counsels, commands, and corrections; cursing, mocking, and all such refractory and scandalous carriage, as proves a shame and dishonor to them and their government.

QUESTION 129

What is required of superiors towards their inferiors?

It is required of superiors, according to that power they receive from God, and that relation wherein they stand, to love, pray for, and bless their inferiors; to instruct, counsel, and admonish them; countenancing, commending, and rewarding such as do well; and discountenancing, reproving, and chastising such as do ill; protecting, and providing for them all things necessary for soul and body: and by grave, wise, holy, and exemplary carriage, to procure glory to God, honor to themselves, and so to preserve that authority which God hath put upon them.

QUESTION 130

What are the sins of superiors?

The sins of superiors are, besides the neglect of the duties required of them, an inordinate seeking of themselves, their own glory, ease, profit, or pleasure; commanding things unlawful, or not in the power of inferiors to perform; counseling, encouraging, or favoring them in that which is evil; dissuading, discouraging, or discountenancing them in that which is good; correcting them unduly; careless exposing, or leaving them to wrong, temptation, and danger; provoking them to wrath; or any way dishonoring themselves, or lessening their authority, by an unjust, indiscreet, rigorous, or remiss behavior.

QUESTION 131

What are the duties of equals?

The duties of equals are, to regard the dignity and worth of each other, in giving honor to go one before another; and to rejoice in each other's gifts and advancement, as their own.

QUESTION 132

What are the sins of equals?

The sins of equals are, besides the neglect of the duties required, the undervaluing of the worth, envying the gifts, grieving at the advancement of prosperity one of another; and usurping pre-eminence one over another.

QUESTION 133

What is the reason annexed to the fifth commandment, the more to enforce it?

*The reason annexed to the fifth commandment, in these words, **That thy days may be long upon the land which the Lord thy God giveth thee**, is an express promise of long life and prosperity, as far as it shall serve for God's glory and their own good, to all such as keep this commandment.*

1. What is it to honor father and mother?

To honor father and mother is to recognize the legitimacy of their authority in the obedience we give to them.

2. What is the extent of authority?

All authority is of God. Authority is not exercised only by father and mother, but by all those who are over us in every area of life.

3. How is authority exercised?

Authority is exercised fundamentally through teaching and secondarily through deciding and directing. The authority of Christ is exercised through the Church in its teaching the nations to obey all he has commanded.[2]

4. Wherein consists the legitimacy of authority?

The legitimacy of authority consists in possessing insight into the good and the means to it; it is not based on might. The authority of insight is rational; it is not merely personal. Insight is historically cumulative; it is not merely individually originated.[3]

5. What is the order of authority within each person?

Man, being made in the image of God, reflects God's order of authority in the relation of knowledge, holiness, and righteousness. Though each aspect is equally in the image of God, there remains an order among them in which the intellect is primary in each person.

6. What is the order of authority within the Church?

Believers, being enabled by the Holy Spirit to carry out Christ's work, do show the unity there is in Christ by observing the order of his ministry as prophet, priest, and king, the work of the prophetic ministry being foundational to the priestly and kingly ministries.

7. What is the order of authority among institutions?

The corporate bodies of family, church, and state, being directly structured and instituted by God, are each, directly and immediately to be submitted to God according to his law. Neither is any institution in any of its forms to be placed under the authority of an institution of another kind.

8. How are we to give honor to whom honor is due?

We give honor to whom honor is due by submission to those who have understanding, by not submitting to those who lack understanding,

---

2. *Matthew 28:18-20.*

3. Gangadean, *Philosophical Foundation*, 221-229.

and by seeking to put into positions of leadership those who, by talent and patience, have gained understanding.

9. What are the blessings of obedience?

As each person seeks to obey God's law in each institution, the joy and peace of righteousness abound, so that the nation is blessed whose God is the Lord.[4] But the people who do not honor God by his law will descend into the pit.

QUESTION 134

What is the sixth commandment?[5]

*The sixth commandment is, **Thou shall not kill.***

---

4. *Psalm 33:12.*

5. Gangadean, *Philosophical Foundation*, 231-243.

QUESTION 135

What are the duties required in the sixth commandment?

The duties required in the sixth commandment are, all careful studies, and lawful endeavors, to preserve the life of ourselves and others by resisting all thoughts and purposes, subduing all passions, and avoiding all occasions, temptations, and practices, which tend to the unjust taking away the life of any; by just defense thereof against violence, patient bearing of the hand of God, quietness of mind, cheerfulness of spirit; a sober use of meat, drink, physic, sleep, labor, and recreations; by charitable thoughts, love, compassion, meekness, gentleness, kindness; peaceable, mild and courteous speeches and behavior; forbearance, readiness to be reconciled, patient bearing and forgiving of injuries, and requiting good for evil; comforting and succoring the distressed, and protecting and defending the innocent.

QUESTION 136

What are the sins forbidden in the sixth commandment?

The sins forbidden in the sixth commandment are, all taking away the life of ourselves, or of others, except in case of public justice, lawful war, or necessary defense; the neglecting or withdrawing the lawful and necessary means of preservation of life; sinful anger, hatred, envy, desire of revenge; all excessive passions, distracting cares; immoderate use of meat, drink, labor, and recreations; provoking words, oppression, quarreling, striking, wounding, and: Whatsoever else tends to the destruction of the life of any.

1. What is it to kill?

To kill is to deny in any way the dignity of man as made in the image of God.

2. Wherein consists the dignity of man?

The dignity of man consists in his capacity to understand.

3. How is the dignity of man denied?

The dignity of man is denied when we do not acknowledge the capacity to understand in ourselves or others; when we do not address the unbelief that divides us; when we use force in place of knowing the truth which sets us free.

4. What are the sanctions for the denial of human dignity?

The denial of the dignity of others begins with the denial of one's own dignity, so that one becomes separated from human society in part or altogether.

5. Is separation a denial of one's dignity?

Separation of those who persist in the denial of the dignity of themselves and others, affirms their dignity by holding them accountable for unbelief.

QUESTION 137

Which is the seventh commandment?[6]

*The seventh commandment is, **Thou shalt not commit adultery.***

QUESTION 138

What are the duties required in the seventh commandment?

The duties required in the seventh commandment are, chastity in body, mind, affections, words, and behavior; and the preservation of it in ourselves and others; watchfulness over the eyes and all the senses; temperance, keeping of chaste company, modesty in apparel; marriage by those that have not the gift of continency, conjugal love, and cohabitation; diligent labor in our callings; shunning all occasions of uncleanness, and resisting temptations thereunto.

---

6. Gangadean, *Philosophical Foundation*, 245-254.

QUESTION 139

What are the sins forbidden in the seventh commandment?

The sins forbidden in the seventh commandment, besides the neglect of the duties required, are, adultery, fornication, rape, incest, sodomy, and all unnatural lusts; all unclean imaginations, thoughts, purposes, and affections; all corrupt or filthy communications, or listening thereunto; wanton looks, impudent or light behavior, immodest apparel; prohibiting of lawful, and dispensing with unlawful marriages; allowing, tolerating, keeping of stews, and resorting to them; entangling vows of single life, undue delay of marriage; having more wives or husbands than one at the same time; unjust divorce, or desertion; idleness, gluttony, drunkenness, unchaste company; lascivious songs, books, pictures, dancings, stage plays; and all other provocations to, or acts of uncleanness, either in ourselves or others.

1. What is the origin of adultery?

Adultery is based on lust, which is based on a false view of the good. It is first of all spiritual toward God, and only subsequently is it natural and outward in its expression.

2. What is the source of fidelity in marriage?

Fidelity in marriage is based on friendship, which is the effect of a mutual commitment to the good. The good is eternal life, which is the knowledge of God.[7]

---

7. *John 17:3;* Gangadean, "Paper No. 4: The Cornerstone: Good & Evil – Life & Death: The Beginning of the Foundation," in *The Logos Papers;* Appendix 4.

3. Is commitment to the good necessary for friendship?

Although persons may for a time share a false view of the good, yet it is not the truth that lasts forever, which truth is necessary for friendship.

4. Is commitment to the good sufficient for friendship?

Since the good is the source of unity within a person, between persons, and between groups of persons in every aspect of life, the good alone is sufficient for friendship.

5. What makes adultery wrong?

Adultery is wrong because it violates the order of unity established by God between body and soul, between the sign and the reality of sex and love, and between male and female becoming one flesh.

QUESTION 140

Which is the eighth commandment?[8]

The eighth commandment is, Thou shalt not steal.

---

8. Gangadean, *Philosophical Foundation*, 255-265.

QUESTION 141

What are the duties required in the eighth commandment?

The duties required in the eighth commandment are, truth, faithfulness, and justice in contracts and commerce between man and man; rendering to everyone his due; restitution of goods unlawfully detained from the right owners thereof; giving and lending freely, according to our abilities, and the necessities of others; moderation of our judgments, wills, and affections concerning worldly goods; a provident care and study to get, keep, use, and dispose these things which are necessary and convenient for the sustentation of our nature, and suitable to our condition; a lawful calling, and diligence in it; frugality; avoiding unnecessary lawsuits and suretyship, or other like engagements; and an endeavor, by all just and lawful means, to procure, preserve, and further the wealth and outward estate of others, as well as our own.

QUESTION 142

What are the sins forbidden in the eighth commandment?

The sins forbidden in the eighth commandment, besides the neglect of the duties required, are, theft, robbery, man-stealing, and receiving anything that is stolen; fraudulent dealing, false weights and measures, removing land marks, injustice and unfaithfulness in contracts between man and man, or in matters of trust; oppression, extortion, usury, bribery, vexatious lawsuits, unjust enclosures and depopulations; engrossing commodities to enhance the price; unlawful callings, and all other unjust or sinful ways of taking or withholding from our neighbor what belongs to him, or of enriching ourselves; covetousness; inordinate prizing and affecting worldly goods; distrustful and distracting cares and studies in getting, keeping, and using them; envying at the prosperity of others; as likewise idleness, prodigality, wasteful gaming; and all other ways whereby we do unduly prejudice our own outward estate, and defrauding ourselves of the due use and comfort of that estate which God hath given us.

1. What is true wealth?

True wealth does not consist in earthly treasures that pass away, but in heavenly treasures that last forever.

2. What is the source of everlasting wealth?

What is of lasting value is derived from the use of one's ability in pursuit of the good, eternal life, the knowledge of God.

3. What is the source of our ability?

All ability is from God. Ability cannot, therefore, be owned absolutely by man, either individually or collectively.

4. For what purpose are we given diverse abilities?

We are given diverse abilities by God for the common good, to exercise dominion, to attain to the fullness of the knowledge of God.

5. What determines regard for ability?

Regard for ability, both in ourselves and in others, is determined by regard for the good.

6. What is stealing?

Stealing is a failure to develop one's ability in pursuit of the good.

QUESTION 143

Which is the ninth commandment?[9]

The ninth commandment is, Thou shalt not bear false witness against thy neighbor.

---

9. Gangadean, *Philosophical Foundation*, 267-275.

QUESTION 144

What are the duties required in the ninth commandment?

The duties required in the ninth commandment are, the preserving and promoting of truth between man and man, and the good name of our neighbor, as well as our own; appearing and standing for the truth; and from the heart, sincerely, freely, clearly, and fully, speaking the truth, and only the truth, in matters of judgment and justice, and in all other things whatsoever; a charitable esteem of our neighbors; loving, desiring, and rejoicing in their good name; sorrowing for, and covering of their infirmities; freely acknowledging of their gifts and graces, defending their innocency; a ready receiving of a good report, and unwillingness to admit of an evil report, concerning them; discouraging talebearers, flatterers, and slanderers; love and care of our own good name, and defending it when need requireth; keeping of lawful promises; studying and practicing of whatsoever things are true, honest, lovely, and of good report.

QUESTION 145

What are the sins forbidden in the
ninth commandment?

The sins forbidden in the ninth commandment are, all prejudicing the truth, and the good name of our neighbors, as well as our own, especially in public judicature; giving false evidence, suborning false witnesses, wittingly appearing and pleading for an evil cause, outfacing and overbearing the truth; passing unjust sentence, calling evil good, and good evil; rewarding the wicked according to the work of the righteous, and the righteous according to the work of the wicked; forgery, concealing the truth, undue silence in a just cause, and holding our peace when iniquity calleth for either a reproof from ourselves, or complaint to others; speaking the truth unseasonably, or maliciously to a wrong end, or perverting it to a wrong meaning, or in doubtful and equivocal expressions, to the prejudice of truth or justice; speaking untruth, lying, slandering, backbiting, detracting, tale bearing, whispering, scoffing, reviling, rash, harsh, and partial censuring; misconstructing intentions, words, and actions; flattering, vainglorious boasting, thinking or speaking too highly or too meanly of ourselves or others; denying the gifts and graces of God; aggravating smaller faults; hiding, excusing, or extenuating of sins, when called to a free confession; unnecessary discovering of infirmities; raising false rumors, receiving and countenancing evil reports, and stopping our ears against just defense; evil suspicion; envying or grieving at the deserved credit of any, endeavoring or desiring to impair it, rejoicing in their disgrace and infamy; scornful contempt, fond admiration;

breach of lawful promises; neglecting such things as are of good report, and practicing, or not avoiding ourselves, or not hindering what we can in others, such things as procure an ill name.

1. Who is a false witness?

A false witness is anyone who fails to know and speak the truth regarding God and man.

2. How is falsehood injurious to my neighbor?

Truth is necessary for justice. Every falsehood, therefore, is injurious to justice for one's neighbor.

3. Who is a faithful witness?

A faithful witness is one who through understanding speaks the whole truth as an activity of the whole of life.

4. What are the consequences of failing to speak the truth?

The consequences of failing to speak the truth are to share in doing injustice and its consequences.

QUESTION 146

Which is the tenth commandment?[10]

The tenth commandment is, Thou shalt not covet thy neighbor's house, thou shalt not covet thy neighbor's wife, nor his manservant, nor his maidservant, nor his ox, nor his ass, nor any thing that is thy neighbor's.

---

10. Gangadean, *Philosophical Foundation*, 277-283.

QUESTION 147

What are the duties required in the tenth commandment?

The duties required in the tenth commandment are, such a full contentment with our own condition, and such a charitable frame of the whole soul toward our neighbor, as that all our inward motions and affections touching him, tend unto, and further all that good which is his.

QUESTION 148

What are the sins forbidden in the tenth commandment?

The sins forbidden in the tenth commandment are, discontentment with our own estate; envying and grieving at the good of our neighbor, together with all inordinate motions and affections to anything that is his.

1. What is the origin of discontentment?

Discontentment arises from a failure to know what is good and God's providence by which the good is brought about. It was manifested in man's first disobedience in turning from the way of life.

2. Is contentment possible apart from the good?

Nothing less than the good can truly satisfy our hearts nor bring unity among men. In misconceiving the good, there arises continual restlessness, selfish ambition, and envy of every kind.

3. What is envy?

Envy is a desire to have for oneself what belongs to another as if it were the good or a mark of one's goodness. There is no envy of the true good.

4. Does suffering hinder our good?

The sufferings of this life, by God's grace, serve to restrain and recall us from and remove from us our sin of not knowing God. Our suffering, therefore, should not be disregarded by hardening, despised as worthless, nor discourage us from seeking God.

5. How is full contentment in God's providence manifested?

Knowing God is our Father and that all things work together for good, the believer, through joy and peace in the Holy Spirit, perseveres in doing good in all circumstances.

Chapter 24

OUR FALLEN CONDITION AND THE CONSEQUENCE OF SIN

QUESTION 149

Is any man able perfectly to keep the commandments of God?

No man is able, either of himself, or by any grace received in this life, perfectly to keep the commandments of God; but doth daily break them in thought, word, and deed.

Of what use is it to know we sin daily in thought, word, and deed?

True knowledge of our sin humbles our pride and magnifies the grace of God; it makes us more gentle and forgiving of others; it increases our understanding of the breadth of God's law and makes us more watchful against sin and diligent in the pursuit of God's kingdom and righteousness.

QUESTION 150

Are all transgressions of the law of God equally heinous in themselves, and in the sight of God?

All transgressions of the law of God are not equally heinous; but some sins in themselves, and by reason of several aggravations, are more heinous in the sight of God than others.

What makes some sins more heinous than others?

That some sins are more heinous than others depends on how directly one sins against the holiness of God, on the influence over others of the person who sins, and on the amount of light one has rejected in that sin.

QUESTION 151

What are those aggravations that make some sins more heinous than others?

Sins receive their aggravations,

1. From the persons offending: if they be of riper age, greater experience or grace, eminent for profession, gifts, place, office, guides to others, and whose example is likely to be followed by others.

2. From the parties offended: if immediately against God, his attributes, and worship; against Christ, and his grace; the Holy Spirit, his witness, and workings; against superiors, men of eminency, and such as we stand especially related and engaged unto; against any of the saints, particularly weak brethren, the souls of them, or any other, and the common good of all or many.

3. From the nature and quality of the offense: if it be against the express letter of the law, break many commandments, contain in it many sins: if not only conceived in the heart, but breaks forth in words and actions, scandalize others, and admit of no reparation: if against means, mercies, judgments, light of nature, conviction of conscience, public or private admonition, censures of the church, civil punishments; and our prayers, purposes, promises, vows, covenants, and engagements to God or men: if done deliberately, wilfully, presumptuously, impudently, boastingly, maliciously, frequently, obstinately, with delight, continuance, or relapsing after repentance.

4. From circumstances of time and place: if on the Lord's day, or other times of divine worship; or immediately before or after these, or other helps to prevent or remedy such miscarriages: if in public, or in the presence of others, who are thereby likely to be provoked or defiled.

QUESTION 152

What doth every sin deserve at the hands of God?

Every sin, even the least, being against the sovereignty,
goodness, and holiness of God, and against his righteous law,
deserveth his wrath and curse, both in this life, and that
which is to come; and cannot be expiated but by the blood
of Christ.

Why does every sin deserve God's wrath?

Every sin, being rooted in the original sin of not seeking God, deserves God's wrath of being given up to one's own way.

Chapter 25

FAITH, REPENTANCE, AND
THE ORDINARY MEANS
OF SALVATION

QUESTION 153

What doth God require of us, that we may escape his wrath and curse due to us by reason of the transgression of the law?

That we may escape the wrath and curse of God due to us by reason of the transgression of the law, he requireth of us repentance toward God, and faith toward our Lord Jesus Christ, and the diligent use of the outward means whereby Christ communicates to us the benefits of his mediation.

What is the wrath of God?[1]

The wrath of God is his infinite justice manifested in giving up the sinner to spiritual death and whatever is the inherent fruit of sin. It is neither imposed externally, nor is it merely future in the afterlife, but is manifested in all without Christ who now are dead in trespasses. It is also in some measure present where sin remains in the believer,

---

1. Gangadean, *The Westminster Confession*. See Question 26.

manifesting itself in meaninglessness, boredom, and guilt, where the means of grace are not diligently used.

QUESTION 154

What are the outward means whereby Christ communicates to us the benefits of his mediation?

The outward and ordinary means whereby Christ communicates to his church the benefits of his mediation, are all his ordinances; especially the Word, sacraments, and prayer; all which are made effectual to the elect for their salvation.

1. What are ordinary means?

Ordinary means are those means God has ordained to achieve his intended purpose. We cannot reasonably expect God's purpose to be achieved apart from the use of ordinary means.

2. How are outward means made effectual unto salvation?

To be made effectual, outward means require both our diligent use and the working of the Holy Spirit in and through them.

3. Are all ordinary means equally effectual unto salvation?

The ordinary means of the Word, sacraments, and prayer are so ordered by God that they are effectual unto salvation when used according to God's order.

Chapter 26

ORDINARY MEANS
OF SALVATION:
THE WORD OF GOD

QUESTION 155

How is the Word made effectual to salvation?

The Spirit of God makes the reading, but especially the preaching of the Word, an effectual means of enlightening, convincing, and humbling sinners; of driving them out of themselves, and drawing them unto Christ; of conforming them to his image, and subduing them to his will; of strengthening them against temptations and corruptions; of building them up in grace, and establishing their hearts in holiness and comfort through faith unto salvation.

Why is the preaching of the Word especially effectual?

Preaching is especially effectual because, by preaching, the Word of God is made more manifest through the efforts of pastor-teachers, who have been prepared for and appointed unto this task by the Holy Spirit.

QUESTION 156

Is the Word of God to be read by all?

*Although all are not to be permitted to read the Word
publicly to the congregation, yet all sorts of people are bound
to read it apart by themselves, and with their families: to
which end, the holy scriptures are to be translated out of the
original into vulgar languages.*

1. Can Scripture be read by all?[1]

The perspicuity of Scripture affirms that basic things about God and
man, and good and evil are clear to all who seek to know. When the
basic truths of Scripture are understood (Biblical Worldview,[2] The Seven
Pillars,[3] and the Principle of Clarity[4]), the less basic truths become
clear in context through the use of good and necessary consequences.

2. Should Scripture be read by all?

All have sinned and come short of the glory of God.[5] All believers are
in need of sanctification, and sanctification is by knowledge of the
truth.[6] Knowledge of the truth is in and by the Word working with the
Spirit. Sanctification is done to the end of the practice of true holiness,
without which no man shall see the Lord.[7]

---

1. Gangadean, *The Westminster Confession*. See Question 9.

2. Gangadean, "Paper No. 13: The Biblical Worldview: Creation–Fall–Redemption (Concise Version)," in *The Logos Papers*; "Paper No. 14: The Biblical Worldview: Creation–Fall–Redemption (Expanded Version)," in *The Logos Papers*.

3. Gangadean, "Paper No. 37: The Seven Pillars: A Brief Summary," in *The Logos Papers*.

4. Gangadean, "Paper No. 3: The Principle of Clarity, Rational Presuppositionalism, and Proof," in *The Logos Papers*.

5. *Romans 3:23.*

6. *John 17:17.*

7. *Hebrews 12:14.*

3. Can Scripture be translated?[8]

Words express concepts and judgments, which are cognitive (true or false). Concepts are universal (the same in all); words are conventional (differ from language to language).[9] Therefore, translations are possible. Since Scripture is meant for all, then translations are necessary and desirable. Translations as desirable are opposed to the use of original languages only, or to the use of one language only, or to paraphrases in the place of translations.

QUESTION 157

How is the Word of God to be read?[10]

The holy scriptures are to be read with an high and reverent esteem of them; with a firm persuasion that they are the very Word of God, and that he only can enable us to understand them; with desire to know, believe, and obey the will of God revealed in them; with diligence, and attention to the matter and scope of them; with meditation, application, self-denial, and prayer.

1. How is the Word attended to with diligence?

The Word of God is attended to with diligence when we set aside a due portion of time to hear it often and regularly.

2. How is the Word attended to with preparation?

The Word of God is attended to with preparation when we hear it without the distraction of the cares of this life and without the hindrances of the lack of learning.

---

8. Gangadean, *The Westminster Confession*. See Question 10.

9. Gangadean, *History of Philosophy*, 28-29.

10. Gangadean, "Paper No. 15: Hermeneutics: Principles of Interpretation: Applied to General Revelation and to Scripture (Concise Version)," in *The Logos Papers*.

3. How is the Word attended to through prayer?

Acknowledging that as creatures and fallen, we are dependent on God for all good, we earnestly pray that our minds would be illuminated to hear, with understanding, the Word of God.

4. How is the Word of God received in faith?

God's Word is received in faith when it is received as the Word of the infallible and all-wise God, when we seek to understand its meaning rather than question its truth.

5. How is the Word of God to be received in love?

God's Word is received in love when we have a love for the truth, when we love God who is the author of truth, and when we delight in God's love revealed in his Word.

6. What is it to lay up God's Word in our hearts?

We lay up God's Word in our hearts when we can at all times call it to mind and when we can meditate upon it day and night.

7. How does the practice of God's Word make it effectual unto salvation?

The practice of God's Word prevents us from being forgetful hearers and deceiving ourselves, brings us to fuller understanding, prepares us to receive more of God's Word, and bears fruit unto holiness and righteousness, pleasing to God and men.

QUESTION 158

By whom is the Word of God to be preached?

The Word of God is to be preached only by such as are sufficiently gifted, and also duly approved and called to that office.

QUESTION 159

How is the Word of God to be preached by those that are called thereunto?

They that are called to labor in the ministry of the Word, are to preach sound doctrine, diligently, in season and out of season; plainly, not in the enticing words of man's wisdom, but in demonstration of the Spirit, and of power; faithfully, making known the whole counsel of God; wisely, applying themselves to the necessities and capacities of the hearers; zealously, with fervent love to God and the souls of his people; sincerely, aiming at his glory, and their conversion, edification, and salvation.

QUESTION 160

What is required of those that hear the Word preached?[11]

It is required of those that hear the Word preached, that they attend upon it with diligence, preparation, and prayer; examine what they hear by the scriptures; receive the truth with faith, love, meekness, and readiness of mind, as the Word of God; meditate, and confer of it; hide it in their hearts, and bring forth the fruit of it in their lives.

---

11. Gangadean, "Paper No. 2: Common Ground: The Necessary Condition for Thought and Discourse (Concise Version)," in *The Logos Papers*; "Paper No. 14: The Biblical World-view: Creation–Fall–Redemption (Expanded Version)," in *The Logos Papers*; "Paper No. 15: Hermeneutics: Principles of Interpretation: Applied to General Revelation and to Scripture," in *The Logos Papers*; "Paper No. 16: The Historic Christian Faith: The Holy Spirit Guides the Church into All Truth," in *The Logos Papers*; "Paper No. 114: The Gospel: For Everyone," in *The Logos Papers*; Appendices 2-9.

Chapter 27

ORDINARY MEANS OF SALVATION: THE SACRAMENTS

QUESTION 161

How do the sacraments become effectual means of salvation?

The sacraments become effectual means of salvation, not by any power in themselves, or any virtue derived from the piety or intention of him by whom they are administered, but only by the working of the Holy Ghost, and the blessing of Christ, by whom they are instituted.

QUESTION 162

What is a sacrament?[1]

A sacrament is an holy ordinance instituted by Christ in his church, to signify, seal, and exhibit unto those that are within the covenant of grace, the benefits of his mediation; to strengthen and increase their faith, and all other graces; to oblige them to obedience; to testify and cherish their love and communion one with another; and to distinguish them from those that are without.

QUESTION 163

What are the parts of a sacrament?

The parts of a sacrament are two; the one an outward and sensible sign, used according to Christ's own appointment; the other an inward and spiritual grace thereby signified.

---

1. Gangadean, *The Westminster Confession*. See Questions 116-118.

QUESTION 164

How many sacraments hath Christ instituted in his church under the New Testament?

Under the New Testament Christ hath instituted in his Church only two sacraments, baptism and the Lord's supper.

1. What are sacraments?

Sacraments are signs and seals of the covenant of grace.

2. How are the sacraments signs?

The sacraments are sensible signs which Christ has ordained to represent God's grace. The sign is not the reality of the grace which it signifies, nor is the grace signified always accompanied by the sign.

3. How are the sacraments seals?

The sacraments, when administered with godly discipline by those who are called to oversight, affirm to faithful recipients the benefits of Christ's redemption.

4. How do the sacramental signs become effectual?

The sacramental signs, administered by Christ's ordinance, become effectual only when they are received by faith, which faith apprehends the invisible grace represented visibly in the signs.

5. Are there more than two sacraments?

The sacraments, as signs and seals of the covenant of grace, are ordained by Christ and so limited. There is, therefore, no warrant for any more than two sacraments, which are, baptism and the Lord's Supper.

6. Have the sacraments changed from the Old to the New Testament?

The Old and New Testaments, being but two administrations of the same covenant of grace, their sacraments have not changed in meaning, but only in outward form.

QUESTION 165

What is baptism?[2]

Baptism is a sacrament of the New Testament, wherein Christ hath ordained the washing with water in the name of the Father, and of the Son, and of the Holy Ghost, to be a sign and seal of ingrafting into himself, of remission of sins by his blood, and regeneration by his Spirit; of adoption, and resurrection unto everlasting life; and whereby the parties baptized are solemnly admitted into the visible church, and enter into an open and professed engagement to be wholly and only the Lord's.

1. Why are we baptized in the name of Christ?

Baptism in the name of Christ signifies our union with Christ in his death, burial, and resurrection. It thereby also signifies our union with God, Father, Son, and Holy Spirit.

2. What does the washing with water signify?

The washing with water signifies our cleansing by the putting off of the sinful nature. The grace of cleansing is realized in regeneration, in which we die unto sin and are raised unto new life in Christ.

---

2. Gangadean, *The Westminster Confession.* See Questions 119-122.

3. How does baptism engage us to be the Lord's?

Baptism signifies our union with Christ. We are, therefore, no longer our own, but must glorify God in all our lives.

QUESTION 166

Unto whom is baptism to be administered?

Baptism is not to be administered to any that are out of the visible church, and so strangers from the covenant of promise, till they profess their faith in Christ, and obedience to him, but infants descending from parents, either both, or but one of them, professing faith in Christ, and obedience to him, are in that respect within the covenant, and to be baptized.

1. What is the visible Church?

The visible church consists of all those throughout the world that profess the true religion; and of their children; and is the kingdom of the Lord Jesus Christ, the house and family of God, out of which there is no ordinary possibility of salvation.

2. What are the marks of a true church?

The marks of a true church are: sound preaching of the Word, proper administration of the sacraments, and godly discipline. Churches differ in degree of purity according as these marks are present.

3. How does one become a member of the Church?

One becomes a member of the Church by a credible profession of faith, which consists in a saving understanding of the person and work of Christ along with obedience to his Word.

4. Why are infants of believers to be baptized?

Because the covenant of grace is one under the Old and New Testaments, and because the promise is to the believer and his household, and because circumcision and baptism signify the same reality of regeneration, the sign of baptism is to be applied to infants of believers.

QUESTION 167

How is our baptism to be improved by us?

The needful but much neglected duty of improving our baptism, is to be performed by us all our life long, especially in the time of temptation, and when we are present at the administration of it to others; by serious and thankful consideration of the nature of it, and of the ends for which Christ instituted it, the privileges and benefits conferred and sealed thereby, and our solemn vow made therein; by being humbled for our sinful defilement, our falling short of, and walking contrary to, the grace of baptism, and our engagements; by growing up to assurance of pardon of sin, and of all other blessings sealed to us in that sacrament; by drawing strength from the death and resurrection of Christ, into whom we are baptized, for the mortifying of sin, and quickening of grace; and by endeavoring to live by faith, to have our conversation in holiness and righteousness, as those that have therein given up their names to Christ; and to walk in brotherly love, as being baptized by the same Spirit into one body.

QUESTION 168

What is the Lord's supper?[3]

The Lord's supper is a sacrament of the New Testament,
wherein, by giving and receiving bread and wine according
to the appointment of Jesus Christ, his death is showed forth;
and they that worthily communicate feed upon his body and
blood, to their spiritual nourishment and growth in grace;
have their union and communion with him confirmed;
testify and renew their thankfulness, and engagement to
God, and their mutual love and fellowship each with other,
as members of the same mystical body.

1. How is the death of Christ shown forth in the Lord's Supper?

In the Lord's Supper, we remember and proclaim, until the end of this age, that Christ our Passover was the Son of God who became flesh, that by his death, he might bear away our sins.

2. How do we discern the body of Christ in the Lord's Supper?

We discern the body of Christ by recognizing and putting away sin, which divides the body of Christ for which he died.

3. How do we partake of Christ in the Lord's Supper?

As Christ lived by every Word of God, so those who hear and obey his Word, which Word is spirit and life, feed on Christ after a spiritual manner.

---

3. Gangadean, *The Westminster Confession*. See Questions 123-128.

QUESTION 169

How hath Christ appointed bread and wine to be given and received in the sacrament of the Lord's supper?

Christ hath appointed the ministers of his Word, in the administration of this sacrament of the Lord's supper, to set apart the bread and wine from common use, by the Word of institution, thanksgiving, and prayer; to take and break the bread, and to give both the bread and the wine to the communicants: who are, by the same appointment, to take and eat the bread, and to drink the wine, in thankful remembrance that the body of Christ was broken and given, and his blood shed, for them.

QUESTION 170

How do they that worthily communicate in the Lord's supper feed upon the body and blood of Christ therein?

As the body and blood of Christ are not corporally or carnally present in, with, or under the bread and wine in the Lord's supper, and yet are spiritually present to the faith of the receiver, no less truly and really than the elements themselves are to their outward senses; so they that worthily communicate in the sacrament of the Lord's supper, do therein feed upon the body and blood of Christ, not after a corporal and carnal, but in a spiritual manner; yet truly and really, while by faith they receive and apply unto themselves Christ crucified, and all the benefits of his death.

QUESTION 171

How are they that receive the sacrament of the Lord's supper to prepare themselves before they come unto it?

They that receive the sacrament of the Lord's supper are, before they come, to prepare themselves thereunto, by examining themselves of their being in Christ, of their sins and wants; of the truth and measure of their knowledge, faith, repentance; love to God and the brethren, charity to all men, forgiving those that have done them wrong; of their desires after Christ, and of their new obedience; and by renewing the exercise of these graces, by serious meditation, and fervent prayer.

1. Why is it necessary to examine oneself before partaking of the Lord's Supper?

Because the Lord's Supper is a sign and seal of our partaking of Christ, and because the deceitfulness of sin remains in us, worthy receivers must examine themselves so that they do not desecrate what the sacrament signifies.

2. For what must we examine ourselves?

We must examine ourselves for holding any doctrine or practice that divides the body of Christ, for our being teachable, and for the genuineness of our repentance in the fruit of new obedience.

3. Why are we judged for eating and drinking unworthily?

The Lord does not hold him guiltless that takes his name in vain,[4] but he chastens us that we should not be condemned with the world.[5]

---

4. *Exodus 20:7.*

5. *1 Corinthians 11:32.*

QUESTION 172

May one who doubteth of his being in Christ, or of his due preparation, come to the Lord's supper?

One who doubteth of his being in Christ, or of his due preparation to the sacrament of the Lord's supper, may have true interest in Christ, though he be not yet assured thereof; and in God's account hath it, if he be duly affected with the apprehension of the want of it, and unfeignedly desires to be found in Christ, and to depart from iniquity: in which case (because promises are made, and this sacrament is appointed, for the relief even of weak and doubting Christians) he is to bewail his unbelief, and labor to have his doubts resolved; and, so doing, he may and ought to come to the Lord's supper, that he may be further strengthened.

QUESTION 173

May any who profess the faith, and desire to come to the Lord's supper, be kept from it?

Such as are found to be ignorant or scandalous, notwithstanding their profession of the faith, and desire to come to the Lord's supper, may and ought to be kept from that sacrament, by the power which Christ hath left in his church, until they receive instruction, and manifest their reformation.

QUESTION 174

What is required of them that receive the sacrament of the Lord's supper in the time of the administration of it?

It is required of them that receive the sacrament of the Lord's supper, that, during the time of the administration of it, with all holy reverence and attention they wait upon God in that ordinance, diligently observe the sacramental elements and actions, heedfully discern the Lord's body, and affectionately meditate on his death and sufferings, and thereby stir up themselves to a vigorous exercise of their graces; in judging themselves, and sorrowing for sin; in earnest hungering and thirsting after Christ, feeding on him by faith, receiving of his fulness, trusting in his merits, rejoicing in his love, giving thanks for his grace; in renewing of their covenant with God, and love to all the saints.

QUESTION 175

What is the duty of Christians, after they have received the sacrament of the Lord's supper?

The duty of Christians, after they have received the sacrament of the Lord's supper, is seriously to consider how they have behaved themselves therein, and with what success; if they find quickening and comfort, to bless God for it, beg the continuance of it, watch against relapses, fulfill their vows, and encourage themselves to a frequent attendance on that ordinance: but if they find no present benefit, more exactly to review their preparation to, and carriage at, the sacrament; in both which, if they can approve themselves to God and their own consciences, they are to wait for the fruit of it in due time: but, if they see they have failed in either, they are to be humbled, and to attend upon it afterwards with more care and diligence.

QUESTION 176

Wherein do the sacraments of baptism and the Lord's supper agree?

The sacraments of baptism and the Lord's supper agree, in that the author of both is God; the spiritual part of both is Christ and his benefits; both are seals of the same covenant, are to be dispensed by ministers of the gospel, and by none other; and to be continued in the church of Christ until his second coming.

QUESTION 177

Wherein do the sacraments of baptism and the Lord's supper differ?

The sacraments of baptism and the Lord's supper differ, in that baptism is to be administered but once, with water, to be a sign and seal of our regeneration and ingrafting into Christ, and that even to infants; whereas the Lord's supper is to be administered often, in the elements of bread and wine, to represent and exhibit Christ as spiritual nourishment to the soul, and to confirm our continuance and growth in him, and that only to such as are of years and ability to examine themselves.

Chapter 28

___

ORDINARY MEANS
OF SALVATION:
PRAYER

QUESTION 178

What is prayer?[1]

Prayer is an offering up of our desires unto God, in the name of Christ, by the help of his Spirit; with confession of our sins, and thankful acknowledgment of his mercies.

1. Why do we offer up our desires unto God?

In offering up our desires to God, we acknowledge every good we receive is a gift from God, and we trust him to give us what is good.

2. Why do we pray in the name of Christ?

We pray in the name of Christ because all our blessings are through his redemption and are sought not for ourselves, but for his kingdom and glory.

___

1. Gangadean, *The Westminster Confession*. See Question 95; Gangadean, "Paper No. 136: On Prayer," in *The Logos Papers*.

3. Why are confession of sins and thanksgiving part of prayer?

We confess our sins in prayer because sin hinders our fellowship with God and his hearing and answering our prayers. We give thanks in prayer to acknowledge that it is of his grace alone that we receive all that we have.

QUESTION 179

Are we to pray unto God only?

God only being able to search the hearts, hear the requests, pardon the sins, and fulfill the desires of all; and only to be believed in, and worshiped with religious worship; prayer, which is a special part thereof, is to be made by all to him alone, and to none other.

QUESTION 180

What is it to pray in the name of Christ?

To pray in the name of Christ is, in obedience to his command, and in confidence on his promises, to ask mercy for his sake; not by bare mentioning of his name, but by drawing our encouragement to pray, and our boldness, strength, and hope of acceptance in prayer, from Christ and his mediation.

QUESTION 181

Why are we to pray in the name of Christ?

The sinfulness of man, and his distance from God by reason thereof, being so great, as that we can have no access into his presence without a mediator; and there being none in heaven or earth appointed to, or fit for, that glorious work but Christ alone, we are to pray in no other name but his only.

QUESTION 182

How doth the Spirit help us to pray?

We not knowing what to pray for as we ought, the Spirit helps our infirmities, by enabling us to understand both for whom, and what, and how prayer is to be made; and by working and quickening in our hearts (although not in all persons, nor at all times, in the same measure) those apprehensions, affections, and graces which are requisite for the right performance of that duty.

QUESTION 183

For whom are we to pray?

We are to pray for the whole church of Christ upon earth; for magistrates, and ministers; for ourselves, our brethren, yea, our enemies; and for all sorts of men living, or that shall live hereafter; but not for the dead, nor for those that are known to have sinned the sin unto death.

QUESTION 184

For what things are we to pray?

We are to pray for all things tending to the glory of God, the welfare of the church, our own or others good; but not for anything that is unlawful.

QUESTION 185

How are we to pray?

We are to pray with an awful apprehension of the majesty of God, and deep sense of our own unworthiness, necessities, and sins; with penitent, thankful, and enlarged hearts; with understanding, faith, sincerity, fervency, love, and perseverance, waiting upon him, with humble submission to his will.

QUESTION 186

What rule hath God given for our direction in the duty of prayer?[2]

The whole Word of God is of use to direct us in the duty of prayer; but the special rule of direction is that form of prayer which our Savior Christ taught his disciples, commonly called The Lord's Prayer.

1. Why do we need a rule to direct us in prayer?

Because prayer is part of the ordinary means whereby Christ communicates to us the benefits of his redemption, we are not left to the imaginations of our hearts; but we are directed by the Word of God on how we should pray so that we may know what we should pray for and what we should expect.

2. How does the Word of God direct us in prayer?

Prayer being offered for things agreeable to God's will, the whole Word of God instructs us in the will of God by precept and example.

3. How does the Lord's Prayer especially direct us in prayer?

The Lord's Prayer, being a form of prayer, summarily comprehends what we should pray for, and that in due order, if our prayers would be effectual.

---

2. Gangadean, "Paper No. 136: On Prayer," in *The Logos Papers.*

QUESTION 187

How is the Lord's Prayer to be used?

The Lord's Prayer is not only for direction, as a pattern, according to which we are to make other prayers; but may also be used as a prayer, so that it be done with understanding, faith, reverence, and other graces necessary to the right performance of the duty of prayer.

QUESTION 188

Of how many parts doth the Lord's Prayer consist?

The Lord's Prayer consists of three parts; a preface, petitions, and a conclusion.

QUESTION 189

What doth the preface of the Lord's Prayer teach us?

*The preface of the Lord's Prayer (contained in these words, **Our Father which art in heaven**), teacheth us, when we pray, to draw near to God with confidence of his fatherly goodness, and our interest therein; with reverence, and all other childlike dispositions, heavenly affections, and due apprehensions of his sovereign power, majesty, and gracious condescension: as also, to pray with and for others.*

1. How are we to draw near to God?

Because God is the sovereign Creator of heaven and earth, because he rules over all in majesty, and because he graciously condescends to receive us as his children, we approach God our Father with reverence and with all other child-like dispositions and with love.

2. What hope is there in approaching God as our Father?

Because God is our Father, we approach him in confidence, as children to a father, knowing he is able and ready to help us.

3. What are we taught in praying to God as our Father?

In praying to God as our Father, we are taught that we are to pray with and for others who are or will be children of God, that we all may be one as the Father and the Son are one.

QUESTION 190

What do we pray for in the first petition?

*In the first petition (which is, **Hallowed be thy name**), acknowledging the utter inability and indisposition that is in ourselves and all men to honor God aright, pray, that God would by his grace enable and incline us and others to know, to acknowledge, and highly to esteem him, his titles, attributes, ordinances, word, works, and whatsoever he is pleased to make himself known by; and to glorify him in thought, word, and deed: that he would prevent and remove atheism, ignorance, idolatry, profaneness, and whatsoever is dishonorable to him; and, by his overruling providence, direct and dispose of all things to his own glory.*

1. What is it to glorify God?

We glorify God when we come to know his glory and make his glory known.

2. How does God make himself known?

God makes himself known in all his works of creation and providence. Man comes to know God as he, by God's grace, exercises dominion in the creation and over sin in himself.

3. Why is this the first petition of the Lord's Prayer?

Hallowed be thy name is the first petition of the Lord's Prayer because man's chief end is to glorify God and because eternal life is to know God.

4. Upon what promise can we hope for this petition?

God has promised in all ages that the earth will be filled with the knowledge of the glory of the Lord as the waters cover the sea.

QUESTION 191

What do we pray for in the second petition?

*In the second petition (which is, **Thy kingdom come**), acknowledging ourselves and all mankind to be by nature under the dominion of sin and Satan, we pray, that the kingdom of sin and Satan may be destroyed, the gospel propagated throughout the world, the Jews called, the fullness of the Gentiles brought in; the church furnished with all gospel officers and ordinances, purged from corruption, countenanced and maintained by the civil magistrate: that the ordinances of Christ may be purely dispensed, and made effectual to the converting of those that are yet in their sins, and the confirming, comforting, and building up of those that are already converted: that Christ would rule in our hearts here, and hasten the time of his second coming, and our reigning with him forever: and that he would be pleased so to exercise the kingdom of his power in all the world, as may best conduce to these ends.*

1. What is God's kingdom of power?

God's kingdom of power consists in his rule over all his works, and all the actions of men and angels, according to his sovereign purpose, for the praise of his glory.

2. What is the kingdom of Satan?

The kingdom of Satan consists in his rule in and through men, by the wisdom of this world, the desires of natural man, and all unjust use of power; which rule is signified as coming through the work of the false prophet, the harlot, and the beast.[3]

3. What is the kingdom of grace?

The kingdom of grace consists of Christ's present rule in and through his people, as prophet, priest, and king, to fill the earth with the knowledge of God.

4. What is the kingdom of glory?

The kingdom of glory is that kingdom of grace which, having grown to its fullness by overcoming the kingdom of darkness, is consummated by the return of Christ and the removal of all evil, forever.

5. How does the kingdom of God come?

The kingdom of God is advanced and hastened as we take every thought captive that is raised up against the knowledge of God,[4] so that we may come into the unity of the faith,[5] and make disciples of all nations.[6]

---

3. Gangadean, "Paper No. 49: Eschatology: Summary and Response to FAQs," in *The Logos Papers*.

4. *2 Corinthians 10:5.*

5. *Ephesians 4.*

6. *Matthew 28:19.*

QUESTION 192

What do we pray for in the third petition?

*In the third petition (which is, **Thy will be done in earth, as it is in heaven**), acknowledging, that by nature we and all men are not only utterly unable and unwilling to know and do the will of God, but prone to rebel against his Word, to repine and murmur against his providence, and wholly inclined to do the will of the flesh, and of the devil: we pray, that God would by his Spirit take away from ourselves and others all blindness, weakness, indisposedness, and perverseness of heart; and by his grace make us able and willing to know, do, and submit to his will in all things, with the like humility, cheerfulness, faithfulness, diligence, zeal, sincerity, and constancy, as the angels do in heaven.*

1. Where is the will of God revealed?

The will of God is summarily comprehended in the moral law, which law is written on the hearts of all men by creation and later given by special revelation in the Ten Commandments.

2. How are we made able to know and obey God's will?

The Spirit of God enables us to know and obey the will of God by bringing us to meditate on the law of God day and night, and to delight in the law of God as the way of life.

3. What is the fruit of obeying the law of God?

By obeying the law of God in its fullness, the kingdom of God is advanced in all the earth, and the name of God is hallowed in all that whereby God makes himself known.

QUESTION 193

What do we pray for in the fourth petition?

*In the fourth petition (which is, **Give us this day our daily bread**), acknowledging, that in Adam, and by our own sin, we have forfeited our right to all the outward blessings of this life, and deserve to be wholly deprived of them by God, and to have them cursed to us in the use of them; and that neither they of themselves are able to sustain us, nor we to merit, or by our own industry to procure them; but prone to desire, get, and use them unlawfully: we pray for ourselves and others, that both they and we, waiting upon the providence of God from day to day in the use of lawful means, may, of his free gift, and as to his fatherly wisdom shall seem best, enjoy a competent portion of them; and have the same continued and blessed unto us in our holy and comfortable use of them, and contentment in them; and be kept from all things that are contrary to our temporal support and comfort.*

1. What is our daily bread?

Our daily bread consists of a sufficiency of the outward blessings of life that we need each day to serve God's holy purpose.

2. Why do we ask God to give us what we need?

Because we cannot merit any of God's goodness, nor enjoy it without his favor, we acknowledge, by asking, that all we have is by his free gift.

3. How are we given what we need?

God gives us what we need, not by the use of unlawful means, nor without the use of ordinary means, but by our waiting upon the providence of God in the use of lawful means.

QUESTION 194

What do we pray for in the fifth petition?

*In the fifth petition (which is, **Forgive us our debts, as we forgive our debtors**), acknowledging, that we and all others are guilty both of original and actual sin, and thereby become debtors to the justice of God; and that neither we, nor any other creature, can make the least satisfaction for that debt: we pray for ourselves and others, that God of his free grace would, through the obedience and satisfaction of Christ, apprehended and applied by faith, acquit us both from the guilt and punishment of sin, accept us in his Beloved; continue his favor and grace to us, pardon our daily failings, and fill us with peace and joy, in giving us daily more and more assurance of forgiveness; which we are the rather emboldened to ask, and encouraged to expect, when we have this testimony in ourselves, that we from the heart forgive others their offenses.*

1. For what must we seek forgiveness?

In this life, we still fail to know God as we ought, and must confess this our sin, so that we may be forgiven and cleansed from it.

2. On what basis does God forgive us?

We are forgiven for Christ's sake only, who bore away our sin by his death on the cross.

3. How can we know that God has forgiven us?

We can know God forgives us if we freely forgive others as we seek to
be forgiven by God.

QUESTION 195

What do we pray for in the sixth petition?

*In the sixth petition (which is, **And lead us not into
temptation, but deliver us from evil**), acknowledging,
that the most wise, righteous, and gracious God, for divers
holy and just ends, may so order things, that we may be
assaulted, foiled, and for a time led captive by temptations;
that Satan, the world, and the flesh, are ready powerfully to
draw us aside, and ensnare us; and that we, even after the
pardon of our sins, by reason of our corruption, weakness,
and want of watchfulness, are not only subject to be tempted,
and forward to expose ourselves unto temptations, but also of
ourselves unable and unwilling to resist them, to recover out
of them, and to improve them; and worthy to be left under
the power of them: we pray, that God would so overrule the
world and all in it, subdue the flesh, and restrain Satan,
order all things, bestow and bless all means of grace, and
quicken us to watchfulness in the use of them, that we and
all his people may by his providence be kept from being
tempted to sin; or, if tempted, that by his Spirit we may be
powerfully supported and enabled to stand in the hour of
temptation; or when fallen, raised again and recovered out
of it, and have a sanctified use and improvement thereof:
that our sanctification and salvation may be perfected,
Satan trodden under our feet, and we fully freed from sin,
temptation, and all evil, forever.*

1. What is it to be tempted?

In every trial of faith, our failure to understand what is good as we ought makes it possible to yield to sin.

2. How are we kept from temptation?

God, who is most wise and righteous, never tests us above what we are able to bear, but shows the way to escape to those who watch and pray.

3. How are we delivered from evil?

To those who by holiness endure the trial of their faith, God is pleased to further make himself known, which knowledge sanctifies us and sets us free from sin.

QUESTION 196

What doth the conclusion of the Lord's Prayer teach us?

*The conclusion of the Lord's Prayer (which is, **For thine is the kingdom, and the power, and the glory, forever. Amen.**), teaches us to enforce our petitions with arguments, which are to be taken, not from any worthiness in ourselves, or in any other creature, but from God; and with our prayers to join praises, ascribing to God alone eternal sovereignty, omnipotency, and glorious excellency; in regard whereof, as he is able and willing to help us, so we by faith are emboldened to plead with him that he would, and quietly to rely upon him, that he will fulfill our requests. And, to testify this our desire and assurance, we say, **Amen.***

1. How can we encourage ourselves in prayer?

We can encourage ourselves in prayer when we enforce our petitions with arguments, which are to be taken not from any worthiness in ourselves or in any other creature, but from God.

2. How is praise fitting to all our prayers?

As the desire of all our prayers is to the praise of God, so we ascribe to him alone eternal sovereignty, omnipotence, and glorious excellence, by which also we plead our requests and trust him to fulfill them.

3. How are we to end our prayers?

To testify to our desire for God's glory and our assurance that he hears us, we say Amen.

—

APPENDICES

—

Appendix 1

―――

THE DISTINCTIVES OF WESTMINSTER FELLOWSHIP

WESTMINSTER FELLOWSHIP AFFIRMS Historic Christianity as it is summed up in the Westminster Confession of Faith of 1648. The Westminster Confession affirms the authority of Scripture, the Tri-unity of God, Father, Son, and Holy Spirit, the sovereignty of God in creation, history, and redemption, the continuity of the Old and New Testaments, the regulative principle of worship, and the law of God for all of life. The Confession of Faith sums up the work of the Holy Spirit, leading the Church into all truth. The Holy Spirit calls and enables the pastor-teachers to respond to challenges to the faith in every age. The modern age has challenged the Church's understanding of general revelation and of the goal of life. Faith has been opposed by reason; Scripture has been opposed by science; focus on heaven has been opposed by focus on this world.

The distinctives of Westminster Fellowship arise from a response to these challenges to the faith.

We affirm that creation and history are revelation of God's glory and that man's purpose is to know God's glory through the work of dominion, given to him in the beginning (*The Goal of the Knowledge of God*).

We affirm that eternal life is knowing God and Jesus Christ, whom he has sent.

We affirm that the eternal power and divine nature of God are clearly revealed, being understood from the things that are made, so that man's unbelief is without excuse (*The Clarity of General Revelation and the Inexcusability of Unbelief*).

We affirm that every thought raised up against the knowledge of God must be taken captive and made obedient to Christ (*Rational Presuppositionalism*).

We affirm the regulative principle and the singing of Psalms in the worship of God.

We affirm that the earth shall be full of the knowledge of the Lord as the waters cover the sea, as Christ subdues all things to himself through the Church (*Postmillennial Eschatology*).

Appendix 2

_____

THE DOXOLOGICAL FOCUS
of the
WESTMINSTER STANDARDS
expresses the
DISTINCTIVES OF WESTMINSTER FELLOWSHIP

THE CONFESSION TEACHES:

Although the light of nature, and the works of creation and providence, do so far manifest the goodness, wisdom, and power of God, as to leave men inexcusable. (1.1)

God hath all life, glory, goodness, blessedness, in and of himself; and is alone in and unto himself all-sufficient, not standing in need of any creatures which he hath made, nor deriving any glory from them, but only manifesting His own glory in, by, unto, and upon them. (2.2)

By the decree of God, for the manifestation of His glory, some men and angels are predestinated unto everlasting life (to the praise of his glorious mercy); and others foreordained to everlasting death (to the praise of his glorious justice). (3.3)

It pleased God the Father, Son, and Holy Ghost, for the manifestation of the glory of His eternal power, wisdom, and goodness, in the beginning, to create or make of nothing the world, and all things therein, whether visible or invisible, in the space of six days, and all very good. (4.1)

God, the great Creator of all things, doth uphold, direct, dispose, and govern all creatures, actions, and things, from the greatest even to the least, by His most wise and holy providence, according to His infallible foreknowledge, and the free and immutable counsel of His own will, to the praise of the glory of His wisdom, power, justice, goodness, and mercy. (5.1)

Our first parents, being seduced by the subtlety and temptations of Satan, sinned in eating the forbidden fruit. This their sin God was pleased, according to His wise and holy counsel, to permit, having purposed to order it to His own glory. (6.1)

THE SHORTER CATECHISM TEACHES:

Man's chief end is to glorify God, and to enjoy him forever. (Q. 1)

The first commandment requireth us to know and acknowledge God to be the only true God, and our God; and to worship and glorify him accordingly. (Q. 46)

In the first petition, which is, *Hallowed be thy name*, we pray that God would enable us and others to glorify him in all that whereby he maketh himself known; and that he would dispose all things to his own glory. (Q. 101)

WE BELIEVE THAT:

We are to glorify God in all that by which he makes himself known, in all his works of creation and providence.

Appendix 3

——

HISTORICAL FOUNDATION

The Work of the Holy Spirit
Leading the Church Into All Truth

ESTMINSTER FELLOWSHIP HOLDS to Historic Christianity. Historic Christianity is the work of the Holy Spirit leading the Church into all truth,[1] through the centuries, through the work of pastor-teachers. Pastor-teachers are given to the Church by Christ to bring believers to the unity of the faith, to the full measure of the stature of Christ.[2]

Challenges occur in every age, to which the Church must respond in order to attain to the fullness of Christ, and to accomplish its task to disciple all nations. Without the teachings of Historic Christianity firmly established in the lives of believers, there is no ordinary basis for hope for attaining maturity in the fullness of Christ.

In every age, as the Church expands, new believers bring into the Church ideas and practices from their culture which challenge the truth of the Gospel. After much discussion, the pastor-teachers come to agreement on the teaching of Scripture in response to these challenges.

The First Church Council was held in Jerusalem in response to the challenge of Judaic legalism.[3] The early gentile converts were influenced by Greek dualism, and raised the challenge of Gnosticism, which was answered by the Apostles' Creed (*ca.* A.D. 180), recited in churches through the centuries. The Council of Nicea (A.D. 325) addressed

---

1. *John 16:13.*
2. *Ephesians 4.*
3. *Acts 15.*

challenges to the doctrine of the Trinity. The Council of Carthage (A.D. 397) identified all the books and only the books that constitute the Scripture of the New Testament. The Council of Chalcedon (A.D. 451) clarified the doctrine of the Incarnation (that Christ is fully God and fully man), and the Council of Orange (A.D. 529) affirmed the doctrine of sin (man is fallen in Adam) and salvation (man is saved by grace) in response to Pelagian and semi-Pelagian error.

The Westminster Confession of Faith (A.D. 1648) is the high-water mark of Historic Christianity at the beginning of the modern era. Building on the work of the pastor-teachers in the early Church councils, it responded to the challenges of systemic distortions in the Church at the time of the Reformation.[4]

It affirmed the authority of Scripture over against all other sources of special revelation. It affirmed the sovereignty of God over all, and its application in salvation through one covenant of grace over against all admixtures of grace with human effort.

It affirmed the work of the pastor-teachers meeting in synods/councils over against hierarchical and independent ecclesiastical authority. And it affirmed the regulative principle of worship, that the worship of God, which God has commanded in Scripture, must be kept pure and entire.

In the modern age, the Church has been challenged in terms of its claim to knowledge (reason and science vs. faith and scripture), and in its view of human purpose (life on earth vs. eternal life in heaven, the secular vs. the sacred).

The Church has not yet come to the unity of faith in meeting these challenges and has steadily been losing ground where it once led the culture in Western Civilization. Current globalization has intensified contact with non-western cultures and worldviews in Asia, Africa, and South America.

The more supernatural forms of Christianity growing in these areas are yet to face the acid tests of skepticism and secularism. By building on Historic Christianity, as summed up in the Westminster Confession of Faith, these challenges can be met.

---

4. Gangadean, "Paper No. 16: The Historic Christian Faith: The Holy Spirit Guides the Church into All Truth," in *The Logos Papers*.

The challenge of reason and science vs. faith and scripture can be met by the Biblical teaching on the clarity of general revelation and the inexcusability of unbelief.[5]

The Westminster Confession opens with the affirmation of this teaching: "The light of nature [reason], and the works of creation and providence do so far manifest the goodness, wisdom, and power of God, as to leave men unexcusable . . ." Believers today are being challenged by skepticism to show the clarity of general revelation and to take thoughts captive which are raised up against the knowledge of God.[6]

Believers today are being challenged by secularism—life in this world vs. eternal life in heaven. This can be met by the Biblical teaching that eternal life is the knowledge of God,[7] and that man's purpose on earth is to fill the earth with the knowledge of God as the waters cover the sea.[8]

The Westminster Confession of Faith affirms that God's purpose in creation and providence is the revelation of his glory;[9] that the first commandment requires us to know and acknowledge God;[10] that the first petition in the Lord's Prayer is that God would enable us and others to glorify him in all that by which he makes himself known;[11] that man's chief end is to glorify God and enjoy him forever.[12]

---

5. *Romans 1:18-20; 2:14.*

6. *2 Corinthians 10:4-5.*

7. *John 17:3.*

8. *Isaiah 11:9.*

9. *WCF 4.1; 5.1.*

10. *SCQ 46.*

11. *SCQ 101.*

12. *SCQ 1.*

Appendix 4

THE GOAL OF THE
KNOWLEDGE OF GOD

PART I:
Creation Is Revelation

1. *God created to make his glory known.* "It pleased God the Father, Son, and Holy Spirit, for the manifestation of the glory of his eternal power, wisdom, and goodness, in the beginning, to create, or make of nothing, the world, and all things therein whether visible or invisible in the space of six days; and all very good."[1] *God rules in history to make his glory known.* "God, the great Creator of all things, doth uphold, direct, dispose, and govern all creatures, actions, and things, from the greatest even to the least, by his most wise and holy providence, according to his infallible, and the free and immutable counsel of his own will, to the praise of his wisdom, power, justice, goodness, and mercy."[2]

2. *This revelation is not bare, but full.* The whole earth is full of his glory.[3] Revelation is not restricted to Scripture. Scripture is not an alternative to general revelation.

3. *Creation is revelation, necessarily.* A being is revealed in its acts; the acts of God in creation and providence reveal the nature of God. Every act of God reveals his nature. No act of God is above, apart from, or against his nature.

---

1. *WCF 4.1.*
2. *WCF 5.1.*
3. *Isaiah 6:3; Psalm 8; Psalm 29.*

4. *Creation is revelation, intentionally.* Creation is by the will of God, by his infinite, deliberate wisdom. What creation reveals, God intends to reveal. What God reveals, he intends to be known. God created and rules to reveal himself.

5. *Creation is revelation, exclusively.* There is no knowledge of God apart from creation and history. There is no direct vision of God, no beatific vision of God in heaven apart from God's self-revelation in creation and history.[4] To see God face to face is to see his revelation clearly, without the distortion of sin. God is a Spirit, immortal, invisible, whom no man has seen nor can see.[5] There is no greater revelation of the glory of God than by his works of creation and providence, which includes Christ's work of redemption.

PART II:
General Revelation Is Clear

1. "Since the creation of the world, God's invisible qualities—his eternal power and divine nature—have been clearly seen, being understood from what has been made, so that men are without excuse."[6] Without clarity of general revelation, there is no inexcusability for unbelief and, therefore, no sin and no need for redemption.

2. The clarity of general revelation includes the existence and nature of God, as well as the law of God which is written on the hearts of all men.[7]

3. Although general revelation is objectively clear, no one, left to himself, sees it. All have sinned and come short of the glory of God.[8] There is no one righteous, not even one; there is no one who understands, no one who seeks God.[9]

---

4. Gangadean, "Paper No. 106: The Good and Heaven: The Good Is Not the Beatific Vision," in *The Logos Papers.*

5. *1 Timothy 1:17; 6:16.*

6. *Romans 1:20; WCF 1.1.*

7. *Romans 2:14-15.*

8. *Romans 3:23.*

9. *Romans 3:10-11.*

4. Without seeking, there is no understanding of what is clear about God. Without understanding what is clear about God, there is no understanding of sin and death, no understanding of the need for Scripture, and no understanding of Christ's redemption.

5. The wages of sin is death.[10] This death is spiritual, not physical. Spiritual death is the destruction of the soul, which is present and inherent in sin.[11] It begins in this life and lasts forever. It is called the second death or the lake of fire.[12] Individually, spiritual death consists in meaninglessness, boredom, and guilt. Corporately, it consists in the death of relationships, institutions, and cultures.

PART III:
Eternal Life Is Knowing God

1. From general revelation, the good for man as a rational being is understanding creation and providence, which reveal God; the good is the knowledge of God. Jesus said: "Now this is eternal life: that they might know you, the only true God, and Jesus Christ, whom you have sent."[13]

2. *Eternal life is the good for man.*[14] It was the good for man before the Fall, as well as after the Fall. Redemption is restoration to life. Eternal life is not heaven. It begins in this life and grows forever. Eternal life is more than salvation; understood as forgiveness of sins and justification.

3. *Man's chief end is to know God.* Man's chief end is to glorify God and to enjoy him forever.[15] To glorify God is to understand his glory (the greatness of his wisdom, power, justice, and goodness) and to make his glory known.

---

10. *Genesis 2:17; Romans 6:23.*

11. *Ephesians 2:1, 4-5.*

12. *Revelation 20:6, 10, 14.*

13. *John 17:3.*

14. Gangadean, "Paper No. 4: The Cornerstone: Good & Evil – Life & Death: The Beginning of the Foundation," in *The Logos Papers*; "Paper No. 42: The Moral Law: The First Commandment," in *The Logos Papers*.

15. *SCQ. 1.*

4. *The first commandment is to know God.* The first commandment requires us to know and acknowledge God to be the only true God, and our God, and to worship and glorify him accordingly.[16]

5. *The first petition of prayer is to know God.* In the first petition of the Lord's Prayer which is *Hallowed be Thy Name*, we pray that God would enable us and others to glorify him in all that by which he makes himself known; and that he would dispose all things to his own glory.[17]

PART IV:
The Knowledge of God Is Through the Work of Dominion

1. "And God said, Let us make man in our image, after our likeness: and let them have dominion over all the earth."[18] The knowledge of God is through the work of dominion. In dominion, man is to be fruitful and multiply and fill the earth and rule over it.[19] The work of dominion is corporate, cumulative, and communal. It requires all of mankind, working together through all of history, to be achieved.[20]

2. *In dominion, man is to rule over the creation.* He is to develop all the powers latent in himself and in the creation.

3. *In dominion, man is to name the creation.* Naming requires grasping the nature of all beings in all their parts and relations so as to make known the glory of God. Man is to know the nature of all things created.

4. In knowing the creation, which reveals the glory of God, man comes to know God.

5. Sin does not cancel God's revelation or the work of dominion, but deepens the revelation and enlarges the work of dominion. The fullness of life is not attained in heaven apart from the completion of the work of dominion.

---

16. *SCQ. 46.*

17. *SCQ. 101.*

18. *Genesis 1:2.*

19. *Genesis 1.*

20. Gangadean, *Philosophical Foundation*, 207-219.

PART V:
The Earth Shall Be Full of the Knowledge of God

1. The Sabbath, from the beginning, signified hope that the work of dominion will be completed. As God completed the work of creation, man will complete the work of dominion. As creation is revelation, so dominion brings knowledge of this revelation.[21]

2. Since the Fall, God calls man back to himself through the curse and the promise.[22] Individually, the curse consists in toil and strife, and old age, sickness, and death. Corporately, the curse consists in famine, war, and plague. The curse is natural evil; it is imposed by God to restrain, recall from, and remove moral evil (sin). Moral evil includes not only not seeking and not understanding, but also self-deception and self-justification for sin.

3. The promise, given in Scripture, is that Christ will *undo* what Adam did, in paying the penalty for sin, and will *do* what Adam failed to do, to fill the earth with the knowledge of God.

4. In Christ, believers must take captive every thought raised up against the knowledge of God.[23] In Christ, believers must make disciples of all nations, teaching them to obey all that he has commanded.[24]

5. As a result of Christ's rule, "The earth shall be full of the knowledge of the Lord, as the waters cover the sea."[25]

---

21. *Genesis 2:1-3.*
22. *Genesis 3:14-24.*
23. *2 Corinthians 10:4.*
24. *Matthew 28:20.*
25. *Isaiah 11:9.*

Appendix 5

Rational

Presuppositionalism

Critically Examining Assumptions for Meaning

RATIONAL PRESUPPOSITIONALISM IS AN epistemological method used to settle philosophical disputes by critically analyzing assumptions for meaning. It applies reason as a test for meaning to what is presupposed in a dispute.

Rational Presuppositionalism (RP) affirms that some things are clear. The basic things are clear. The basic things about God and man and good and evil are clear to reason.[1] RP is an answer to skepticism and fideism. It is an alternative to rationalism and to empiricism, both of which make uncritically held assumptions.[2]

Thinking is presuppositional. We think of the less basic in light of the more basic. We think of truth in light of meaning, experience in light of basic belief, conclusions in light of premises, and the finite and temporal in light of the infinite and eternal. If we understand what is more basic, we can understand what is less basic; if we agree on what is more basic, we can agree on what is less basic.

RP seeks to avoid needless disputes by examining if there is agreement on what is more basic. It seeks to avoid straining at gnats while swallowing camels. It looks at both the objective and the subjective aspects of knowledge and dialogue. Dialogue presupposes a commitment to reason along with an understanding of the nature of reason.

---

1. Gangadean, *Philosophical Foundation*, 287-292.
2. Gangadean, *History of Philosophy*, 131-149.

Having knowledge presupposes a concern to know, which presupposes integrity as a concern for consistency, both theoretically and personally. If there is commitment to reason, with integrity, disputes can be settled.[3]

Skepticism claims that knowledge is not possible. It is rooted in uncritically held assumptions, that if rationalism (for example, Descartes) and empiricism (for example, Hume) cannot give knowledge, then no knowledge is possible.[4] Consistently held, skepticism leads to nihilism, in which no distinction is clear, including the distinction of *a* and *non-a*, being and non-being, true and false, and good and evil.

Skepticism denies reason, makes dialogue impossible, and leads to silence as well as a cessation of all thought. It dissolves the meaning of its terms—*knowledge* and *possible*. Pragmatism cannot overcome the meaninglessness of skepticism.[5] And fideism (appeal to faith apart from proof based on understanding) becomes an arbitrary affirmation of one view from among many.

RP affirms that sense experience gives knowledge of appearance but not of reality, and that the data of experience (common sense, scientific or mystical) must be interpreted in order to be meaningful. RP does not allow the post-modern skeptical view that "it is all a matter of interpretation." Philosophy does not end with interpretation, but begins here.

Every interpretation can be, and must be, tested for coherence and meaning. RP affirms that the self-evident truths of rationalism (Descartes' *cogito* or Jefferson's self-evident truths) are not logically basic, even though they are taken as properly basic. The alternatives of absolute idealism and naturalism require a response.

Rational Presuppositionalism is to be distinguished from fideistic presuppositionalism, in which one moves from Scripture (the Triune God of the Bible) to reason. RP is to be distinguished from axiomatic presuppositionalism, in which one begins with the Scripture as one's set of axioms.

RP is to be distinguished from reformed epistemology, in which one begins with what is taken as properly basic beliefs.[6] RP is to be

---

3. Gangadean, *Philosophical Foundation*, 287-292.

4. Gangadean, *History of Philosophy*, 9-12.

5. Gangadean, *Philosophical Foundation*, 117-118.

6. Gangadean, *History of Philosophy*, 175-179.

distinguished from evidentialism, in which one seeks to argue from miracles to God. RP is to be distinguished from common sense realism, in which the objective existence of the external world is assumed.[7]

RP affirms that the clarity of general revelation is necessary for the inexcusability of unbelief and undertakes to show what is clear from general revelation by showing the alternatives of unbelief are contrary to reason.[8] It is to be distinguished from all attempts to answer historical criticism of the Scriptures without first establishing the clarity of general revelation.

RP begins with an affirmation of the nature of reason based on the reality of thought. Reason is to be defined in itself, in its use, and in us.[9]

Reason in itself is the laws of thought. Most basically, these are the law of identity: *a* is *a*; the law of non-contradiction: not both *a* and *non-a*, at the same time and in the same respect; and the law of excluded middle: either *a* or *non-a*. Other laws of thought are based on these laws. To doubt these laws is to lose all distinctions and to cease to think.

Reason in its use is formative, critical, interpretive, and constructive. Reason is used to form concepts, judgments, and arguments, which are the forms of all thought. Whenever there are thoughts, reason is being used formatively. Reason is used critically as a test for meaning. It is applied especially to basic beliefs as a test for meaning. If a belief, upon analysis, violates a law of thought, it lacks meaning and cannot be true. Reason is used to interpret experience in light of one's basic beliefs. No experience is meaningful without interpretation, and every interpretation can and must be tested for meaning. And lastly, reason is used to construct a coherent world and life view upon one's basic belief. Worldviews are manifest in cultures. They are held more or less consciously and more or less consistently and, therefore, continually face the internal and external challenges of reason.[10]

Reason is always being used formatively. It is often used constructively, without first being used critically. It is sometimes used interpretively

---

7. Gangadean, "Paper No. 3: The Principle of Clarity, Rational Presuppositionalism, and Proof," in *The Logos Papers*.

8. Gangadean, "Paper No. 3: The Principle of Clarity, Rational Presuppositionalism, and Proof," in *The Logos Papers*; Gangadean, *Philosophical Foundation*, 71-161.

9. Gangadean, *Philosophical Foundation*, 10-15.

10. Gangadean, "Paper No. 19: Foundation for Philosophy of History," in *The Logos Papers*.

without realizing it. Reason in itself is not fallible, but a person may fail to use reason critically and fully.

Reason does not succeed only if it persuades subjectively, but if it answers objections with an objectively sound argument. Many objections against reason and rationalism are really against what amounts to a failure to use reason.[11] Reason in itself must therefore be distinguished from reason in its use.

Reason in us is natural, ontological, transcendental, and fundamental. Reason is natural, not conventional. It is universal, the same in all persons. Reason as the laws of thought is the common ground among all thinkers. What distinguishes us is not reason, but the willingness to use reason. What distinguishes us is not our assumption, but the willingness to critically examine our assumption for meaning.

Reason is ontological. It applies to being as well as to thought. There are no square-circles, no uncaused events, no being from non-being. It applies to all being, including the highest being. God is not both eternal and not eternal, at the same time and in the same respect. Matter is not both extended and not extended, at the same time and in the same respect.[12] There is no noumenal realm or dimension in which reason does not apply, but to which faith gives access.[13] While the mysteries of faith do not originate in reason, they do not go against reason. Miracles are not against the laws of reason, but against a law of nature. Reason, as an aspect of God's being, is eternal. The laws of nature are created. Paradoxes are puzzling to reason insofar as assumptions present and at work are not yet critically examined and corrected. Finite beings cannot have exhaustive or comprehensive knowledge of anything, but the unknown is not against the laws of reason.

Reason is transcendental. It is authoritative and self-attesting. It is transcendental in that it stands above thought and makes thought possible. It cannot be questioned, but makes questioning possible. Statements about general and special revelation (Scripture) can and must be questioned, by reason, but reason itself as the laws of thought cannot be questioned. As transcendental, it cannot be argued for, even in a circular manner. In thought, what is of highest authority

---

11. Gangadean, *History of Philosophy*, 131-137.

12. Gangadean, *History of Philosophy*, 38.

13. Gangadean, *History of Philosophy*, 151-153; Gangadean, *Philosophical Foundation*, 109-110.

is self-attesting, and only reason is self-attesting.[14] Scripture assumes reason as that by which Scripture is to be understood. Scripture, if it is to be received, must be spoken in the name of God; that is, it must be consistent with the nature of God known from general revelation. There is not and cannot be any conflict between reason, general revelation, and Scripture. Scripture is set against all other forms of special revelation, not against reason and general revelation.

Reason is fundamental. It is fundamental to other aspects of human personality. Feelings are directed by belief about the good, and thought and feeling move the will to act. Feeling and will are not independent of or contrary to belief. Conflicts within the understanding are manifest in conflicts in feeling and will. Unnoticed, these misunderstandings, as conflicts within our thoughts, lead to apparent conflict between thought and feeling, etc. Our deepest need is for meaning. Our deepest misery is in the awareness of the lack of meaning. Meaninglessness is a fundamental aspect of spiritual death, and, sometimes, physical death is sought as an escape from spiritual death. Boredom comes from meaninglessness, in which the creation, apart from or in place of the Creator, cannot satisfy. Failure to be rational is experienced as guilt, from which escape is sought in the unending rationalizations of self-justification. Our greatest happiness is from the use of reason in understanding the creation, when this understanding leads to the knowledge of God.

The first application of RP is to the question *what is real?* It clarifies the subjective factors of integrity and commitment to reason as preconditions to knowledge. It prevents further discussion, which would be fruitless if these preconditions are not in place.

We begin with the question *what is real?* because existence is our most basic concept, and eternal existence (without beginning) is more basic than temporal existence (with beginning).

To show that *some is eternal* is true, we show that the contradiction *none is eternal* cannot be true. *None is eternal* implies that *all is temporal, all had a beginning, all came into being.* If all came into being, it would have come into being from non-being, which is impossible.

---

14. Gangadean, *Philosophical Foundation*, 298-299.

Hence, *none is eternal* cannot be true, and its contradiction *some is eternal* must be true. *All came into being from non-being* is not the same as creation *ex nihilo*, in which God is eternal and acted to create.[15]

By *non-being* is meant the absence of all being whatsoever, not just the absence of all visible being. An unending series of finite and temporal beings having the power to create *ex nihilo*, is not an objection that has been (or, upon analysis, can be) made.

If it is agreed that it is clear to reason that there must be something eternal, we can go on to the next step in showing what is clear.[16]

15. Gangadean, *Philosophical Foundation*, 61-68.
16. Gangadean, *Philosophical Foundation*, 71-284.

Appendix 6

_____

THE CLARITY OF
GENERAL REVELATION

*God's Eternal Power and Divine Nature,
and the Moral Law*

G ENERAL REVELATION IS WHAT MAY BE KNOWN of God by all men,
everywhere, at all times. What is clear from general revelation is
his eternal power and divine nature and the moral law.[1]

The clarity of general revelation is the basis of the inexcusability of
unbelief and of the necessity of redemptive revelation in Scripture.[2]
Because general revelation is clear, those in unbelief regarding the
existence and nature of God and of the moral law have no reason for
their unbelief.

To deny what is clear requires the denial of reason. The clarity of
general revelation, under the condition of moral and natural evil, leads to
recognition of the necessity, content, origin, and existence of Scripture.
This further leads to the recognition of the transmission, completion,
translation, clarity, sufficiency, and interpretation of Scripture.[3] The
clarity of general revelation is necessary in order to avoid misinterpre-
tation of Scripture.

If non-believers are responsible for seeing through the inexcusability of their unbelief, believers are all the more so. If we have come to

---

1. *Romans 1:18-20; 2:14-15.*

2. Gangadean, "Paper No. 12: The Necessity for Scripture: General Revelation Requires Special
Revelation," in *The Logos Papers*.

3. Gangadean, "Paper No. 11: From General Revelation to Special Revelation: Prologue to
Scripture," in *The Logos Papers*.

understand what is clear, we should be able to show what is clear.[4] We should be able to take thoughts captive that are raised up against the knowledge of God.[5]

But believers still have sin and have to contend with the noetic effect of sin in themselves. Believers have to struggle to avoid being taken captive by prevailing unbelief in the culture in which they live. But by recognizing the need for the renewal of one's mind, by benefiting from the understanding already achieved in Historic Christianity, and by engaging with the remaining internal and external challenges to the Faith, believers can come to a mature understanding of the clarity of general revelation.

Rational Presuppositionalism is an epistemological method which seeks to settle disputes by thinking of the less basic in light of the more basic and critically analyzing assumptions for meaning. By Rational Presuppositionalism, we can understand the major steps in showing the clarity of general revelation.

1. Show the necessity for clarity in general against skepticism, and the necessity for clarity in particular for Christian theism, against fideism.

2. Show, by ontological argument, that there must be something eternal. This is a paradigm of what is clear to reason. Rational Presuppositionalism requires agreement here before going any further in metaphysics. If this cannot be known, nothing can be known and dialogue is not possible.

3. Show, by cosmological arguments, that only some (God) is eternal; that is, show theism vs. all forms of non-theism. This requires showing that matter exists and that matter is not eternal; that the soul/spirit exists and the soul is not eternal.

   To show the material world is not eternal, it must be shown that the material world is not self-maintaining (vs. material monism—all forms of scientific materialism and cosmological naturalism).

   To show that the soul exists, it must be shown that the mind is not the brain. To show the individual soul exists, it must be shown that

---

4. Gangadean, "Paper No. 110: On Clarity: Concern for Consistency in Thought and Action," in *The Logos Papers*; "Paper No. 39: Clarity: And Its Application," in *The Logos Papers*.

5. *2 Corinthians 10:4-5.*

there is not one mind only and its ideas (vs. spiritual monism—absolute or Vedantic idealism).

To show that the material world exists (vs. ordinary idealism), it must be shown that the cause of what is seen is not my mind or another mind, but outside all minds.

To show that the soul is not eternal (vs. all forms of dualism—Greek, Indian, Persian, and Mormon, and reincarnation), it must be shown that the soul experiences unique events.

4. Show, by teleological argument, that the natural order is by design (that is, show special creation) vs. all forms of evolution—natural and theistic.

5. Show, by teleological argument, that, in divine providence, moral and natural evil serve the divine purpose (that is, show the Ironic Solution to the problem of evil) vs. naturalistic and free will solutions.

6. Show the moral law, structured into human nature by creation, is clear, comprehensive, and critical, the same in content as the law given by special revelation.

7. Show the necessity, content, origin, and existence of special revelation (vs. deism). Further, show the transmission, completion, translation, clarity, sufficiency, and interpretation of special revelation.

8. Show Christian theism (vs. all forms of non-Christian theism—that is, Judaic and Islamic theism), based on general and on special revelation.

9. Show the response to past challenges to Christian theism, based on general and on special revelation, and summed up in the ecumenical and historical creeds (Gnosticism, Trinity, Incarnation, predestination).

10. Show the response to continuing external and internal challenges to Christian theism (faith vs. reason, otherworldliness and secularism vs. knowledge of God, continuing divisions within theism vs. unity of the faith).

Appendix 7

———

THE NOETIC EFFECT OF SIN

The Effect of Moral Evil on the Mind of Man

I T IS THE NATURE OF SIN (MORAL EVIL) TO NOT SEEK the good, to misunderstand the good, in ignorance to call good evil and evil good, to oppose the good in light of one's misconception, and to avoid and resist correction by self-deception and self-justification. The effect of moral evil on the mind of man is called the noetic effect. It began with the Fall of man and is removed gradually in the redemption of man.

Scripture (the biblical worldview of creation–fall–redemption) assumes the clarity of general revelation.[1] Sin begins in the failure to seek and understand what is clear about God. This sin is universal.[2] This sin is deep.[3] This sin is destructive.[4] The neglect of not seeking is set against the necessity for seeking: he that comes to God must believe that he is and that he is the rewarder of those that diligently seek him.[5] The reward of diligently seeking God is knowing him. Eternal life is knowing God.[6]

The noetic effect of sin is first seen in the Garden of Eden. Man is called to know God through the work of dominion. Left to himself, man turns from the knowledge of God as the good. When tested (regarding

———

1. *Romans 1:20.*
2. *Romans 3:10-11.*
3. *Jeremiah 17:9.*
4. *Romans 6:23.*
5. *Hebrews 11:6.*
6. *John 17:3.*

his understanding of good and evil, and life and death) he failed. He believed the falsehood: "You shall not surely die . . . you shall be like God knowing good and evil."[7] The outward act of eating of the tree of the knowledge of good and evil revealed the inward state of not seeking and not knowing God. He lost sight of the radical difference between God as Creator and man as creature in knowing good and evil. He had put himself in the place of God to determine good and evil.

Good for a being is based on the nature of that being. God knows good and evil, not by discovery, but by determining the nature of beings by the act of creation. Adam was to know good and evil by discovering the nature of beings. Man cannot be like God in knowing good and evil because man is a creature, not the Creator. He cannot determine the nature of things. Adam, by not seeking the knowledge of God as the good, failed to understand what is clear about God—that God is the infinite and eternal Creator, and that man is a finite, temporal creature. This, the original sin, is the origin of all sin in all men. Sin is the failure to understand what is clear about God.

As the inward act of sin of not seeking and not understanding is exposed by the outward act of unrighteousness (eating), man experiences shame in his nakedness. Shame is the first natural and inward call back from sin. It is the call of conscience. Man avoids this call back through self-deception, by covering his nakedness. God calls man back a second time, outwardly, by a call to self-examination in asking: where are you? Man resists the second call by self-justification, blaming the woman and God himself for his own disobedience. God calls man back a third and final time by imposing on man the curse (toil and strife, and old age, sickness, and death) and by the giving of the promise (the seed of the woman will crush the head of the serpent).[8] Man responds to the third call by repentance and faith. He is justified by God in being covered with the coats of skin (forgiveness through the death of another), and is to be sanctified through suffering, by expulsion from the Garden to live under the curse.

Sin is permitted by God and is made to serve his purpose. It deepens the revelation of his justice and mercy. If it is removed abruptly, the revelation will not be deepened. If it is not removed, the revelation will

---

7. *Genesis 3:5.*

8. *Genesis 3:15.*

not be seen. Sin, as unbelief, is permitted to work itself out in human history in every form and degree of combination with belief. In this age-long and agonizing conflict, good overcomes evil. The seed of the woman crushes the head of the serpent, according to the promise.[9]

Although forgiven in Christ, sin remains in believers, along with its noetic effect. Believers continue to fail to understand what is clear about God from general revelation. This failure to seek and to understand the clarity of general revelation is overlooked in self-deception and resisted in self-justification. Natural evil (the curse) continues to call men back from moral evil (sin). Suffering calls men to stop and think about basic things, about meaning and purpose, about God and man, about good and evil, about life and death. Suffering the curse and agonies of the spiritual war of belief vs. unbelief continues as long as the noetic effect of sin remains.

The clarity of general revelation cannot be denied without denying the inexcusability of unbelief. But clarity cannot be affirmed without being required to show the clarity of general revelation. As a result, the doctrine of clarity has been left in the dark. Believers continue to show a disregard for the clarity of general revelation and a disinclination to show the inexcusability of unbelief.[10] This, and other closely connected doctrines, has been held more or less consciously, and more or less consistently.

Self-deception about diligently seeking to know God continues; self-justification for not knowing what is clear about God continues; the suffering of toil and strife, and old age, sickness, and death continues as God's call back to stop and think. Insofar as we do not stop and think, our understanding remains in darkness. What we profess to believe becomes emptied of meaning or filled with misunderstanding. One's entire worldview is affected by one's understanding of good and evil.

The failure to understand what is clear from general revelation continues in the failure to understand what is clear from special revelation. The divisions in the Church in understanding Scripture reflect the divisions in understanding general revelation. Sin has affected the entire Christian worldview by distorting understanding of foundational

---

9. Gangadean, *Philosophical Foundation*, 156-161.

10. Gangadean, "Paper No. 61: The Present and Future State of the Church: To and For the Church," in *The Logos Papers*; "Paper No. 62: The Next Reformation: Prepare the Way of the Lord," in *The Logos Papers*.

teachings. The following briefly mention some of this misunderstanding, with further explanation below.

Moral evil is not seen as the failure to understand what is clear about God. It is seen as a willful act of disobedience of a command of God. Faith is not seen as based on understanding and evidence. It is seen as a choice to believe above, apart from, or against evidence. The wages of sin is not seen as spiritual death, present and inherent in sin. The wages of sin is seen as hell, which is future and imposed. Eternal life is not seen as the knowledge of God. It is seen as the absence of the curse in heaven.

1. The noetic effect affects our understanding of sin (moral evil).

Sin is the failure to seek and to understand what is clear about God (divine nature) and man, and good and evil (moral law). Sin is not fundamentally the willful outward act of disobedience of a command of God.[11] Adam believed what was false about God and about sin and death before he ate; and he ate because of his unbelief. Sin is coming short of seeing the glory of God. This is the sin which is universal, and of which all must repent. Yet, personally and corporately, the Church repents of fruit sin, but not root sin. We think of ourselves as concerned to know the truth even when we fail to know what is clear. We resist responsibility for knowing what is clear by denying clarity (no one knows), or making it impossible to know (reason is finite/fallen), or irrelevant to faith (deep down everyone knows). The noetic effect of sin is covered by hypocrisy through self-deception and self-justification. Integrity, by self-examination and by discipline, is necessary and sufficient to overcome hypocrisy, and to know what is clear about God.

What can be known of God is revealed by the Word of God. Man, in his fallen state, resists and rejects the Word of God in every form: in himself as reason;[12] in creation as general revelation;[13] in history as special/redemptive revelation;[14] in person as Jesus Christ, the Word incarnate.[15]

---

11. Gangadean, "Paper No. 120: Contra Voluntarism: The Will Is Not Independent of the Intellect," in *The Logos Papers*.

12. *John 1:4-5.*

13. *John 1:10.*

14. *John 1:11.*

15. *John 1:14.*

2. The noetic effect affects our understanding of spiritual death.

The wages of sin is death,[16] not hell as is commonly conceived. Death here is spiritual, not physical. Spiritual death is present and inherent in sin, whereas hell, as a literal lake of fire, is future and imposed. Hell, in biblical language, is a symbolic representation of spiritual death. It is called the second death.[17] Taken literally, hell, as a lake of fire, is without meaning. Spirits are not affected by physical fire. To appeal to a continual miracle in order to make the literal hell possible is to deny God's justice and to invite blasphemy.[18] The fear of hell (avoiding natural evil) is not the fear of God (avoiding moral evil). There is a necessary connection between sin (not seeking, and not understanding) and death (meaninglessness, boredom, and guilt). Understanding the connection between sin and death creates the fear of the Lord, which moves us to diligently seek him. Thus, the fear of the Lord is the beginning of wisdom.

3. The noetic effect affects our understanding of the curse (natural evil).

The curse of toil and strife, and old age, sickness, and death, is God's call back from sin, not punishment for sin. There are two kinds of death as well as two kinds of resurrections: physical and spiritual.[19] The wages of sin is spiritual death, not physical death. It is part of the noetic effect of sin to avoid and resist the curse as God's call to repentance of failing to see what is clear.

Physical death is not original in the creation. Physical death is not inherent in sin. Physical death is imposed because of sin. It is the third and last call back from sin. (The first call back of shame is avoided by self-deception, and the second call back to self-examination is avoided by self-justification.) The noetic effect of self-deception and self-justification objectively require the curse and at the same time subjectively resist the curse. Although the curse is sometimes referred to as punishment and sometimes as chastening, it is not punishment in the strict or absolute

---

16. *Romans 6:23; Genesis 2:17; Ephesians 2:1.*

17. *Revelation 20:14.*

18. *Romans 2:24.*

19. *John 5:24-29; John 11:25; Revelation 20:6.*

sense of the term. Physical death cannot (in the strict sense) be considered punishment for sin, in this life or the next. If physical death were punishment for the believer, then Christ did not bear the full penalty of sin. If physical death were punishment for the non-believer, there would be no resurrection for the bodies of non-believers. If the curse were punishment for both believers and non-believers, there would be some proportionality in its manifestation. But the most righteous, for example Job, often suffer more than others, and the wicked often prosper more than the righteous.[20]

The curse serves several purposes in relation to sin. Its serves to restrain all from sin, to recall non-believers from sin, and to remove the sin remaining in believers. In all the suffering of the curse, there is a call to stop and think deeply about good and evil, about the meaning and purpose of life. It is a call to know God. The curse is intensified in history to become famine, war, and plague. At death, there is no further call back. A person continues in the condition in which they died. The curse is fully removed, not at death, but at the end of this age in the resurrection, when all things have been subdued to Christ.[21] The last enemy to be destroyed is death.

4. The noetic effect affects our understanding of eternal life.

Eternal life is to know God.[22] Eternal life is not heaven. Eternal life begins in this life, at regeneration. Heaven begins after this life. God makes himself known through his works of creation and providence (providence includes redemption in history). God is a Spirit, immortal and invisible, whom no man has seen nor can see.[23] God cannot be seen directly in heaven apart from his works. Creation is revelation, necessarily, intentionally, and exclusively. In heaven, after death, and before the resurrection, in the intermediate state, the fullness of blessing is not received, but is awaited. Departed believers await the completion of the work given to man in history.[24] Through the work of dominion,

---

20. *Psalm 75.*
21. *1 Corinthians 15:25-28.*
22. *John 17:3.*
23. *1 Timothy 6:16.*
24. *Hebrews 11:13, 39-40.*

the earth is to be filled with the knowledge of God as the waters cover the sea.[25]

Dominion (developing the powers latent in the creation—in one's self and in nature) is necessary for knowledge of the creation. And knowledge of the creation is necessary for the knowledge of God. The fullness of life is not absence of the curse, but the fullness of the knowledge of God. To expect life without knowledge of God is contrary to human nature. To expect fullness of life apart from the completion of dominion is false hope. To expect the work of dominion to be done by Christ at the Second Coming, supernaturally, apart from the Church, is to misunderstand the nature of knowledge through dominion.[26] To expect the knowledge of God through the work of dominion is true hope.

Due to sin and its noetic effect, the work of dominion is not set aside, it is deepened. The noetic effect is opposed by a spiritual war. With the curse in natural evil is given the promise in redemptive revelation: between good and evil (light and darkness, truth and falsehood, belief and unbelief), there is a spiritual war, which is age-long and agonizing, in which good eventually overcomes evil.[27] Every thought raised up against the knowledge of God will be made subject to Christ. Dominion now extends over sin.[28] The spiritual war is fought asymmetrically. Truth uses reason to persuade; falsehood uses threat and slander and the entire range of pseudo-arguments commonly called informal fallacies.[29] There is enmity, hostility, and hatred toward what exposes falsehood. Removal of this hostility requires a redemptive change of heart by regeneration. Truth prevails: "the light shines in the darkness and the darkness cannot overcome it or withstand it."[30] The rational requirements of human nature cannot be eradicated. The need for meaning, found only in the knowledge of God (eternal life), remains.

---

25. *Isaiah 11:9.*

26. Gangadean, *Philosophical Foundation*, 207-219.

27. *Genesis 3:15.*

28. *2 Corinthians 10:4.*

29. Gangadean, *Philosophical Foundation*, 45-48.

30. *John 1:5.*

5. The noetic effect affects all our basic beliefs.

The noetic effect affects our understanding of faith and reason and the inseparability of the two. It affects our interpretation of Scripture and of literature. It affects our understanding of good and evil, and why there is evil, and how evil serves the good. It affects our understanding of the moral law written on the hearts of all men and how the law serves the good. It affects our view of world history and Church history and human propensity toward apostasy. It affects our understanding of human conflicts and is the source of all conflicts and of every kind and degree of evil (in and between persons, in each household, in and between churches, in and between nations, and most comprehensively summed up between two ways, two kingdoms, two cities: the City of God and the City of Man). It affects our eschatology and our interpretation of all of life.

We can progress in overcoming the noetic effect:

1. by acknowledging the nature of sin at its root and its continued existence in us.

2. by acknowledging the curse (toil and strife, and old age, sickness, and death) as imposed by God as a continuing call to stop and think.

3. by acknowledging the good as the knowledge of God and the goal of filling the earth with the knowledge of God.

4. by acknowledge the work of the Holy Spirit leading us into all truth through the work of the pastor-teachers and summed up in the creeds of the Church.

5. by acknowledging the continuing internal and external challenges to the faith as God's call to take all thoughts captive which are raised up against the knowledge of God.

Appendix 8

———

POSTMILLENNIAL ESCHATOLOGY
The Earth Shall Be Full
of the Knowledge of God

ESCHATOLOGY HAS TO DO WITH THE END. It has to do with our hope. It has to do with what we can expect in the future. Eschatology has a broader and a narrower aspect. The broader aspect has to do with the goal, or end, of human existence.

The first question of the Shorter Catechism is: "What is the chief end of man?" It is the more basic aspect of eschatology. The narrower aspect has to do with how and when this chief end of man is realized. If we understand what is more basic, we will understand what is less basic.

If we agree on the chief end of man, we can overcome the divisions regarding premillennial, amillennial, and postmillennial eschatologies. If we keep in mind the method of Rational Presuppositionalism and the problems of the noetic effect of sin, we can come to the unity of the faith in relation to eschatology.

From general revelation, from Scripture, and from Historic Christianity (summed up in the Westminster Confession of Faith) we can know that eternal life—the good for man—is the knowledge of God,[1] and that the earth shall be full of the knowledge of God as the waters cover the sea.[2]

We know that creation reveals the glory of God[3] and that knowledge of God's glory comes through the work of dominion given to man in the

———

1. *John 17:3.*
2. *Isaiah 11:9.*
3. *Isaiah 6:3.*

beginning. The hope of life in knowing God is assumed and affirmed throughout Scripture from the beginning to the end.

1. Sabbath

The Sabbath is the single, greatest, continuing affirmation of hope for mankind. Man is made in the image of God. As God worked and completed his work of creation, so man will work and complete his work of dominion. As creation is revelation, dominion brings knowledge of this revelation. As a result of the corporate work of mankind through the ages in ruling over the creation, the earth will be filled with the knowledge of God as the waters cover the sea.

2. The seed of the woman

In sin, man turned away from knowing God as the good. He put himself in the place of God to determine good and evil. God permits evil to serve the good—to deepen the revelation of his glory, especially his justice and mercy. His mercy is seen in the promise of redemption, and in the curse which restrains, recalls from, and removes moral evil. God established a spiritual war between believer and non-believer which is age-long and agonizing, with the promise that good (the seed of the woman) will overcome evil (crush the head of the serpent).

3. Noah

In the first age of human history, God permits evil to come to maximum expression. Yet his purpose is not frustrated. Noah, in faith and hope, builds the ark in which he preserves the promise of redemption and the work of dominion attained thus far. In doing so, he comforts us (mankind) in the labor and painful toil of our hands caused by the ground the Lord has cursed. Hope is preserved through the greatest darkness, and continues, with further restraints on evil by increased toil and diminished lifespan.

4. Abraham and the patriarchs

Apostasy has become worldwide again at Babel and further restrained by the division of mankind. While mankind is left to go on in apostasy,

God chooses to fulfill the promise of redemption for all of mankind through Abraham. In Abraham's seed all the families of the earth will be blessed. The promise continues through Isaac and Jacob and his sons, who are seeking the City of God, a city with foundations, which is the kingdom of God on earth, in the Promised Land.

5. Moses

Moses sought this City too. He left the power and glory of Egypt for the promise in Christ. He led the people out of Egypt by God's power and gave them the Law of God for the Kingdom of God. The way of life through atonement, sanctification, and service is taught, culminating in the feast of ingathering (of all peoples) and the full removal of all debt (jubilee).

6. Joshua

After the first generation leaving Egypt did not enter the Promised Land because of their unbelief, Joshua leads the next generation in the conquest of Canaan. Joshua's conquest is a pattern for the Church to overcome all worldviews of the nations raised up against the knowledge of God, rather than fear the giants of opposing systems of thought, and wander in the wilderness in unbelief.

7. David and the Psalms

David and others in the Psalms sing of the person and work of Christ, both in his suffering and his glory. Christ is raised from the dead and appointed to reign now.[4] All the ends of the earth will remember and turn to the Lord and all the families of the nations will bow down before him. All of creation is brought to praise the Lord whose splendor is above the earth and the heavens.

8. The Prophets

All the prophets speak of God's judgment of famine, war, and plague on sin, and of God's restoration of His people. This restoration extends beyond the near future into the Gospel age, in which the nations are

---

4. *Psalms 2, 22, 67, 72, 110, 148,* and *150.*

brought into the house of God. All nations stream to it[5] until the earth is filled with the knowledge of God.[6] The comfort of restoration extends to the new heavens and the new earth.[7] Ezekiel sees the restoration in the vision of the dry bones[8] extending as a river from the Temple to all mankind.[9] Daniel sees the kingdom of God grow from the Rock that struck the image of the worldly kingdoms and became a huge mountain that filled the whole earth.[10] Jonah's life prefigures the resurrection of Christ and the call of the nations to repentance. Joel anticipates the outpouring of the Spirit on multitudes in the Valley of Decision.

9. Jesus

Jesus is the seed of the woman who came to destroy the works of the devil. He is the seed of Abraham in whom all the families are to be blessed. He is the Lamb of God who takes away the sin of the world. He is the anointed prophet, priest, and king, whose kingdom is to rule over all the earth. He is the Word of God, the Son of God, incarnate. He taught the character of the kingdom and the law of the kingdom in his Sermon on the Mount. He taught that the goal of the will of God and the coming of the kingdom is that the name of God would be hallowed (that God would be glorified in all that by which he makes himself known). He taught that the kingdom will grow gradually to its fullness (as a mustard seed, and as leaven). Though few at first are saved, and though Jerusalem will be destroyed,[11] he commanded his followers to make disciples of all nations, and he sent the Holy Spirit to enable them to do this work.

---

5. *Isaiah 2.*

6. *Isaiah 11.*

7. *Isaiah 40; 66.*

8. *Ezekiel 37.*

9. *Ezekiel 47.*

10. *Daniel 2:34-35.*

11. *Matthew 23-24.*

10. Paul

The apostle Paul taught that where sin increased, grace increased all the more.[12] He taught that God placed all things under Christ who, through his body the Church, is to fill everything in every way,[13] that through the work of the Spirit in the ministry of pastor/teachers, the Church is to attain to the unity of the faith, to the whole measure of the fullness of Christ.[14] He taught that all Israel will be saved when the fullness of the gentiles has come in;[15] that Christ will reign until he has put all his enemies under his feet, the last enemy to be destroyed, at his second coming, is death.[16]

11. Peter

Peter exhorts his readers to be patient in suffering for the cause of Christ; that although false teachers are bold and arrogant, God rules, as in the days of Noah, when he brought that world to a sudden end. So too now the world of wickedness will be destroyed. Believers are to speed the coming of that day by their witness. The rule of spiritual forces of evil in the heavenly realms (the heavens) will be destroyed and the fundamental principles (the elements/*stoicheia*) of the world will be destroyed suddenly. In the place of the old, believers look for a new heaven and a new earth, in which the will of God is done.

12. John

John's Revelation brings the blessing of hope to all who read it and take it to heart. The time is near to readers in every age. After a seven-fold description of the state of the Church in John's age, the rule of God through the curse and the promise in an age-long spiritual war is unveiled in a seven-fold vision: the seven seals, the seven trumpets, the woman and the dragon, the seven bowls, the woman on the beast, the age-long spiritual war (Armageddon—fought with the sword coming

---

12. *Romans 5.*

13. *Ephesians 1.*

14. *Ephesians 4.*

15. *Romans 11.*

16. *1 Corinthians 15.*

out of the mouth), the thousand-year rule of believers (the millennium, in which all rule, who are raised from the dead spiritually—the first resurrection). Each vision covers the entire period of Christ's rule, from the first to the second coming. Each vision depicts the spiritual war between believers and non-believers under different aspects. Each vision shows the conquest of the kingdom of God over the kingdom of darkness. John's Revelation ends with the consummation of the kingdom of God. The work given to mankind in the Garden of Eden is completed by Christ through the Church. The City of God, perfected in beauty, comes down from heaven to earth. The river of life flows through the middle of the city, bringing blessing to all nations, life in its fullness. The hope of the Sabbath, of work and rest, is fully realized. The earth is filled with the knowledge of God as the waters cover the sea.

Appendix 9

_____

THE REGULATIVE PRINCIPLE

OF WORSHIP

According to the Revealed Will of God

GENERAL REVELATION, SCRIPTURE, AND Historic Christianity (the Westminster Confession of Faith) call us to worship God as he is in truth, and not according to our own imagination. They call us to worship God with all the heart and not merely outwardly, in vain.

"The light of nature shows that there is a God, who has lordship and sovereignty over all, is good, and does good unto all, and is therefore to be feared, loved, praised, called up, trusted in, and served, with all the heart, and with all the soul, and with all the might. But the acceptable way of worshipping the true God is instituted by himself, and so limited by his own revealed will, that he may not be worshipped according to the imaginations and devices of men, or the suggestions of Satan, under any visible representation, or any other way not prescribed in the Holy Scripture."[1]

The principle which regulates worship limits worship to the revealed will of God. The second commandment requires the receiving, observing, and keeping pure and entire, all such religious worship and ordinances as God has appointed in his Word.[2] It forbids the worshiping of God by images, or any other way not appointed in his Word.[3] The second commandment affirms the regulative principle of worship which limits worship to what God has revealed in his Word. The regulative

---

1. *WCF 21.1.*

2. *SCQ. 50.*

3. *SCQ. 51.*

principle includes what is commanded; it does not include what is not commanded as well as what is explicitly forbidden. Jesus taught that God is Spirit, and his worshipers must worship in spirit and in truth.[4]

The book of Psalms in the Scriptures is given for singing, which is an ordinary part of public worship. "The reading of the Scriptures with godly fear, the sound preaching and conscionable hearing of the Word, in obedience unto God, with understanding, faith, and reverence, singing of psalms with grace in the heart . . . are all parts of the ordinary religious worship of God."[5]

The Psalms alone, and not any songs of human composition, are to be used in singing in the corporate worship of God. Our own heart, which in this life remains affected by sin and comes short of the glory of God, is not sufficient to represent the truth of God, to be confessed immediately in singing by all. A broken and a contrite heart will not put its fallible thoughts of God in place of God's revelation of himself.[6]

Biblical piety is in contrast to zeal without knowledge. We are sanctified by knowing the truth of God.[7] Singing the Psalms with understanding develops true spirituality. The Psalms affirm the nature of God as both just and merciful. They affirm the Biblical worldview of creation, fall, and redemption in all aspects. They affirm the will and purpose of God in history in his law and kingdom. They affirm, with hope, the full force of spiritual warfare faced by believers in every age. They are intimately acquainted with the whole range of human emotions. They are always God-centered and not self-centered. They are Christ-centered in his person and his work, on earth and at God's right hand.

Through singing the Psalms, the Word of Christ comes to dwell in us richly,[8] and we are filled with the Spirit.[9] The Psalms are to be sung, not as a matter of prudence or preference merely, but as the expression of love for God as he is in truth, not as we might imagine him to be.

---

4. *John 4:24.*

5. *WCF 21.5.*

6. *Job 42:5-6.*

7. *John 17:17.*

8. *Colossians 3:16.*

9. *Ephesians 5:18-19.*

Appendix 10

_____

DISCIPLESHIP AT
WESTMINSTER FELLOWSHIP

"Go and make disciples of all nations . . ."
Matthew 28:20

The Church is the people of God, the body of Christ, the Kingdom of God expressing itself in all of culture. The Church consists of all those who make a credible profession of the Historic Christian Faith, and their children.

The Pillar and Ground of the Truth: Christ is the eternal Word of God (the Logos) incarnate who makes God fully known. The Logos is Truth in its fullness. The Church as the body of Christ is, therefore, the pillar and ground of the Truth to all mankind.

Man's Chief End: God created and rules over all things for his own glory. Man is created in the image of God. Man's chief end is to glorify God and to enjoy him forever. Through the work of dominion given to mankind at creation, man is to fill the earth with the knowledge of God as the waters cover the sea.

Fall and Redemption: Mankind is fallen in Adam. Although they knew God, they glorified him not as God.[1] Christ comes in the place of Adam to undo what Adam did (he is the Lamb of God who takes away the sin of the world) and to do what Adam failed to do (he is the Lord who rules to make God known).

_____

1. *Romans 1:21.*

Worship and Discipleship: To worship God is to know and acknowledge him as he has revealed himself, and not in the imagination of one's own heart. The Church is gathered out of the world to worship God in spirit and in truth and to make disciples of all nations.

Salt and Light: The Church is the salt of the earth and the light of the world. As Christ makes known the Truth of God to the Church, the Church makes that Truth known to the world. Without the Truth, there is division and apostasy in the Church and decay and collapse in the culture.

Marks of a True Church: The marks of a true church are doctrine (Truth), sacraments (signs and seals of the Truth), and discipline through its oversight (upholding the practice of Truth in the Church). Churches are more or less pure according to the presence of each of the marks of a true church.

Truth in the Church: Christ, the Word of God (the Logos) incarnate, sends the Holy Spirit to lead the Church into all Truth: by reason, by the clarity of revelation in creation, and by Scripture; by its councils and creeds, by regeneration of unbelievers, and by the sanctification of believers.

From the Garden to the City of God: The Church is to grow from the Garden of Eden to the City of God, the Kingdom of God in its fullness. The Church must be taught to obey all that Christ has commanded. The Church is to take captive every thought raised up against the knowledge of God to the obedience of Christ.

The Discipline of Instruction: The Church is to be instructed in all knowledge, understanding, and wisdom, at every stage in the lives of its members in order to do its work. The Church is to be established on its philosophical, theological, and historical foundation by the discipline of instruction as called for by all vows made by its members. The Church must express the worldview built upon its foundation in all of culture, until man's work of dominion is completed.

Appendix 11

———

VOWS

MEMBERSHIP VOW

1. Do you believe the Scriptures of the Old and New Testaments to be the Word of God, the only infallible rule for faith and life?

2. Do you believe in the one living and true God—Father, Son, and Holy Spirit, as revealed in the Scriptures?

3. Do you repent of your sin; confess your guilt and helplessness as a sinner against God; profess Jesus Christ, Son of God, as your Savior and Lord; and dedicate yourself to his service? Do you promise that you will endeavor to forsake all sin, and to conform your life to his teaching and example?

4. Do you promise to submit in the Lord to the teaching and government of this Church as being based upon the Scriptures and described in substance in the Bylaws of Westminster Fellowship? Do you recognize your responsibility to work with others in the Church and do you promise to support and encourage them in their service to the Lord? In case you should need correction in doctrine or life, do you promise to respect the authority and discipline of the Church?

5. To the end that you may grow in the Christian life, do you promise that you will diligently read the Bible, engage in private prayer, keep the Lord's Day, regularly attend the worship services, observe the appointed sacraments, and give to the Lord's work as he shall prosper you?

6. Do you purpose to seek first the kingdom of God and his righteousness in all the relationships of your life, faithfully to perform

your whole duty as a true servant of Jesus Christ, and seek to win others to him?

7. Do you make this profession of faith and purpose in the presence of God, in humble reliance upon his grace, as you desire to give your account with joy at the Last Great Day?

BAPTISMAL VOW

1. Do you believe this child is a possession of God entrusted to your care?

2. In this light, do you promise to provide for his/her temporal well-being, to teach him/her to love God and his Word, the Bible, and to provide him/her with a God-centered education?

3. Do you promise to teach him/her of his/her sinful nature, of the plan of salvation which centers in Jesus Christ, and his/her own personal need of a relationship with Christ?

4. To the end that he/she may grow in the Christian life, do you promise to pray for him/her, and to train him/her to read the Bible, to pray, to keep the Lord's Day, and to understand the nature of the Church, the value of its worship and fellowship, and his/her need to seek communicant Scriptural Membership in the Church?

5. Do you promise to lead him/her by your example and parental discipline exercised in love, to seek first the Kingdom of God and his righteousness in all the relationships of life?

6. Do you make these promises in the presence of God, in humble reliance upon his grace, as you desire to give your account with joy at the Last Great Day?

ABOUT THE AUTHOR

DR. SURRENDRA GANGADEAN (1943–2022) was a professor of Philosophy at Phoenix College and at Paradise Valley Community College for forty-five years. Additionally, he taught from the pulpit at Westminster Fellowship for almost 30 years and taught courses at Logos Theological Seminary for over 25 years. Courses he taught include Introduction to Philosophy, Logic, Ethics, Philosophy of Religion, Eastern Religions, World Religions, Introduction to Christianity, Introduction to Humanities, Philosophy of Art, The Great Books, Philosophical Theology, Biblical Worldview, Biblical History, Church History, Systematic Theology, Biblical Hermeneutics, and Existential Hermeneutics. He received an M.A. degree in Literature from the University of Arizona, an M.A. degree in Philosophy from the University of Arizona, and a Ph.D. in Natural Theology from Reformed International Theological Seminary. He presented academic papers and public lectures on Natural Theology and the Moral Law. Dr. Gangadean was the organizing President of The Logos Foundation, which serves academic education in Liberal Arts and Theology.